JAMES FITZJAMES STEPHEN AND THE CRISIS OF VICTORIAN THOUGHT

James Fitzjames Stephen, from a portrait by G. F. Watts

James Fitzjames Stephen and the Crisis of Victorian Thought

James A. Colaiaco

© James A. Colaiaco 1983
Softcover reprint of the hardcover 1st edition 1983

All rights reserved. No part of this publication may be reproduced or transmitted, in any form or by any means, without permission

First published 1983 by
THE MACMILLAN PRESS LTD
London and Basingstoke
Companies and representatives
throughout the world

ISBN 978-1-349-16989-4   ISBN 978-1-349-16987-0 (eBook)
DOI 10.1007/978-1-349-16987-0

To my Mother and Father and T.

Contents

James Fitzjames Stephen	*frontispiece*
Preface	ix
A Chronology of the Life of Sir James Fitzjames Stephen	xii
1 Culture and Democracy	1
2 The State	26
3 The Politics of Literature	49
4 Towards a Science of Society	61
5 The Criminal Law	74
6 India	97
7 *Liberty, Equality, Fraternity*	122
8 An Honest Doubter	167
9 The Last Sanction	191
10 Epilogue	214
Notes	218
Bibliography	245
Index	257

Preface

Among the many pleasures which the study of intellectual history affords, perhaps none is greater than the discovery of a person whose writings shed valuable light upon his time but who has been forgotten or underestimated. James Fitzjames Stephen distinguished himself in the field of criminal law and as a thinker on political, moral and religious subjects. In the course of his career, he engaged in vigorous controversy with the great minds of Victorian England – John Stuart Mill, Matthew Arnold, Cardinal Newman, Carlyle, Dickens and Gladstone. A devout disciple of the extremely influential Utilitarian philosophy of Jeremy Bentham, Stephen also spent a great part of his life advocating legal reform in England, especially codification. During the heyday of the British Empire, he served for a time in India, codifying its criminal, evidence and contract law.

Stephen's writings illuminate what may be called a crisis of Victorian thought. The second half of the nineteenth century was marked by a breakdown of the political, social and religious ideas that had long supported English civilisation. The passage of England from an oligarchy to a democracy and the decline of orthodox Christianity led to a failure of confidence among the intellectual class. Like many of his contemporaries, Fitzjames Stephen was concerned with preserving liberty and culture at a time when political power was being transferred to the unenlightened multitude and the religious sanction for morality was dwindling. The inability of the English to combine political education with the increasing suffrage led Stephen to become one of the most powerful critics of democracy during the Victorian age.

Throughout his life, Fitzjames Stephen was devoted to the principles of classical liberalism. Nevertheless, because he was the most penetrating critic of John Stuart Mill – who holds the highest place within the pantheon of nineteenth-century liberals – Stephen's political thought has been misunderstood. Many have falsely assumed that anyone who attacked Mill so thoroughly could not himself be a liberal. This misconception existed in Stephen's time and persists today in books on Mill. Needless to say, one may be a liberal and still be critical of liberalism. The essence of the liberal point of view, and here Mill remains the best-known authority, is the willingness to subject one's beliefs to continual examination.

It will become clear in this study that, although both Stephen and Mill were part of the liberal consensus which characterised mid-nineteenth-century England, Stephen's liberalism differed significantly from that of Mill. Their opposition can be seen most dramatically in Stephen's strenuous attack upon Mill's famous essay *On Liberty*. Despite its obvious appeal, *On Liberty*, as Stephen brilliantly demonstrates, suffers from overstatement, ambiguity and serious logical flaws. Stephen also attempts to show that Mill's work, if its principle were fully applied in the social realm, would ultimately cause the dangers it was intended to prevent. In refuting Mill, Stephen offers a major reinterpretation of *On Liberty* which should be of great interest to those who are concerned about the fate of modern liberalism.

Unlike many of his contemporaries, Stephen was able to transcend narrow partisanship and subject the assumptions of both liberals and conservatives to telling criticism. He paid the price of unpopularity for shattering their complacency; and today he still has not received his due recognition. In this book I intend to establish that Fitzjames Stephen has remained in the shadows too long and deserves to be ranked among the great minds of Victorian England. Though not always correct in his conclusions, he induced many to re-examine their thinking on such fundamental questions as the nature of the State, the role of morality and religion in society, the development and reform of the law, and the utility of the British Empire. Moreover, Stephen's unrelenting attack upon the new liberalism in the name of the old remains relevant as the liberal philosophy is again under fire throughout the Western world.

The present study is an intellectual biography. I attempt to show the unity of Stephen's thought and its relation to the political and intellectual events of his day. The excellent biography of Fitzjames by his brother Leslie Stephen in 1895 remains the best source of information about his life, but no full-scale assessment of his thought has been published. The material on Stephen published during this century consists of some brief discussions of his work in India and his contribution to the criminal law. His political and religious thought, though noticed, has not been given the full treatment that it warrants. We are fortunate in that his major political work, *Liberty, Equality, Fraternity* – which deserves to rank as a classic – was reprinted in 1967. The biography by Leslie Stephen was reissued in 1972. In the present work, I make ample use of the Stephen papers, which contain much material which has never before been published.

In the course of my research and writing, I have incurred several debts which it is my pleasure to acknowledge. This study was first undertaken as a dissertation at Columbia University under the guidance of Professor Jacques Barzun. I am deeply grateful for his readings and criticisms. Professor Robert Nisbet was of assistance in reading an early version of the manuscript. Professor Joseph H. Smith, of the Columbia Law School, read the chapter on criminal law and saved me from some errors. I have profited from the discussions on political thought that I have had with my friend Brian Heffernan, who also gave the chapters on politics a critical reading. I wish to thank my father, Alfred Colaiaco, for typing the first draft and for his invaluable assistance in preparing the manuscript for publication. I am also thankful to Dorren Heffernan for typing a draft in record time. I owe a profound debt to the late Professor Arthur M. Wilson, a great scholar and teacher, who will always be a source of inspiration to me. Needless to say, though this book has benefited from the reading and kind suggestions of others, I alone bear responsibility for what errors remain. Finally, I am grateful for the aid that I have received from the libraries of the following institutions: Columbia University, the Association of the Bar of the City of New York, the New York Public Library, Cambridge University, and the London School of Economics and Political Science.

Whitestone
New York
September 1980

J. A. C.

A Chronology of the Life of Sir James Fitzjames Stephen

1829	Born in London on 3 March, son of Sir James Stephen (1789–1859)
1847–50	Attends Trinity College, Cambridge; member of the 'Apostles'.
1854	Called to the Bar; joins the Midland Circuit.
1855–68	Writes 'middles' for the *Saturday Review*.
1855	Marriage to Mary Richenda Cunningham.
1858–61	Secretary for the Duke of Newcastle's Education Commission.
1859	Appointed Recorder of Newark.
1861	Counsel for Rowland Williams.
1862	*Defence of the Reverend Rowland Williams; Essays by a Barrister*.
1863	*A General View of the Criminal Law of England*.
1865–75	Writes for the *Pall Mall Gazette*.
1865	Stands unsuccessfully for Parliament as a Liberal for Harwich.
1867	Employed by the Jamaica Committee in its attempt to prosecute Governor Eyre.
1869–72	Legal Member of Council in India.
1872	*The Indian Evidence Act*. Elected to the Metaphysical Society.
1873	*Liberty, Equality, Fraternity*. Stands unsuccessfully for Parliament as a Liberal for Dundee.

1874	Homicide Law Amendment Bill.
1875–9	Professor of Common Law at the Inns of Court.
1876	*A Digest of the Law of Evidence.*
1877	*A Digest of the Criminal Law.*
1878	Draft of a Criminal Code.
1879–91	Judge, Queen's Bench.
1883	*A History of the Criminal Law of England*, 3 vols; *A Digest of the Law of Criminal Procedure in Indictable Offences.*
1885	*The Story of Nuncomar and the Impeachment of Sir Elijah Impey*, 2 vols.
1889	Trial of Mrs Maybrick.
1891	Retires from judgeship because of ill health.
1892	*Horae Sabbaticae*, 3 vols.
1894	Death at Ipswich.

1 Culture and Democracy

I

G.K.Chesterton once remarked, with his usual discernment, that the most important event in the history of nineteenth-century England was an event that never occurred: an English revolution along the lines of the French Revolution.[1] Fear of such a catastrophe induced the ruling oligarchy to fortify the State by passing a number of moderate and gradual reforms. The Reform Act of 1832 was a characteristic example of English political adaptation, in which the aristocracy took the first step towards democracy by consenting to the enfranchisement of nearly half the middle classes. The fear of revolution, clear enough in the first part of the century, diminished as gradual reforms continued to be made and as Victorian prosperity gave rise to an almost universal faith in improvement. England was a land of growing progress, the fruits of which were triumphantly proclaimed at the Great Exhibition in 1851.

Although most were no longer haunted by the spectre of an English revolution, many liberal intellectuals feared that the emerging democracy would lead to a tyranny of the majority. Nineteenth-century liberalism was very different from that of today. While the Victorian liberal believed in freedom, the rule of law and representative government, he was also sceptical of democracy, unabashedly elitist, jealous of the right of property and an advocate of a limited suffrage. He thought that in a democracy people tend to promote equality of condition and big government at the expense of liberty, and were, therefore, easy prey for the demagogue and the despot. Unless reform was restrained and properly directed, the Victorian liberal concluded, the result would be disastrous. With increasing concern, many envisioned the subjection of England's most cherished institutions to the whims of the ignorant multitude.

As a liberal, James Fitzjames Stephen endorsed the major political and social reforms of the first part of the nineteenth century. He also accepted that a growing suffrage would be an inevitable result of the vast economic and social changes which were occurring in England of his day. Yet Stephen also shared the apprehension of many of his contemporaries. With the threat of democracy looming on the horizon, he was convinced that England was in the midst of a crisis. The challenge was to reconcile democracy with culture, by which he understood enlightenment, tolerance, responsibility and high standards of excellence. During the mid- and late Victorian period, men such as John Stuart Mill, Matthew Arnold and Thomas Carlyle were also concerned with the preservation of culture. During the 1850s, Stephen engaged in a vigorous campaign for culture which sometimes brought him into intellectual conflict with these illustrious contemporaries. Yet their disagreement was over means rather than ends, as they all sought to prepare their countrymen for the democratic age.

By the time of his birth in London on 3 March 1829, the family of Fitzjames Stephen had attained considerable distinction and belonged to what Noel Annan has christened the 'intellectual aristocracy' of England.[2] Fitzjames's grandfather, James Stephen (1758–1832), held a seat in Parliament and was an original member of the Evangelical reformist group known as the Clapham Sect, with which he worked for the abolition of slavery. Sir James Stephen (1789–1859), Fitzjames's father, was a famous colonial administrator who became Under-Secretary of State, drafted the bill abolishing the slave trade in the British Empire in 1833, and later became Regius Professor of Modern History at Cambridge. Jane Catherine Venn, the mother of Fitzjames, was a daughter of the Rector of Clapham, John Venn, and a descendant of one of the first Evangelicals.

Fitzjames Stephen was educated at Eton, at King's College, London, and then at Trinity College, Cambridge, where he achieved what can only be described as modest academic success. His desire for independent study and his disregard for scholastic distinction led to his failure to win a fellowship. As he later admitted, he was 'the most unteachable of human beings', preferring to go his own way in the pursuit of knowledge.[3] Nevertheless, his intellectual talent was recognised by his teacher, the great jurist Henry Maine, and he was invited to become a member of the select Cambridge Apostles. Stephen's powerful oratory was displayed in several debates at the Cambridge Union with

William Harcourt, the future Liberal statesman and Home Secretary.

Having failed to secure a fellowship for further study at Cambridge, Stephen, after much deliberation, decided upon a legal career. He studied at the Inner Temple, was called to the Bar in 1854, and joined the Midland Circuit. He also earned a Bachelor of Laws degree at the University of London, where he won a scholarship, his only university success. In 1855 he married Mary Cunningham, the daughter of a clergyman, who would become the devoted mother of his children. To support his family, Stephen found it necessary to supplement his legal practice by writing for a number of periodicals. Throughout most of his life he was therefore engaged in two professions: journalism and the bar. Journalism gave him a welcome opportunity to speak his mind on a variety of important issues, especially the state of culture in his day, which exclusive devotion to the bar would not have permitted him.

The principal means by which Stephen conducted his campaign for culture was the *Saturday Review*. Founded as a weekly journal in 1855, it soon emerged as the leading organ of critical opinion for the educated and propertied classes.[4] As an advocate of culture, the *Saturday* embarked on a relentless war upon popular cant. Though it regarded reform as necessary, it welcomed only that which was consistent with the preservation of English institutions. From its inception until the Reform Act of 1867, its refrain was that 'freedom depends on the political supremacy of the upper and middle classes'.[5] Fearing that democracy might lead to the destruction of the social and cultural fabric, it maintained that 'in every age and in every people the offspring of Democracy is Tyranny'.[6] It reserved its severest criticism for the radical John Bright, attacking him as a revolutionary and a demagogue. Bright responded by dubbing the review the 'Saturday Reviler',[7] an appellation the staff thoroughly enjoyed.

The first editor of the *Saturday* was John Douglas Cook. A man of great managerial skill, he recruited his contributors from Oxford and Cambridge, and from the ranks of the London barristers. Stephen, a graduate of Cambridge and a recent member of the bar, was introduced to Cook by Henry Maine in 1855, and he immediately became a regular contributor. Within a few years, he also began to write pieces for the *Cornhill Magazine*. Stephen's earliest experience as a journalist had come from a brief stint of writing for the *Christian Observer* and the *Morning Chronicle*. During his association with the *Saturday*, the staff included such famous names as E. A. Freeman, J. R. Green, Vernon Harcourt, M.E.Grant Duff, Stephen's younger brother Leslie, and Henry Maine. There were also occasional contributions from Walter Bagehot, George Henry Lewes and Mark Pattison. The staff comprised perhaps the greatest concentration of ability of any journal of the Victorian age. The legal historian Frederic Maitland later said: 'As memoirs are published, it becomes always more evident that any-one who never wrote for the *Saturday* was no one.'[8] Lord Bryce believed that 'there surely never was a journal which enlisted so much and such varied literary talent as the *Saturday* did between 1855 and 1863'.[9]

As a journalist, Stephen quickly attained renown. Anthony Trollope said that Stephen was 'the most conscientious and industrious' newspaper writer of the day.[10] A sense of the great influence that he exercised over the men and opinions of the *Saturday* is conveyed by the words of T. H. S. Escott, who was acquainted with Stephen and a friend of the journal:

> As a journalist, Fitz-james Stephen did not only help to make the *Saturday Review*. He *was* the *Saturday Review*. His views of life set forth in casual conversation, if they could have been correctly reported, would have run naturally into *Saturday Review* articles. The most characteristic expressions of Cook's best contributors on ethical or serious social themes were echoes of Stephen's mind, bodying themselves forth in articulate expression.[11]

The recent historian of the *Saturday*, Merle Bevington, has concurred with Escott's judgement.

Stephen continued to write for the journal until 1868, except for a two-year hiatus from February 1861 to February 1863 when, for reasons which remain inexplicable, he and a number of other contributors withdrew from the staff. Leslie Stephen speculated that they objected to Cook's attempt to restrict their writing for other periodicals.[12] According to Bevington, Stephen was Cook's greatest loss: 'He was not as profound a scholar as Maine, but he was a more representative exemplar of the *Saturday* attitude. His every admiration and enthusiasm was tempered by the critical spirit.'[13]

Stephen left a deep impression upon most with whom he came in contact. Even those who vehemently disagreed with him conceded that he was a man of immense mental power. A portrait of Stephen as he appeared in the late 1860s is found in the London correspondence of Charles Eliot Norton, the American scholar and man of letters:

> Fitzjames Stephen strikes me as the clearest and strongest-minded man I have met here. He has a big frame and a big, solid head, and already wears the look of a Chief Justice or Lord Chancellor. There is a most satisfactory air about him of capacity for doing hard work easily. He is simple in manner without pretense, and without overbearingness. He talks well, and tells a good story with effect. Although intellectualized to a degree of hardness common among English, or rather London men who are much in society, he has a heart, and shows it now and then in a dash of humour in which sentiment if it be not present is at least implied. He is a great friend of Carlyle's, and walks with him often on Sunday afternoons.[14]

Despite Stephen's considerable influence, it would be a mistake to think that Cook gave his views free rein. In accord with the editor's design to steer the journal along a moderate course, the more trenchant and liberal writers – which included Stephen, his brother Leslie and John Morley – were kept from writing leading articles, editorials commenting on current politics, and were confined to book reviews and the so-called 'middles', articles of broad, general application.[15] Leslie Stephen characterised the middle as 'a kind of lay sermon', to which the educated English public at that time was very receptive.[16] Though Fitzjames was excluded from the writing of 'leaders', he was allowed to contribute many pieces attacking popular nostrums and defending culture. Some of these he republished anonymously in 1862 as *Essays by a Barrister*. In addition, he wrote articles on political and religious thinkers of the past that show the general philosophy which underlay his incisive social criticisms. These were later collected and published under his name as the three-volume *Horae Sabbaticae* (1892).

Some account must also be given of Stephen's connection with the *Pall Mall Gazette*. Founded in 1865 as an evening newspaper by George Murray Smith, its first editor was Frederick Greenwood. In addition to Stephen, its contributors included his brother

Leslie, G.H.Lewes, R.H.Hutton, Matthew Arnold, Trollope and Sir Henry Maine. As John Morley, who became editor of the paper in 1880, later recalled, Greenwood did his best 'to encourage a vigorous all-around reaction against the Liberalism associated with Mill in one field and Gladstone in another'.[17] Stephen joined the staff in 1865 and for the first time was permitted to write 'leaders'. He greatly valued this opportunity to comment directly upon politics from day to day. His industry and talents were immediately recognised. As Greenwood wrote:

> With the second number Fitzjames Stephen began the long fast-following series of articles which were a delight to him to write and to us no small credit to print. No journalist that I have known took so much pleasure in his work or brought more conscience to it or more eagerness and endeavour. Leading articles were the main of his contributions and he also wrote in what we call the literary columns of the paper.[18]

Unfortunately, no record survives of the editorials Stephen wrote, for anonymity was the rule which then governed most of the journalism of the day. We do know that between 1865 and 1873 his contributions totalled over a thousand articles. Leslie Stephen gives us an idea of his brother's toil: 'Making allowances for Sundays, it will be seen that in 1868 Fitzjames wrote two-thirds of the leaders, nearly half the leaders in 1867, and not much less than half in the three other years (1865, 1866 and 1869).'[19] It is not necessary to try to identify here the articles Stephen wrote, because the ideas they contain are fully developed in the hundreds of identifiable pieces which he contributed to other periodicals.[20] Except for the well-known series collected in *Liberty, Equality, Fraternity*, written during the latter part of 1872 and January 1873, Stephen's almost daily pieces for the *Pall Mall* did not deal with first principles. Indeed, when this series first appeared, Leslie Stephen confessed his surprise that Greenwood permitted such a theoretical discussion in his newspaper.[21]

In pursuing his two professions, Stephen necessarily wrote under difficult conditions. Besides having to meet deadlines, he had to work during the free moments he could spare while handling briefs on the Midland Circuit. Nevertheless, even by Victorian standards his output was immense. Writing became almost a compulsion with him. He often rose early to write before breakfast; at other times he worked late into the night. He even managed to dash off pieces in court while waiting for his cases to be heard. His enormous energy astounded his friends and irritated his adversaries. Physically strong and an inveterate walker, he made several Alpine tours, and a fifty-mile walk from Cambridge to London was not for him unusual. Leslie Stephen, himself a man of uncommon stamina, related that once, when the two brothers were climbing the Alps, Fitzjames, during the most arduous part of the ascent, began to expound an article which he projected for the *Saturday Review*. Leslie recalled his exasperation: 'I consigned that journal to a fate which I believe it has hitherto escaped.'[22]

II

In 1862 Fitzjames Stephen took the fight for culture to the pages of the *Cornhill Magazine*, with his essay 'Liberalism'. Founded in 1860, with Thackeray as its editor, the *Cornhill* sought to combine the virtues of a critical review with the pleasures of serial novels. Like the *Saturday*, it appealed to a highly literate audience. During 1867 and 1868, it published the articles which eventually became Matthew Arnold's *Culture and Anarchy*. Within its pages could also be found the fiction of such luminaries as George Eliot, Hardy, Trollope and Thackeray.

Throughout the 1850s the Liberal Party under Lord John Russell had unsuccessfully tried to reform the franchise. Nevertheless, many viewed an increase of the suffrage towards democracy as inevitable. Fearing that without adequate preparation democracy would become the enemy of culture, Stephen proposed a definition of liberalism which he hoped would guide his countrymen. Early in the nineteenth century, the word 'liberal' referred to those who sought to reconstruct the established order upon what they regarded as broader and more tolerant principles.[23] It was thus initially conceived in a negative, critical, emancipating sense. Liberals wished to extend individual freedom in all aspects of life. They were opposed by those who assailed their idealism and insisted that the imperfections of human nature made certain restraints upon liberty necessary. Both groups, the liberal and the conservative, balanced and checked each other by their alternate and partial success. The result, Stephen contended, was that the English, by promoting yet restraining and directing reform, had managed to reconcile progress and stability: 'The deep changes which have been made in our institutions have made no permanent and fundamental change in the sentiments or conduct of the nation. Nothing in the history of England is more striking than its continuity.'[24] This belief was widespread in Stephen's day. Ever since Edmund Burke's denunciation of the French Revolution, the English had prided themselves on the fact that they had avoided revolutionary solutions to political and social questions.

Stephen was convinced that by the mid-nineteenth century the negative aspect of liberalism had done its work. As a liberal and a Utilitarian, he applauded the reforms of the past generation. Individual freedom had been extended in the political, social and economic realms. Now that these freedoms had been won, the new challenge was to harmonise the rights of the individual with the needs of society. Stephen insisted that it was imperative to emphasise 'the positive side of liberalism', that which is consistent with culture. In the proper sense, liberalism ought to denote 'generous and high-minded sentiments upon political subjects, guided by a highly instructed, large-minded, and impartial intellect. Liberalism, in a word, ought to mean the opposite of sordidness, vulgarity, and bigotry.'[25] Stephen lamented that instead of following this standard, liberalism was becoming popularly understood as denoting majority rule or democracy. He shared the apprehension of those who believed that democracy, by elevating the masses to power, would subject England to a tyranny of the majority. Once political and social equality were achieved, he argued, the nation would be governed according to the prevailing tastes of the uneducated multitude. Stephen deplored a growing tendency among certain politicians and popular writers to curry favour by deifying the uninformed opinions of the working classes. A correct conception of liberalism was necessary, he asserted, because the paramount political question of the age was not whether democracy would be attained – he viewed it as inevitable — but whether the liberals in increasing the power of the people would at the same time succeed in 'raising thereby the general tone of life, and in causing it to be pervaded by a higher conception of the objects of national existence'.[26]

Such a task, Stephen believed, demanded that the liberals supply the necessary leadership. In the past, England had been ruled by a landed aristocracy. But the political and social changes of the first half of the nineteenth century had greatly diminished the power and influence of this old ruling elite. Stephen held that the duty of the new generation of liberals was to ensure that the old aristocracy be replaced by an aristocracy of merit: an intellectual and moral elite derived from the educated and professional classes which would guide England into the democratic age. He declared:

> The highest function which the great mass of mankind could ever be fitted to perform . . . would be that of recognizing the moral and intellectual superiority of the few who, in virtue of a happy combination of personal gifts, with accidental advantages, ought to be regarded as their natural leaders, and of following this guidance, not slavishly but willingly, and with an intelligent co-operation.[27]

Stephen's conception of rule under the guidance of an aristocracy of merit paralleled that of Mill. Their mutual pessimism concerning the competency of the sovereign people to govern themselves should be stressed, since Stephen has been interpreted as a reactionary, while Mill is hailed as the great liberal. As Mill declared in his essay *On Liberty*:

> No government by a democracy or a numerical aristocracy, either in its political acts or in the opinions, qualities, and tone of mind which it fosters, ever did or could rise above mediocrity, except in so far as the sovereign may have let themselves be guided (which in their best times they always have done) by the counsels and influence of a more highly gifted and instructed Few. The initiation of all wise or noble things comes and must come from individuals; generally at first from some one individual. The honour and glory of the average man is that he is capable of following that initiative; that he can respond internally to wise and noble things, and be led to them with his eyes open.[28]

III

Stephen was not the first to point out the dangers of democracy. As early as the 1830s Alexis de Tocqueville, in his now classic *Democracy in America*, argued convincingly that democracy poses a serious threat to individual freedom and makes high cultural standards difficult to maintain. The book converted John Stuart Mill, who welcomed it with two lengthy and generally approving reviews.[29] A proponent of universal suffrage since his youth, Mill came to advocate a franchise weighted to favour those with education and property. In his widely celebrated essay *On Liberty* of 1859, Mill echoed Tocqueville by drawing attention to the evils of popular rule – the subversion of individual liberty by a tyranny of the majority and a general levelling of excellence. Mill's essay aroused considerable debate, and was reviewed by Fitzjames Stephen in two successive issues of the *Saturday*.[30]

With warm approbation, Stephen indicates that the general tone of the work corresponds entirely with the frame of mind which the *Saturday* wished to inculcate amongst its readers.[31] He then summarises Mill's fundamental argument. To counter the dangers of democracy, Mill asserts 'one very simple principle' to govern absolutely the relations between the individual and society: the sole end for which men are warranted, individually or collectively, in interfering with the liberty of action of any of their number, either by law or public opinion, is self-protection. Stephen saw value in this principle – though he would later contest it vigorously – and he agreed with Mill that democracy posed a threat which the English could not afford to ignore:

> Trite as this doctrine may appear to some persons, Mr. Mill is obviously prompted to assert it by a fear that it is by no means universally accepted in practice, and by a feeling – which we are afraid is but too well grounded – that notwithstanding our political freedom, many causes are at work which tend to subject us to a tyranny more searching, infinitely more powerful, and much more difficult to resist, than any which depends on merely material force; for it arises from the gradual destruction of all the peculiarities of individuals, and the general adoption of a sort of commonplace ideal of character, to which everyone is forced to conform, by a vast variety of petty sanctions applying with a leaden invariable persistency to all the common actions of life.[32]

Stephen's praise for Mill's second and third chapters, those defending liberty of thought and discussion and extolling individuality, is effusive; he detects echoes of Milton: 'We know of nothing in English literature since the *Areopagitica* more stirring, more noble, better worthy of the most profound and earnest meditation, than these two chapters of Mr. Mill's essay.'[33] He also finds the essay an effective reproof of the characteristic smugness of the day, a 'complacent optimism' which regards the progress of knowledge and civilisation as inevitable, independent of individual effort.

But this praise did not go unqualified. At first, Stephen was obviously impressed by the bracing moral appeal of Mill's work. Mill had already achieved the status, which he still retains, of an oracle among English liberals. Stephen readily espoused the contents of his *System of Logic* (1843) and the *Principles of Political Economy* (1848), but he had some reservations about the essay *On Liberty*. In his second article, Stephen dissents as to the degree to which the dangers to freedom and individuality had begun to pervade English society. While these dangers were indeed present in an age of growing democracy, Mill unfortunately overstated his case and drew an extremely negative picture of his country, unwarranted by the facts. Stephen observes that Mill's essay is marred by a tone of 'melancholy', a 'want of humour'. To judge from Mill's argument, mediocrity reigns and individuality is declining in England.[34] Reviewing Mill's *Dissertations and Discussions*, Stephen alleges that it is impossible to read them without receiving the impression that 'his general opinion of England at the present day is a very mean one'. Mill failed to perceive 'what an immense scope for the development of individual character is afforded in one direction by the very social arrangements which appear to forbid it in another'.[35] Though there does exist a general conformity among the various classes in England, it is more 'external', pertaining to the less serious concerns of life, such as dress and conversation. But what a man reads, what he thinks, how he educates his children, and his religious beliefs, are questions left to the individual to decide for himself.[36]

Stephen was not alone in his disagreement with Mill over the waning of individuality in England. The historian Thomas Henry Buckle, a firm believer in progress, also thought that Mill had overstated his case.[37] Macaulay, after reading *On Liberty* in one sitting, declared that Mill's plea was tantamount to someone exclaiming 'Fire!' in the midst of Noah's Flood.[38] One scholar has surveyed the reception of the essay in the contemporary periodicals and concluded:

> Very few of them [Mill's contemporaries] . . . shared his anxiety about the impending eclipse of individual character. The

majority of those who discussed the essay during his lifetime were either decidedly against him or strangely silent on an issue which he took to be so fundamental. Furthermore, they demurred both in respect of the magnitude of the phenomenon he deplored and as to the causes of such evidence for it that they were themselves prepared to concede.[39]

In the third chapter of *On Liberty*, 'Of Individuality', Mill argued that Calvinism, which he apparently equated with English Evangelicalism, was to blame for the loss of originality among his countrymen. Its exaggerated emphasis upon obedience as a virtue, and its negative view of human nature, served merely to repress individual character. This charge brings out a deeper rift between Stephen and Mill, stemming from their differing conceptions of human nature, and underlying their later dispute over liberty and equality. Stephen believed that restraints, both religious and legal, were essential to the maintenance of public order. He therefore held that obedience was necessary for the development of character, since it enables men to forgo immediate and transitory ends for enduring ones.[40]

The danger threatening England, according to Stephen, came not from Calvinism, but from the uneducated masses, whose occupations 'engross the attention without developing the intellectual or moral powers of those who pursue them'.[41] England at that time had no national system of education. The Newcastle Commission of 1858 was the first of three instituted during the second half of the nineteenth century to investigate the condition of popular instruction in the country. This was the same investigative body that sent Matthew Arnold to report on the quality of education on the Continent. Stephen, then only twenty-nine years of age, served with distinction as its secretary. The Revd William Rogers, a member of the commission, testified that he 'brought to the task a combination of talents rarely found in any one individual. To his keen insight, wide grasp, accurately balanced judgment, and marvellous aptitude for details, was due much of the success with which we were able to lay down the future lines of popular education.'[42] The commission dissolved in 1861, its six volumes of reports having been prepared by Stephen. It recommended that, instead of establishing a State system, the current practice of voluntary effort should be extended and improved.

The absence of a universal system of State education before

1870 is one of the great failures of Victorian England. Since the 'public' (that is, private) schools and universities were also in drastic need of reform, even the education among the middle and upper classes was in a deplorable state. Not until the Forster Act of 1870 was a national primary school system created, and then only where the voluntary system was wanting. Throughout the nineteenth century, education reform was continually frustrated by the prevalent liberal philosophy, and by the dispute between Anglicans and Dissenters over the kind of religion which should be taught. Only after the Reform Act of 1867, which enfranchised the urban workers, did reform in this matter make real headway. The former obstacles were virtually swept away by the sense of urgency expressed in the famous slogan attributed to Robert Lowe: 'We must educate our masters.' Because at the time Mill wrote his essay the uneducated class was 'the most numerous, increasing and influential in the country', Stephen believed that England had more to fear from them than from Calvinism.[43] Indeed, in an age when law and order were threatened, Calvinism helped supply the restraint that was needed.

When Stephen first read *On Liberty* it is clear that, like Mill, he was principally concerned with preserving liberty from the dangers which he saw inherent in democratic rule. In later years he concluded that, though liberty must be cherished and preserved, Mill erred in making it an end in itself. He argued that Mill's doctrine of liberty is actually contrary to utility since, if consistently carried out, it would lead to the destruction of the entire political and social order. Mill had therefore departed from the Utilitarian tradition. It is significant that at first Stephen found no objection to Mill's attempt to distinguish between those actions which affect the individual alone, which should remain absolutely free, and those which affect society and are therefore subject to compulsion. The majority of the contemporary reviews believed that this demarcation was specious and untenable.[44] Though the distinction was to become a subject of contention between Mill and himself, Stephen did not challenge it at this time. Not until more than a decade later, after much reading and reflection, and after the experience of India, was he moved to launch a more penetrating criticism of Mill in his great *Liberty, Equality, Fraternity*.

IV

No discussion of the emergence of democracy in England would be complete without mentioning the name of Thomas Carlyle. Stephen was his friend for many years and, along with the historian James Anthony Froude, executor of his will. The circumstances of Stephen's introduction to Carlyle were a cause of embarrassment. When he first called at Carlyle's house on Cheyne Row, Mrs Carlyle, thinking him an American celebrity hunter, ordered him away. After learning his name, however, she ushered him inside to speak with her husband.[45] The two men soon became close friends.

Carlyle was an imposing figure. In a review of his collected works for the *Saturday*, Stephen observes that among his readers Carlyle enjoys an 'almost mystical reputation',[46] and that he is 'far the most popular preacher to which this generation has listened'.[47] From an artistic point of view, his works rank 'at the head of contemporary literature'. His *French Revolution* (1837), which established his reputation, is characterised by brilliant style and vivid portraiture. In dramatic fashion, he depicts the Revolution as the descent of God's wrath upon the French governing classes. His pictures are 'so distinct, so life-like, that they make it almost impossible to remember the scenes which they describe through any other medium'.[48]

If Stephen could extol Carlyle's artistry, he could also subject his thought to telling analysis. Though they remained intimate until Carlyle's death in 1881, Stephen's honesty prevented him from relaxing his critical powers. As a journalist, he was well aware of the power of the written word to persuade, a talent Carlyle possessed in abundance. He alleged that Carlyle falsified history not by an inaccurate rendering of events, but by an excess of imagination.[49] The sheer brilliance of his style lent his interpretations a verisimilitude which they did not deserve. John Holloway, in his book *The Victorian Sage*, has drawn attention to the power of Carlyle's writing – his idiosyncratic language, his esoteric metaphors, and his masterly use of paradox and humour.[50] It was this great flair for writing, the ability to persuade by rhetorical device and imaginative diction, that Stephen believed distorted the truth in Carlyle's works and led many readers to accept as true what they would perceive as false if presented by a less skilful author. Though the *French Revolution* is an artistic masterpiece, it is not reliable history:

Mr. Carlyle is, we fully believe, quite incapable of the slightest distortion of a matter of fact, and indeed, his native and national shrewdness and honesty entitle him to the praise of great accuracy and critical discernment, but his imagination is so enormously powerful that no amount of fact can ballast it. Whenever he writes, he creates a whole set of people who are in one sense real enough, but whose identity with the historical personages whom they represent is very doubtful. His readers must feel as if they had known personally the Robespierre, the Danton, the Camille Desmoulins and all the other personages who figure in Mr. Carlyle's pages; but they can have no confidence at all that their acquaintances are identical with the men who once went by those names. Mr. Carlyle's conception of the Revolution itself is quite intelligible, and there is no doubt a true epic consistency and unity about it; but it does not follow that the thing itself was really so because a very able man can so conceive it; and if, in point of fact, the conception is false, it must be mischievous also.[51]

Stephen was also extremely critical of Carlyle's political and social writings: those dealing with the questions of how England ought to be governed, and how the great issue of the poor ought to be handled. Like all but a few Victorian thinkers, Carlyle feared the spread of democracy; yet for him the means to preserve culture lay in abolishing the nation's most venerated institutions. In several works – *Chartism* (1840), *On Heroes and Hero Worship* (1841), *Past and Present* (1843) and *Latter-Day Pamphlets* (1850) – he excoriated Benthamite liberalism and *laissez-faire* economics for bringing on the evils of the age. He showed great concern for the poor; indeed the opening chapter of *Chartism*, on the 'Condition of England Question', referring to the plight of the nation's impoverished, supplied a phrase that retained its appeal throughout the nineteenth century. But his sympathy stopped short of favouring the participation of the working classes in government. To Carlyle, the solution to England's difficulties lay in scuttling parliamentary institutions and vesting power in a Hero ruling through an aristocracy of talent.

Stephen maintained that Carlyle's political and social works, like his history, were ingenious but inaccurate representations of English society. 'Probably no man of genius, being at the same time a good and honourable man, ever wrote two books so unjust and injurious as *Past and Present* and the *Latter-Day Pamphlets*.'[52] He declared that Carlyle was 'one of the greatest wits and poets, but the most untrustworthy moralist and politician of our age and nation'.[53] His writings contain little that is new. The virtues which he sought to inculcate – truth, honesty, industry, and attention to facts – have always been generally acknowledged, though not necessarily followed. Stephen argued that, despite his widespread popularity, Carlyle had no significant influence upon English political, moral or religious ideas. The greatest influence had been exercised by the Utilitarians. Consequently, 'Mr. Carlyle is certainly entitled to the praise of having preached on a very old subject in such a manner as to arrest the attention of his congregation and to keep them wide awake, but it does not follow that he has, as so many people seem to think, made any wonderful discoveries in morality.'[54]

Stephen's defence of Benthamism and liberalism was reserved for the first part of a long review article for *Fraser's Magazine* in 1865, occasioned by the publication of Carlyle's *Frederick the Great*. In the *Latter-Day Pamphlets* Carlyle had disparagingly characterised Benthamism as 'pig-philosophy', and derided parliamentary government and popular institutions as slow and inefficient. The only solution lay in relinquishing power to a Hero. At first Carlyle thought that Sir Robert Peel would fill the bill; but the untimely death of the former prime minister in 1850, after a fall from his horse, foreclosed that hope. After owning that he was a disciple of the so-called porcine creed that Carlyle scorns, Stephen charged that he altogether misunderstood the character and merits of popular institutions and parliamentary government. Indeed, they 'constitute collectively a most vigilant, active, powerful, and benevolent government, which has done, and is doing in this country and elsewhere, one of the greatest works that ever was done in the world'.[55]

Stephen then came to the defence of his own intellectual forbears. Benthamism, he contended, by means of the principle of 'the greatest happiness of the greatest number', had been eminently successful. This principle was 'the guiding and ruling spirit of the government for the whole of the present and during part of the last century', and instrumental in effecting a number of beneficial political, legal and administrative reforms. [56] Though it is true that parliaments spend much time talking and proceed laboriously, their results are more often substantial. 'A worshipper of fact and veracity ought to see something eminently respectable and satisfactory in the slow irresistible elephantine manner in which the English Parliament and cognate institutions do their work.'[57] Nor would Stephen have anything to do with Carlyle's Hero. He defended the idea of representative government with popular sovereignty as opposed to vesting power in one man. English parliamentary government was far more benevolent than that in France under Napoleon III:

> The truth is that the commonplaces about the advantages of parliamentary government, a free press, and all the rest of it, are in the main true. Downing-street, Westminster Hall, and the Houses of Parliament, with all their babblements, . . . are collectively a far better king that any Cromwell or Frederick could possibly be. Will anyone compare King Parliament to King Louis Napoleon?[58]

Stephen found the politics of Thomas Macaulay more palatable than Carlyle's. During his youth, the *Essays* were among Stephen's favourite books, and throughout his life he continued to read them with pleasure. Macaulay loved the Victorian age as much as Carlyle hated it. He praised the liberal reforms of the day and was a fervent preacher of the gospel of improvement. When the great historian died in 1859, Stephen spent the night composing a eulogy. He paid tribute to 'a true Englishman. A truer and more hearty lover of his country never lived.'[59] Macaulay's most engaging quality, Stephen alleged, was the substantial unity of his life. The Whig views that he eloquently set forth in Parliament were the very same views which permeate his famous *History of England*. His rejection of natural rights in favour of empirical facts and historical precedent made him 'the greatest, and indeed almost the only great, advocate and expounder of Whig principles since the time of Burke'.[60] Though Stephen conceded that the Whig philosophy was subject to some 'limitations and additions',[61] he also insisted that it had been largely responsible for England's greatness. Stephen was proud of the fact that England had been able to reconcile liberty and order, and that by means of the Whig principle of moderate reform it had avoided the revolutions that had convulsed the Continent. Though he later found fault with Macaulay for not probing deeply into speculative matters, he praised the *History* for its accurate portrayal of English history.[62]

V

Like Mill, Carlyle and Stephen, Matthew Arnold believed that the English were ill prepared for the emerging democracy. Arnold was undoubtedly the most famous advocate of culture in Victorian England. He is known today as a literary and social critic, and as one of the most urbane exponents of the humanistic tradition. By his own admission, much of his conception of culture derived from the liberal education he had received from his famous father Thomas Arnold at Rugby, and from the legacy of 'sweetness and light' which he had absorbed during his years at Oxford. His appointment to the post of inspector of schools in 1851 enabled him to observe the political and social ills of England at first hand. Like Stephen, Arnold was disturbed because his countrymen were set on blindly pursuing democracy without regard to social order.

In 'The Function of Criticism at the Present Time', published in 1864, Arnold directs some harsh words at the English, alleging that they are provincial, deficient in reasoning power, and inaccessible to general ideas. He reserves praise only for Burke: 'Almost alone in England, he brings thought to bear upon politics, he saturates politics with thought.'[63] The English poverty of thought stems from their preoccupation with material wealth and their emphasis upon means at the expense of ends. The remedy — to which he believes his countrymen are singularly ill disposed — lies in 'disinterested' criticism, endeavouring 'to know the best that is known and thought in the world, and by in its turn making this known to create a current of true and fresh ideas'.[64] In contrast to the English, the French live by ideas, recognising that 'the prescriptions of reason are absolute, unchanging, of universal validity'.[65] As proof, Arnold points to the example of the French Revolution. He considers it remarkable 'that a whole nation should have been penetrated with an enthusiasm for pure reason, and with an ardent zeal for making its prescriptions triumph'.[66] The fatal mistake of the Revolution — and here Arnold believes the French might learn from the English — was in attempting to give these general ideas immediate application, disregarding moderation and tradition. Arnold also denigrates the British Constitution as 'a colossal machine for the manufacture of Philistines'.[67]

Stephen found these criticisms disturbing and unjust. While he shared Arnold's concern over the English devotion to material comforts, he rejected the notion that it was owing to inferior mental ability. Accordingly, he hurried off a retorting 'middle' to the *Saturday*, entitled 'Mr. Matthew Arnold and His Countrymen'. Though the article was anonymous, the authorship was an open secret, as Arnold referred in his letters to 'a long, elaborate attack on me, of nearly four columns. It is by Fitzjames Stephen, and is due partly to his being Colenso's advocate, partly also to his ideas being naturally very antagonistic to mine.'[68] As in the case of Carlyle, the fact that Stephen engaged in a lively controversy with Arnold did not prevent them from remaining on good terms – another characteristic of the great Victorian age of free thought. After beginning his article with the usual amenities, praising Arnold as 'always brilliant, good-natured, entertaining, and even instructive',[69] Stephen moves to the offensive:

> Like all that he writes, his article is very pretty reading, but from first to last, it appears to us to be fundamentally wrong, and in particular, it totally fails to apprehend that against which it is directed. The truth is that ... Mr. Arnold has quick sympathies and a great gift of making telling remarks; but ... he has hardly any power of argument.[70]

Stephen then disposes of Arnold's underlying premise with the penetrating observation that his claims for the so-called immutable prescriptions of absolute reason assume the truth of the transcendental or idealist school of philosophy. But the English, schooled in the sober empiricism of Mill's *Logic*, have already considered, understood and found wanting the transcendental philosophy that Arnold applauds. He overlooks, Stephen says, that the English have an empirical and Utilitarian tradition from Hobbes to John Stuart Mill which 'thoroughly understands and on theoretical grounds deliberately rejects the philosophical theory which Mr. Arnold accuses the English of neglecting'. Stephen believes that the English are opposed not to general ideas as such, but only to those, such as natural law, without a basis in experience. Contrary to Arnold's denigrations, the English have amply demonstrated their ability to be inspired by, and to follow, general principles:[71]

> In fact no nation in the world is so logical as the English nation. Once get it well convinced of the truth of a general principle ... and it will do anything. For instance, the English nation believes

in political economy, and the consequence is that it is the only nation in the world which has established free trade. The New Poor Law and the Bank Charter Act were based upon the principles of the same science. Bentham persuaded the English nation that the greatest happiness of the greatest number was the true rule for legislation, and every part of the law has been reformed by degrees by the application, more or less skillful and complete, of that abstract principle. Newton persuaded the English nation that the force of gravity varies inversely as the square of the distance, and this doctrine, with its consequences, was accepted and worked out to its practical results by the English nation before any other people fully took it in. Mr. Mill has persuaded the English nation that men ought to argue, not from universals to particulars, but from particulars to particulars, and the practical influence of this highly abstract principle is seen in that state of criticism to which Mr. Arnold objects. Our modern Indian policy has been governed by the abstract principle that the natives ought to be civilized on the English pattern. When abstract principles like these are embraced by and do influence the English people most deeply, is it just, or even decent to talk about 'British Philistines' because we English do not choose to recognize as eternal truths a set of platitudes which may be proved to be false?[72]

Arnold directly acknowledged his critic in the preface to his *Essays in Criticism* in 1865. Though he refused to reply to the specific charges against him, he still managed some glancing blows at the Benthamism which the *Saturday* supposedly professed, and linked the periodical with middle-class philistinism. Stephen, who always relished a genial but hard-hitting dispute, prodded Arnold to come out fighting by rejoining that the preface was 'too good natured. There is no pleasure in hitting a man who will not hit you back again.'[73]

Stephen got his wish, for Arnold's reticence was only a pose. In 1866, Arnold wrote an extensive reply in an article for the *Cornhill*, 'My Countrymen' – the title obviously a reference to Stephen's earlier attack. The result was a brilliant *tour de force*. Ostensibly penitent, Arnold begins by confessing that by virtue of the criticisms levelled by the *Saturday*, he has come to recognise the flagrant injustice of his description of England as a nation replete with Philistines, inaccessible to ideas, and destitute of the higher mental faculties. After vowing that he will mend his ways, he cleverly embarks upon what amounts to a reprise of his criticisms by recounting the unfavourable views of foreigners about England which he allegedly heard during a recent tour of the Continent in his capacity as school inspector. To this, Stephen composed a riposte, 'Mr. Arnold on the Middle Classes', calling upon his readers to consider not the opinions of foreigners, but the historical facts. He perorates with solemn praise for England's greatness: its political and religious freedom; its civilising and benevolent Empire.[74]

As an instrument to prepare for democracy, Arnold introduced a conception of culture, the unifying idea of his entire social criticism. Throughout 1867 and 1868 he composed a set of brilliant articles for the *Cornhill*, which were later collected and published as *Culture and Anarchy* in 1869. The first, entitled 'Culture and its Enemies', was his valedictory lecture as Professor of Poetry at Oxford. Casting the light of culture upon English complacency and materialism, he urges restraint and intelligence to counteract the anarchical tendencies of the era. As he sees it, his countrymen must choose between culture and anarchy. By culture, Arnold means something analogous to Stephen's conception of liberalism. It is an 'internal condition', characterised by 'the pursuit and study of perfection', which 'consists in becoming something rather than in having something'.[75] This perfection is at once general, 'developing all parts of our society', and harmonious, 'developing all sides of our humanity'.[76] His conception of culture is modelled, Arnold tells us, on that of the Greeks, and consists of what Swift, in his *Battle of the Books,* calls the happy conjunction of 'the two noblest of things, sweetness and light',[77] or beauty and intelligence.

According to Arnold, the English can avoid political and moral anarchy only by following the dictates of culture and instituting some centre of authority in society. He rejects as futile the attempt to find this centre in any of England's classes. Analysing each of them, to which he applies the labels 'Barbarians', 'Philistines' and 'Populace', signifying, respectively, the aristocracy, the middle class and the masses, he finds them deficient.[78] The Barbarians are dismissed because of their inaccessibility to ideas; the Philistines because of their passion for material comfort; the masses because of their destitution and poor education. The only recourse, Arnold insists, is to transcend the class spirit and seek the nucleus of authority in the State. Once this is achieved, social classes would disappear and men would live in a condition of equality.

Culture and Anarchy may be interpreted as an indirect refutation of Mill's *On Liberty*.[79] For Arnold, the degree to which Mill wished to extend liberty was inconsistent with culture and, therefore, conducive to anarchy. Arnold considered himself a liberal; yet he believed that, in an era of growing democracy, culture, order and authority were most needed and most threatened. In later years, Stephen would argue along the same lines. Though he did not have an opportunity to review all of *Culture and Anarchy* when it first appeared, we can assume that Stephen had serious reservations regarding its political philosophy. He probably viewed Arnold's attempt to abolish social classes as dangerously visionary. A classical liberal, Stephen could not conceive of society except as stratified; indeed, he thought that English liberty depended upon a class system. In true liberal fashion, he was also wary of Arnold's desire to increase State power. Stephen held that the State should be limited to protecting private property and providing for the common defence.

Stephen did manage to write a critique of Arnold's article 'Culture and its Enemies', the first chapter of *Culture and Anarchy*. He conceded the article's obvious merits, and regretted that the lesson which Arnold imparts is one which the English 'have the least inclination, and the greatest need to learn'.[80] Yet Stephen held that Arnold's conception of culture was too Olympian and one-sided to be the sole solution to England's problems. The pursuit of culture 'unaccompanied by an active interest in the social or moral problems that surround us, is more likely to enervate and demoralize our mental energies than to brace them'.[81] In stressing culture as an internal perfection, Arnold neglects the importance of practical activity: 'What a man is matters more than what he does; but then, again, what he is depends fully as much on what he does as on what he knows. Culture alone will not give sweetness nor even "flexibility", though it is an immense, and ordinarily an indispensable assistance to acquiring those qualities.'[82] But Stephen's stricture is unfair. Arnold never intended to divorce culture from conduct. Having devoted the greatest part of his life to the proposition that 'literature is a criticism of life', he conceived of culture as promoting the disinterested frame of mind necessary for the solution of practical problems. Stephen, no champion of the mental capacity of the common man, would

Culture and Democracy 23

undoubtedly retort that this notion rested upon the ingenuous assumption that there lies a Socrates deep in the recesses of every human breast. Despite all reservations, Stephen preferred 'the liberalism of the apostles of culture' to the radicalism of such men as John Bright and Edmond Beales.[83]

VI

The years 1865 to 1867 convinced Stephen, Mill, Arnold and Carlyle that what they had feared for England was on the verge of becoming a reality. A combination of economic distress and popular discontent brought the reform issue to the fore. Many members of the upper and middle classes realised that only prosperity had saved them from the radical Chartist movement in 1848. In 1866 the Liberal Ministry, led by Russell and Gladstone, introduced a bill to extend the suffrage. It was defeated because of a Conservative opposition expertly managed by Disraeli and aided by the secession from the Liberal ranks of a group of anti-reformists led by Robert Lowe and known, in Bright's word, as the 'Adullamites'. Shortly after the failure of the bill, with a Conservative Ministry in power, the volume of popular agitation increased as the middle-class Reform Union and the working-class Reform League initiated a clamorous campaign for a more equitable franchise. Edmond Beales was president of the League, and its other leaders included Ernest Jones, G. J. Holyoake and Charles Bradlaugh.

On 23 July 1866 came a dramatic showdown between the Government and the reform agitators.[84] The Reform League had scheduled a demonstration to take place in Hyde Park. The Home Secretary, Spencer Walpole, ordered the park gates to be closed. The League, led by Beales, marched with thousands of supporters to the Marble Arch. When they were refused admittance to the park, Beales and part of the crowd decided to proceed to Trafalgar Square. But the majority remained, and in defiance of the Government, they stormed the gates, knocking over the park railings and trampling the lawns and flowerbeds. This outcome had a shocking effect upon the middle and upper classes. As one writer has concluded: 'It is scarcely too much to say that the fall of the Park railings did for England in July 1866 what the fall of the Bastille did for France in July 1789. The shooting of Niagara was seen to be inevitable.'[85] Walpole was forced to resign in disgrace; indeed, a story circulated, probably apocryphal, that on one occasion he had burst into tears while remonstrating with a delegation from the Reform League. Mill met with the leaders of the League and persuaded them not to resort to violence, arguing that force was justified only if they were convinced that conditions were so intolerable as to warrant a revolution. Actually, a revolution at that time was unlikely. The Hyde Park rioters sought not to overthrow the Government, but to participate in it. Arnold was immensely disturbed by the whole affair, and responded by writing *Culture and Anarchy*, in which he derided the 'Hyde Park rough'. Leslie Stephen said that the behaviour of the Conservative Government at the time aroused his brother's 'hearty contempt'.[86]

Meanwhile, in the provinces, the radical John Bright was spreading the reform rhetoric in city after city. Finally, as the popular demonstrations continued and the economic depression took its toll in unemployment, the Conservatives, led by Derby and Disraeli, perceived that reform could no longer be delayed. To seize the initiative for their party and 'dish the Whigs' in the process, they proposed a moderate reform bill in March 1867, which they hoped would gratify the workers. The ensuing months, from March to August, were occupied by numerous debates in the Commons on the substance of the bill, and the conjunction of Liberal attacks and popular agitation transformed it far beyond the intent of its original framers. In May 1867 there was another large demonstration in Hyde Park; this time the Government did not interfere. Finally, in August, after five months of heated debate, Disraeli surprisingly assented to a series of Liberal amendments and the bill was passed. What had initially been intended as a minor concession to the working classes had been transformed into the historic Reform Act of 1867, which more than doubled the electorate. England was now irrevocably committed to democracy. Disraeli could only hope that his party would be credited with this accomplishment and win the support of a majority of the newly enfranchised urban workers. Lord Derby quipped that the capitulation of the Conservative Party to the reform movement was 'a leap in the dark', born of necessity and hope. Carlyle published his apocalyptic article 'Shooting Niagara: And After?', in which he viewed the extension of the suffrage as a mad plunge into a maelstrom of devastation. What is ironic is that the bill was passed not by the Liberals, but by the Conservatives. Yet, as Asa Briggs has observed, it is more correct to speak of England in 1867 as being divided between optimists and pessimists.[87]

Needless to say, Stephen was a pessimist. He shared the view of many of his contemporaries that, once the lower classes were given the vote, politicians would pander to their tastes in exchange for votes. Government by wisdom and knowledge would give way to government by ignorance and mediocrity. Politics would fall victim to the demagogue. England was entering the age of organised parties dependent upon mass support. Upon this fact Walter Bagehot expressed the best Victorian thought in the Preface to the second edition of his classic work *The English Constitution* in 1872:

> In plain English, what I fear is that both our political parties will bid for the support of the workingman; that both of them will promise to do as he likes if he will only tell them what it is; that, as he now holds the casting-vote in our affairs, both parties will beg and pray him to give that vote to them. I can conceive of nothing more corrupting or worse for a set of poor ignorant people than that two combinations of well-taught and rich men should constantly offer to defer to their decision, and compete for the office of executing it. *Vox populi* will be *Vox diaboli* if it is worked in that manner.[88]

Stephen himself experienced this new popular politics in the 1870s, when his legal codification efforts, despite strong support from qualified sources, failed largely because the subject never became a popular concern. Hence neither party was interested in making codification a part of its platform. This is undoubtedly what Stephen meant when he said that under a democracy many worthy and necessary schemes would fall by the wayside.

The change in national politics towards the new liberalism was prophetically outlined in the *Pall Mall Gazette*. When Lord Palmerston died in October 1865, a eulogy appeared – it may have been written by Stephen – lamenting the former prime minister's death as marking the passing of an era. For Palmerston, with his urbane, detached and open-minded approach to politics, was the last of the great race of 'the politicians of the salon'. Replacing him was a new breed, those identified closely with specific popular causes, the sectarian 'politicians of a creed'. The future of the nation depended upon the answer to this question: 'Will the new school of narrower doctrine, more scrupulous conscience, more anxious temperament, accomplish as much for England or for freedom?'[89]

2 The State

I

In the course of the mid-1860s, during the debates over parliamentary reform, Stephen wrote a number of expository and critical articles for the *Saturday* which dealt with the works of great thinkers of the past on moral, religious and political subjects. These articles, ranging from Hooker and Hobbes to Burke and Paine, display his broad speculative interests and his characteristic common-sense. They were later collected and published as the three-volume *Horae Sabbaticae* (1892), which Stephen believed to comprise 'all the best things I ever wrote'.[1] Traversing ground familiar to many of his readers, the articles contain little that may be described as original. But one should not ask of Stephen what he did not intend to give. It is not easy to be original on speculative questions that have preoccupied the greatest minds for centuries. Nevertheless, no reader of Stephen's works can fail to be impressed by the power of his mind and the penetration of his judgements. Writing the articles entailed a great deal of reading on Stephen's part, and enabled him to rethink his own positions on important issues. He formulated many of the ideas which he would continue to ponder during his work in India and which form the basis of his attack on John Stuart Mill in *Liberty, Equality, Fraternity*.

Leslie Stephen faulted his brother for not considering the historical position of the books he discussed, and for neglecting to compare his own impressions with those of other nineteenth-century critics.[2] Most likely, Leslie would have preferred the method that he himself employed in his brilliant *History of English Thought in the Eighteenth Century* (1876), a masterpiece of intellectual history. But the merits of Fitzjames Stephen's articles lie in these supposed faults. He was concerned not with relating the views of men such as Hobbes and Burke to their eras, but with pointing out truths in their writings for his own time. Books are great because they speak to all ages, striking responsive chords in successive generations of readers. Besides, Stephen's neglect of the opinions of other modern critics bestowed upon his articles an engaging freshness. The reader of *Horae Sabbaticae* is taken on a tour, as it were, of the great books, with a penetrating intellect as his guide. In the process, Stephen clarifies many difficult points, and provides valuable insight on such questions as the nature of the State and political change. We shall see that, in addition to Bentham, Stephen's mentors were Thomas Hobbes and Edmund Burke. From Hobbes he learned the science of politics and the nature of sovereignty; from Burke he derived sound principles of political reform and a deep reverence for the English Constitution.

II

Soon after graduating from Cambridge in 1850, and while reading for the bar, Stephen was converted to the Utilitarianism of Jeremy Bentham. At that time Bentham was at the height of his reputation and, as Leslie Stephen attests, Fitzjames became 'a thorough Benthamite with certain modifications'.³ During the first half of the nineteenth century, Utilitarianism exercised a great influence upon the reform movement in England. Stephen adopted Bentham's famous principle of utility: the test of the morality of an action or the validity of an institution is its tendency to produce the greatest happiness of the greatest number. Armed with this principle, Bentham and his followers waged war against an outmoded political and social system. According to these liberal reformers institutions must be founded not upon abstract ideas or tradition, but upon social utility. While Utilitarianism supplied an important critical instrument for reform, Stephen agreed with John Stuart Mill that Bentham's philosophy must be supplemented by a broader understanding of human nature and society.⁴ Stephen therefore found it necessary to draw upon thinkers such as Hobbes and Burke for a comprehensive theory of the State.

The most profound influence upon Stephen's political and social thought was exerted by Thomas Hobbes. In fact, with due allowance for Stephen's liberalism, he might be characterised as a Hobbes of the nineteenth century. Hobbes's *Leviathan* (1651) is perhaps the greatest systematic treatment of politics in the English language. Nevertheless, he fell into disrepute in his own day. His support of the Monarchy against Parliament during the Civil War was naturally looked upon with disfavour by those who had espoused the cause of the triumphant Parliament. At the same time, the Royalists viewed Hobbes's rejection of divine-right kingship as atheism. Consequently, his work was eclipsed by John Locke's *Second Treatise on Civil Government*, written before the Glorious Revolution but not published until 1690. Locke quickly became the hero of the Whigs in their opposition to the Monarchy. Not until the late eighteenth and early nineteenth centuries were the liberal implications of Hobbes's thought sufficiently recognised. His writings were then revived by the Utilitarians. They saw, correctly, that his political philosophy could be used to support parliamentary government as well as absolute monarchy. Bentham's *Principles of Morals and Legislation* (1789), James Mill's *Essay on Government* (1820) and John Austin's famous lectures *The Province of Jurisprudence Determined* (1832) were dependent upon Hobbesian conceptions of law and sovereignty. And it was a Utilitarian, Sir William Molesworth, who undertook to edit Hobbes's complete works.[5]

Stephen maintained that Hobbes deserved to be ranked as the father of modern English philosophy, and of the Utilitarian school of which John Stuart Mill was the most prominent member. Stephen had the highest regard for the *Leviathan*, and often read it during his leisure hours while travelling on circuit. He believed it to be

> one of the ripest, the most complete, and the most perfectly well-written books of the sort in the whole range of literature. Hardly any *magnum opus* of the speculative kind has been so maturely weighed, so completely thought out, and so deliberately fashioned to express in every point the whole mind of its author.[6]

Stephen contended that, despite obvious merits, the works of Hobbes remained unpopular because their true character was misunderstood. He therefore undertook to make clear Hobbes's thought by recasting it in modern form.[7] Stephen singled out as Hobbes's greatest achievement his founding the science of politics upon a secular basis. Hobbes attempted to apply to the study of civil society the empirical method of natural science, which had undergone extraordinary progress during the late sixteenth and seventeenth centuries. He based the State not upon tradition or religion but upon utility: the only justification for the State is its capacity to keep order. Unlike the conventional natural law theorists, he distinguished between politics and ethics. Right and wrong, in the legal sense, are what the State permits and forbids. To confuse law and morals, therefore, leads to imprecise, sentimental and dangerous political and legal thinking. While Hobbes retained the notion of natural law in his thought, for him it denoted less a transcendent norm by which positive law may be judged than a set of general rules, dictates of reason, by which men may satisfy the basic need of self-preservation. Hobbes's political philosophy, as Stephen understood, constituted a shift from the traditional metaphysical conception of natural law as a system of eternal God-given laws toward a more secular conception rooted in human nature.

For a correct understanding of Stephen's thought it is necessary to recognise that he belongs to the tradition of thinkers, which includes Machiavelli and Hobbes, that separated the study of politics from morals. Not that Stephen believed morals to be unimportant; indeed, the principle of utility was a moral standard by which all actions and institutions were to be judged. He perceived that Bentham furnished the safeguard against abuses of power that might arise in the name of Hobbes. As one astute writer put it: 'The formula of the greatest happiness is made a hook to put in the nostrils of Leviathan, that he may be tamed and harnessed to the chariot of utility.'[8] Stephen agreed with Bentham that the role of the legislator is to promote the happiness of society. But he contended that the treatment of politics and law as sciences necessitated that they be mentally abstracted from ethics.

Hobbes deduces the State from a theory of human nature. Man is egoistic, moved only by the pursuit of pleasure and the avoidance of pain. Hobbes rejects Aristotle's view that man is by nature a social animal. Men enter civil society only because it provides the security requisite for the pursuit of self-interest. Man lives in a condition of perpetual striving. Hobbes's classic sentence deserves repeating: 'I put for a general inclination of all mankind, a perpetual and restless desire of power after power, that ceaseth only in death.'[9] As Stephen explains, the universal desire for power is 'only a name for this continual striving' for the satisfaction of personal ends.[10] Hobbes concludes that the power of every man is opposed to that of every other man. Human character being such, the state of nature – the condition prior to the institution of civil society – must be a 'war of every man against every man'. Consequently, there is no culture, no society, and the life of man so deprived is 'solitary, poor, nasty, brutish, and short'.[11]

According to Hobbes, in order to escape the precarious state of nature, the people are induced by the desire for self-preservation and the dictates of reason to vest all political power in the hands of a single person, or a group of persons, who thereby becomes the sovereign, 'that great Leviathan . . . that mortal god'.[12] By means of the social contract, men form a civil society and surrender their rights (except that of self-preservation) to the sovereign, who is appointed to act for them in their collective capacity. The State, then, originates in utility. The power of the sovereign is absolute, irrevocable and indivisible. Though the sovereign is created by the contract, he is not a party to it; he has no duty but to protect. The subjects enjoy no legal rights against the sovereign, for such rights cannot exist anterior to law, which is dependent upon his will. But he is under a moral obligation to preserve the social order and the safety of those under his rule. To disregard this duty is to court rebellion. Because of his attempt to separate politics from morals, Hobbes's political thought presents an interesting paradox. Since all law is dependent upon the sovereign, revolution is never legal. But, once a revolution succeeds, its very success makes the new government legitimate.

In the study of the State and society, as in the study of the law, Stephen advocated a combination of the historical and analytical methods. Largely because the materials for an historical study of the origin of the State were still unavailable in his day, Hobbes confined himself to the analytical method, applying it to arrive at clear and definite notions of law, liberty, right and sovereignty as they exist within the State. Stephen observed that the historical method dominated the current school of moral and political speculation. Although a champion of this prevailing tool, he insisted that the merits of the analytical method should not be underestimated, for 'the breath and the generality' of its conclusions 'were of the greatest value as a step in speculation'.[13]

Stephen knew that Hobbes's contract theory could not withstand historical investigation. Bentham's earliest work, *A Fragment on Government* (1776), and the writings of Hume had demolished it as a mere fiction. Yet Stephen contended that the contract theories of Hobbes, Locke and Rousseau, though historically unfounded, were useful as 'analogies and hypotheses'.[14] Stephen realised that these theorists were concerned with the logical deduction of the State, and not with tracing its historical development. He agreed with the conclusion reached by Sir Henry Maine in his *Ancient Law* (1861), that the notion of contract is a relatively late development in the history of Western civilisation. Stephen knew also that the contract theorists underrated the importance of tradition and habit in the formation of human institutions. Yet he believed that the real issue was not historical truth, but the grounds upon which the coercive power of the State may be justified. The prime concern of the liberal tradition has been to reconcile the rule of law with individual freedom. Translating Hobbes's contract into modern language, Stephen asserted that it contains a basic truth – the fact that without the State, without the rule of law, anarchy would prevail:

> If no one or more men had the power of issuing to others such commands as appeared reasonable to themselves, there would be no such thing as society amongst men. Everyone would be able to make whatever use he pleased of whatever faculties he possessed, and the only guide which he would have for the regulation of his conduct would be his own notions of what it was desirable for him to do. The existence of that kind of commands which we call laws is what stands between us and this state of things, which would be a state of general confusion. This appears to be the true interpretation of the well-known paradox that the state of nature is a state of war – a most inoffensive and perfectly true proposition which became offensive only by the way in which it was put.[15]

Stephen thought that Hobbes's conception of sovereignty, his 'great contribution to systematic politics',[16] shed light upon current political controversy: 'It would tend considerably to clear various matters connected with the question of the extension of the suffrage, if we bore in mind the fact that the question is one, not of liberty, but of the distribution of political power.'[17] This interpretation is important for an understanding of Stephen's later dispute with John Stuart Mill in *Liberty, Equality, Fraternity*. The degree of liberty in a State depends not upon the form of government, but upon the extent of the laws. As Hobbes correctly perceived, 'the distinction between monarchy and democracy lies, not in the amount of liberty which the subjects enjoy – which is an accidental matter dependent on the quantity of ground (so to speak) covered by the laws at a given time – but in distribution of power'.[18] Those who argue that an extension of the suffrage in England will enhance liberty are therefore mistaken. Democracy has no necessary correlation with liberty.

Further implications for the debate over parliamentary reform may be drawn from Hobbes's political thought. Reformers should bear in mind that the State depends ultimately upon restraint, in the form of law, for its survival. Individual rights should be protected, but they do not exist prior to or independent of the State. Liberty, which the reformers claim would be enhanced by increasing the franchise, is not an absolute. For Hobbes, as for Stephen, liberty is defined as the absence of restraint, or whatever the law permits. Liberty is therefore a negation. Stephen praises Hobbes for seeing 'clearly, what very few people see even now, that liberty is a negative idea, and that what is usually claimed under that name is not liberty, but dominion. That part of our life as to which the law issues no commands is the province of liberty.'[19]

Liberty, moreover, is dependent upon the rule of law. In the state of nature, not even the strong are secure. The degree of compulsion to which an individual is subject in this condition far exceeds that in the State. Law – that is, restraint – actually enhances liberty because it substitutes a definite and systematic compulsion in civil society for the arbitrary and indefinite compulsion of the state of nature. One of the foremost interpreters of Hobbes, Michael Oakeshott, has written that in Hobbes's political philosophy law implies liberty. He concludes that 'Hobbes, without being himself a liberal, had in him more of the philosophy of liberalism than most of its professed defenders.'[20] He was not an apologist for tyranny, but a rigorous supporter of the autonomous individual.

Stephen's negative conception of liberty is entirely consistent with classical liberal theory. Not only Hobbes, but also Locke and the early Utilitarians, understood liberty to be dependent upon the rule of law. As Locke wrote, 'Wherever law ends, tyranny begins.' As far back as Magna Carta, English common law conceived of liberty as the right of all men to due process. Stephen was also in accord with classical liberalism in holding that liberty and equality are contradictory. This belief would play an important role in *Liberty, Equality, Fraternity*, in which he undertook to refute the new school of egalitarian liberalism that became prominent in the latter part of the Victorian era. In the common law, liberty and property were regarded as virtually synonymous; Coke closely linked them in his famous *Institutes* (1628–44). And what is property but a source of inequality? Locke maintained that government is instituted to protect property – broadly conceived to include life, liberty and material possessions. As Stephen saw it, liberty leads inevitably to inequality. Liberalism values individualism and liberty promotes differences among men, while equality tends to reduce men to a common norm:

> Liberalism is in many respects an aristocratic creed, inasmuch as the essence of it is to produce a condition of things in which the energies of every individual will have the fullest scope, and produce the most permanent results. The vigorous man will, under this system get a maximum of advantage from his superior strength, and will transmit to his descendants the advantages which he has acquired. The apparent tendency of unrestricted free-trade and unlimited competition is to throw wealth and everything that depends upon and is derived from it, into comparatively few hands. What the average man likes is an artificial system which provides as large a number of persons as possible with a reasonable level of comfort.[21]

Despite his great admiration for Hobbes, Stephen was not an uncritical disciple. As a liberal, he found fault with Hobbes's thought regarding political reform. Political and social order being for Hobbes the end of the State, he failed to provide sufficiently for change. Consequently, said Stephen, his work is a study of 'political statics', which unfortunately neglects the 'dynamics of government'.[22] Stephen's conception of liberalism, seeking to harmonise culture and democracy, saw the necessity of both order and reform. He speculated that it was horror of the English Civil War which led Hobbes to view changes in government as sinister:

> There are few more curious instances in literary history of the prodigious effect of contemporary events and personal prejudices, even on the most powerful mind, than the effect which the civil wars produced on Hobbes, and the horror which he felt of disturbance and danger, as the greatest of all evils.[23]

To ensure political stability, Stephen said, sovereign power must reside either in one man or in one group of men. For, if there exist in any State more than one man or body claiming legislative power, the body politic is in the condition of 'dormant anarchy', which will eventually break out into the open kind.[24] Stephen was careful to distinguish between *de jure* and *de facto* sovereignty, between sovereignty in a purely legal sense and sovereignty as a historical fact. Not only Hobbes, but also the early Utilitarians, tended to neglect the influence of history. But Stephen's study of the past confirmed for him that sovereignty was ultimately a question of fact: 'He is sovereign who actually is supreme, and by whose consent the laws actually are enforced; not he whom some one or other, at some time or other, has agreed to consider supreme.'[25]

Stephen believed that Hobbes erred in failing to perceive that his doctrine of sovereignty was merely an ideal type:

> The propositions which it states are propositions which are suggested to the imagination by facts, though no facts completely embody and exemplify them. As there is in nature no such thing as a perfect circle . . . or a state of society in which men act simply with a view to gain, so there is in nature no such thing as an absolute sovereign in Hobbes's sense of the word.[26]

Yet Stephen insisted that this does not imply that the doctrine of sovereignty is false:

> As the non-existence of the set of things first mentioned does not prevent both mathematics and political economy from being sciences of the greatest importance in everyday life, so the fact that sovereignty never is absolute in fact does not diminish the value of Hobbes's speculations.[27]

Stephen, then, believed that Hobbes's abstract theory was subject to correction and qualification when measured against existing facts. He also noted that Hobbes failed to make the necessary distinction between society and government.[28] As a liberal, Stephen saw the importance of separating the State from society, in order to limit the former's power. He therefore emphasised the social part of man's nature. Society would, he contended, exist independently of government. Life might be less pleasant, but its principal affairs would continue. Hobbes, he submitted, had an imperfect understanding of human nature. The social motives are sufficiently strong to insure that, in most cases, contracts would be honoured, and individuals would refrain from injuring one another. Thus society depends not merely upon legal sanctions – for the law restricts man in but a small portion of his behaviour – but also upon common social values: 'Society is the work of law in some proportion, but in a much greater proportion it is the work of very different agents – love of companionship, curiosity, the desire of all sorts of advantages which are to be derived from mutual assistance founded on mutual good will.'[29] What Stephen neglected to point out is that Hobbes's identification of society and the State goes a long way towards explaining his inordinate fear of anarchy. Had he made a distinction between them, he would have recognised that a change of government is not tantamount to the dissolution of society.

The question of sovereignty was for Stephen the overriding issue in politics, one that cannot go unresolved in any State for long. For ultimate power must reside somewhere; compromises only postpone the final resolution. Taking his cue from Hobbes, Stephen insisted that sovereignty is indivisible. The English Constitution, he observed, is in theory mixed, or based on a balance of power. But English history refutes this theory. Though a balance has existed theoretically, in fact ultimate power has resided in either the King or Parliament at various periods of English history. He pointed to the example of the American Constitution. In the United States, the question of sovereignty was postponed, and power was shared among the individual states and the Federal Government. This gave rise to a condition of dormant anarchy, which persisted until the issue of ultimate power was temporarily resolved by the Civil War.[30] Stephen maintained that, because of the current agitation for parliamentary reform, a condition of potential anarchy existed in England. One detects an ominous tone in his words:

> The divergence between the state of facts which exists among us at the present day, and the abstract notion of a State, is probably greater than it ever was before in any great country, and it is possible that it may one day have to be considerably reduced, by methods, which may not be pleasant to our feelings, or flattering to our national vanity.[31]

Unlike Hobbes, Stephen did not view anarchy as an unmitigated evil. 'Anarchy, properly speaking, is not only not necessarily a bad thing, but it may be very good; for anarchy is only the absence of restraint – in other words, it is another name for liberty.'³² Committed to the liberal principle of progressive reform, Stephen saw anarchy, in the sense of conditions of uncertain sovereignty, as inevitable. It might indeed be useful in solving the question of sovereignty. Practically speaking, compromise among the various powers within a State is often necessary. The United States, for instance, could not have been founded had the issue of states' rights not been postponed. Likewise, England was ruled benevolently despite the fact that until the late seventeenth century it was the scene of a struggle between the Monarchy and Parliament. Stephen accepted changes in the English Constitution as the inevitable product of social progress; he did not share Hobbes's inordinate fear of the disruption that invariably attends such changes. Yet he knew that the English had but two alternatives with regard to parliamentary reform – either a democracy wedded to culture and enlightenment, or a democracy subject to the tastes of the masses. That his countrymen might choose the wrong path was a matter of concern.

One of Hobbes's gravest mistakes was his incorrect understanding of the extent of the State's power. Stephen agreed with him that in a legal sense the power of the sovereign is unlimited; but there are certain natural checks which Hobbes underestimated.

> Being a man, or a body of men, the sovereign is always more or less ignorant, weak, and irresolute. He may be deceived, or avoided, or dissuaded from his purpose. Hence his threats are always more or less uncertain. There is always a great chance of impunity, and this diminishes their effect to an incalculable degree. In the last resort, he may even be successfully resisted by open force or by passive disobedience, and this again puts a limit to his power, not the less because it is tacit, and because its extent cannot be precisely ascertained.³³

Moreover, Hobbes overlooked the fact that the sovereign cannot alter human nature. The ruler cannot make beneficial what is injurious to man. No amount of coercion can induce people to regard bad laws as good, or prevent them from judging that a condition of anarchy is preferable to submitting to them. Thus Stephen believed that the power of the State is always balanced by the threat of popular rebellion or revolution.

III

Like the classical liberals, Stephen knew of the love men have for power, and the need therefore to limit carefully the sphere of government. The restrictions that he wished to place upon the power of the State are best illustrated by his role in the celebrated Governor Eyre case.[34] Edward John Eyre had been appointed Governor of Jamaica in 1864. Throughout the first part of the nineteenth century, the West Indies had been suffering economic decline. Its sugar economy received serious competition from Cuba and Brazil, and the islands had been beset with labour problems since the emancipation of the slaves in 1833. In Jamaica, the largest island of the British West Indies, the economic wane produced political unrest. In the early 1860s, George Gordon, a mulatto member of the Jamaican legislature and a political enemy of Eyre, led a number of blacks in agitating against the Government for higher wages and improved working conditions. In October 1865, at Morant Bay, a riot was started by some of Gordon's followers, and several white residents were killed. Governor Eyre responded by declaring martial law and dispatching troops to quell the rebellion. The outcome was that nearly a hundred blacks were summarily shot without a trial, and over 300 were executed after court-martial. Gordon, though he had taken no part in the rebellion, was tried and hanged.

The incident aroused a storm of protest in England. Eyre's conduct was vigorously and eloquently debated in Parliament, and the press divided over the question of whether he had exceeded his authority. A Royal Commission was appointed, and in April 1866 it reported that, though Eyre was right in putting down the disruption, his actions had been excessive. He was subsequently recalled to England.

Late in 1865, the critics of Eyre formed a Jamaica Committee, with John Stuart Mill as chairman, to campaign for the prosecution of the Governor. For three arduous years the Committee attempted without success to bring Eyre to trial for murder. England's intellectual community was sharply split on the issue. The Jamaica Committee had the support of Darwin, Bright, Frederic Harrison, Spencer and T. H. Huxley. At the same time, there was an Eyre Defence Committee, which included Carlyle, Ruskin, Tennyson, Dickens and Charles Kingsley. Those who defended Eyre maintained that the preservation of the British Empire depended upon a firm rule. The matter was complicated by the fact that during this time England was also the scene of agitation for parliamentary reform. In July 1866, while the Jamaica Committee was engaged in advocating Eyre's prosecution, the working classes were storming the railings of Hyde Park. The two movements quickly became identified. Middle-class radicals, members of the working classes and Evangelical organisations sided with the Committee. On the other hand, many of the propertied middle and upper classes, fearing that a wave of democracy would endanger existing institutions at home and subvert the Empire, tended to sympathise with Eyre. Public opinion was split, passions were aroused, and friendships were strained.

Fitzjames Stephen was appointed to serve as barrister for the Jamaica Committee. His correspondence reveals that he believed that, in executing Gordon, Eyre had unjustly exercised his authority. Though he sympathised with the Governor, he insisted that 'he has been in this matter, violent, tyrannical, and imprudent to a degree which I hardly imagined to be possible, if I had not seen it'.[35] Early in 1866, Stephen drew up the opinion of the Jamaica Committee, charging that Eyre had abused his authority and was guilty of murder. In January 1867, Stephen made an application on behalf of the Committee before the magistrates at the Bow Street Police Court to commit for trial the officers responsible for the court-martial. He eloquently argued before the court that the issue was whether the British Empire was to be ruled by law or by arbitrary despotism. For Stephen, justice required that no one should be above the law. The case was eventually thrown out by the grand jury. In March, Stephen made a similar application, this time regarding Eyre, to the magistrates of the Market Drayton Petty Sessional Division in Shropshire. He argued that martial law is justifiable only as a means to restore civil order, and that, once stability is established, the exercise of force is no longer warranted. Here again, the case was dismissed when the magistrates decided that the evidence presented did not establish a probable assumption of guilt. After these two failures, Stephen reluctantly recommended, to Mill's disappointment, that the Jamaica Committee drop the case. He reasoned that it would be fruitless to pursue the matter further, and that if it did the Committee would run the risk of appearing to engage in a vindictive persecution of the Governor. As far as Stephen was concerned, the matter was over, and he quickly extricated himself from the case.

The Committee persisted in its efforts until ultimate failure in 1868.

IV

Agreeing with Hobbes that the State is based upon utility rather than natural rights, Stephen was necessarily opposed to the political philosophy expressed in Locke's *Second Treatise on Civil Government*. Stephen perceived that Locke's politics was inconsistent with his metaphysics.[36] As an empiricist, Locke rejected the notion of innate ideas on the basis that all knowledge is the product of experience. Yet he founded his political thought upon such *a priori* conceptions as natural law and natural rights. His work, Stephen declared, is 'an illustration of the great truth, that the founders of a powerful school seldom draw the inferences which naturally flow from their principles'.[37]

Stephen pointed out the danger of allowing *a priori* general principles to overrun political philosophy. He might very well have had in mind Coleridge's dictum that only fiends or angels could regulate their lives in accord with abstract reason. Unverifiable notions such as natural rights had often been employed to justify the wholesale adjustment of society in accord with fixed formulas. Stephen expressed the utmost contempt for radicals such as Thomas Paine who refused to show respect for the English Constitution. 'He is, and always will be Tom – the wretched, uneducated plebeian who dared to attack Church and State.'[38] It was, Stephen alleged, abstract ideas like those of Paine about the universality and absoluteness of liberty and equality that led to the excesses of the French Revolution. Stephen had learned from Mill the peril of attempting to found the State upon unverifiable general principles. 'There is, indeed, no branch of speculation in which Mr. Mill's observation on the syllogism is more to the point than in politics.'[39] Stephen believed that the failure to heed the lessons of Mill's *System of Logic* vitiated much of the political speculation of the day. In a striking passage in his *Autobiography*, Mill wrote that truths independent of experience served as 'the great support of false doctrines and bad institutions'.[40] For the belief in innate ideas enables those who employ them to dispense with the obligation of justifying their beliefs according to the rigorous canons of reason.

What made abstract ideas even more sinister was that they could also be employed to support dangerous reactionism. In the seventeenth century, Bossuet had invoked revealed truth to support the absolutism of Louis XIV. Indeed, his vigorous attack upon Protestant claims for the independence for human reason in religious matters paved the way for the revocation of the Edict of Nantes. 'Intolerance,' Stephen declares, 'civil as well as ecclesiastical, is the cornerstone of Bossuet's system.'[41] In the wake of the French Revolution there arose in France a reactionary movement, in support of monarchy, Church and nobility, led by Joseph de Maistre. Basing his politics on what Stephen thought were unverifiable generalities, de Maistre contended that constitutions were the work not of men, but of God; man could never write a constitution. Moreover, de Maistre maintained that the State derived its sovereignty only from God, the author of all laws. As a Utilitarian who espoused the Hobbesian conceptions of law and sovereignty, Stephen believed that Maistre's works were riddled with sophistry.[42] Though opposed to the natural-rights-of-man theory of Paine, Rousseau and the French Jacobins, as contributing to the excesses of the French Revolution, Stephen never denied the necessity of that revolution. Accordingly, he confessed his preference for the general principles of the radicals to those of the reactionaries:

> If we wish to do justice to the revolutionists of the last century, we must remember that their declarations of the Rights of Man and other dithyrambs were levelled not against calm Benthamite philosophers, or English constitutional lawyers nourished on the Bill of Rights and the Habeas Corpus Act, but against gross tyrannies which had been in the memory of living men as fierce and cruel as became their principles. First principles of all kinds are bad things, but we infinitely prefer the Rights of Man to the doctrines of de Maistre and Bonald, or even to [Bossuet's] *Politique tiree de l'Ecriture Sainte*.[43]

V

Stephen also drew some important lessons from Edmund Burke. Because he supported the English and American revolutions while opposing the French, Burke has often been charged with inconsistency. But Stephen saw correctly that the great British statesman had remained faithful to his principles. As John Morley later said, Burke changed his front, but he never changed his ground.**44** Stephen shared both Burke's profound reverence for the English Constitution, and his belief that government should be adjusted to human needs rather than to metaphysical principles. Like Burke, he also held that a government should exhibit both a willingness to reform and a disposition to preserve. As early as 1858, in an article for the *Saturday Review*, Stephen lauded the statesman for having laid the foundations of 'modern Liberal Conservatism', and for protesting against government according to abstract theory 'long before the French Revolution inoculated the world with a spurious and morbid Liberalism'.**45**

Stephen believed that his countrymen had much to learn from Burke. Parliamentary reform, like all other, ought to proceed in conformity with his touchstones of prudence, prescription and utility. To Stephen, Burke's method was essentially Utilitarian: 'Expediency is thus the basis of all his speculation, and the first rule of expediency is to set off from existing facts, and to take all measures whatever with respect to them.'**46** Stephen viewed any departure from this empirical foundation as dangerous. He thus belongs to the nineteenth-century tradition of liberal interpreters – which included Buckle, Morley, Lecky and Leslie Stephen – who regarded Burke as a forerunner of modern English Utilitarianism.

But Stephen, with his usual sagacity, perceived the conflict in Burke's thought. While his method is empirical, Burke shared with Locke a reliance upon *a priori* ideas such as natural law. Stephen therefore accused Burke of starting unwittingly from the same sentimental basis as the revolutionaries he condemned.**47** Unlike Hobbes and Bentham, Burke proceeded from conceptions of antecedent justice and rights, independent of and prior to the State, and thereby had more in common with his opponents than he would have us believe:

> No one ever wrote more earnestly, strange as it may appear, about the rights of man. The question between him and the Jacobins was not whether men had natural rights, but whether they had the rights which were claimed by the Revolutionists, and especially the right of cashiering governments, and altering the whole existing distinctions of property and authority at the will of the majority.**48**

Stephen concluded that 'Hobbes and Bentham are in principle further from Burke than Rousseau or Voltaire . . . . '**49**

Some scholars have attempted to demonstrate that there is no conflict in Burke's thought, that he was not a Utilitarian, but a natural-law theorist who attempted to distinguish between false or revolutionary natural rights and valid natural rights in the traditional sense of natural law. Thus one must not misconstrue Burke's repudiation of eighteenth-century natural rights as a rejection of the entire natural-law tradition.[50] In any case, the effect of Stephen's argument is that, even if Burke's thought is internally consistent, natural law is an improper basis for politics.

Stephen believed that a strong point of Burke's political thought was his recognition of the true nature of sovereignty. For Burke clearly perceived that constitutional questions are questions not of law, but of power:

> Legal questions are those which can be decided by a common superior according to a fixed rule, but the question whether such and such functions belong to the Crown, to the House of Lords, or to the House of Commons, cannot possibly be decided by reference to a common superior. If neither party will give way, they can be decided only by an appeal to force, by a *coup d'état* in one shape or another – the deposition, it may be the execution of a King, or the turning of the Parliament out of doors by an armed force.[51]

Stephen applauded Burke's defence of the American Revolution, observing that 'when we read his arguments the wonder is how anyone could ever be so insane as to doubt their soundness'.[52] In eloquent statements, such as the *Speech on American Taxation* (1774) and the *Speech on Conciliation with America* (1775), Burke appealed to utility and prescription. Eschewing subtle philosophical distinctions and abstract theories of sovereignty, he contended that the dispute between Britain and its colonies over taxation should be settled according to the dictates of expediency and mutual advantage. In advocating conciliation with America, Burke was in direct conflict with the designs of George III and his prime minister, Lord North. He was, in fact, instrumental in forging the Rockingham Whigs into an effective parliamentary opposition to the Monarchy. Stephen noted that it was Burke who saw party government as implicit in parliamentary rule, for politicians can best implement their goals by uniting with those among them who share their views.[53]

Though Stephen shared Burke's solicitude for the English Constitution, he believed that, like Hobbes, Burke failed to provide sufficiently for political change. Stephen speculated that Burke's fear of the French Revolution and his detestation of abstract rights precluded his having 'a broad and open view of expediency' and 'prevented him from encouraging the development of what was contained in old and accepted principles'.[54] Burke's failure was that, though he began with a sound theory for conducting politics, he became too attached to a particular set of institutions. Stephen subscribed to the Utilitarian belief that all institutions are relative, dependent upon and reflecting ever-changing social conditions:

> Constitutions are made for empires and nations, empires and nations are not made for constitutions; and as the social constitution of Great Britain, and of the various members of the British Empire changed, it was absolutely essential that the Constitution, both of the Empire and the nation, should change also.[55]

The English Constitution had been considerably altered since the eighteenth century, when 'that noiseless revolution which has made the House of Commons the only real depository of all political power had not taken place and could scarcely be anticipated'. Since that time 'the Constitution has grown into a shape which Burke's theory cannot be made to fit'.[56] Stephen illustrated that Blackstone's discussion of the separation of executive and legislative powers did not reflect the Constitution. He referred to 'a very luminous writer', obviously Walter Bagehot, who had pointed out that during the nineteenth century there had been a virtual fusion of the executive and legislative powers through the Cabinet. Stephen also observed that Parliament, especially the Commons, had greatly exceeded the merely deliberative function which it exercised in Burke's day, and that Cabinet government had grown to a dimension unforeseeable to a politician of the eighteenth century. Burke had simply misunderstood the nature and durability of the British Constitution. For politicians, Stephen added, no longer idealise it to the extent of considering it unalterable. 'If we had had several generations of statesmen passionately intent upon keeping up a proper balance between the three elements of the Constitution, where should we all have been at the present moment?'[57] Stephen acclaimed the emergence of popular sovereignty in England during the nineteenth century as a fact which Burke would have to accept as consistent with his political principles:

> If Burke was right (as no doubt he was) as to the importance of prescription and passion, the respect due to existing facts, and the flimsiness of some of the metaphysical theories which he so much detested, still, on the other hand, the fact – for it is a fact – of the sovereignty of the people in the broadest sense of the words, has been established in this country by the general course of events, in a manner which is altogether unquestionable and conclusive. Nor can the struggles which led to its recognition, both in France and England, be denied to have been justified by the result, awful as they undoubtedly were in some of their details.[58]

Burke's view of representation was also deficient. He saw nothing wrong with the fact that during the eighteenth century many areas of England were under-represented in Parliament. As a product of the great age of liberal reform, and a supporter of the Reform Act of 1832, Stephen demurred: 'No reasonable politician of to-day would dream of denying . . . that it is in so far an evil to any borough to be without its own representative, and to any individual to be without his fragment of political power.'[59] Consequently, 'the more reasonable opponents of Reform in the present day can scarcely count Burke as an ally, or an authority on their side. He goes too far, or, we should perhaps say, he stays too far behind.'[60] Stephen contended, moreover, that Burke failed to see that a restricted House of Commons actually hindered good government. Burke's extreme veneration of the Constitution led him to fail to appreciate what Stephen believed was 'an obvious commonplace – namely, that the wider the base of representation within certain limits, the more likely it is that the public business will be well done'.[61] Accepting an extension of the suffrage as inevitable, Stephen concluded that 'the contest of modern politics turns upon what these limits are, whether any wise extension of them, is possible now, and in what direction an extension might be most advantageously made'.[62] Of one thing he was certain: only by granting the vote to those fit to have it could parliamentary reform be reconciled with culture.

VI

The differences between Burke and Stephen may be illustrated by comparing their attitudes towards the French Revolution. Its outbreak in 1789 horrified Burke, inducing him to set down in elaborate form his political thought in the famous *Reflections on the Revolution in France* (1790). Proceeding from his reverence for constituted society and the principles of expediency and prescription, he embarked upon a passionate condemnation of the Revolution, its theory of natural rights, and its sweeping schemes to alter the State and society in accordance with general principles. The work was an eloquent defence of the French monarchy, the Church and the nobility.

Though Stephen feared and detested the abstract theory of rights which it fostered, he believed that the French Revolution was necessary, inevitable and justified. Burke had contended that the Revolution was unnecessary, since the constitution was repairable, and compromise possible. Instead of building upon old and tested foundations, the French chose to destroy all and build anew. Stephen argued that Burke failed to understand the political and social condition of France on the eve of the Revolution. For the nation had already passed the point of no return, making a revolution unavoidable and peaceful change no longer feasible. Had it been possible to reform the Old Regime by peaceful measures, the French would probably have done so, since 'no one pulls down his house when it is obvious that nothing is required beyond ordinary repairs'.[63] In the final analysis, Burke misinterpreted French history by imposing upon it an English standard of gradual reform: 'To have got a British Constitution out of the Revolution, the history of France ought to have been the history of England.'[64]

For a correct understanding of the French Revolution, Stephen suggested that we supplement Burke's *Reflections* by Alexis de Tocqueville's celebrated work *The Old Regime and the French Revolution* (1856). This study of pre-revolutionary France is still regarded highly today, though some of its judgements have been refuted or qualified by subsequent research. Stephen thought that Tocqueville was the first to study the Old Regime with a view to interpreting the Revolution. He contended that Tocqueville's shrewd perception of the situation in France served to confirm, amplify and correct a number of Burke's conclusions. For Burke never really answered the question of why France had a revolution.

Instead, he merely insisted that it was unnecessary. Though Burke failed to explain the Revolution satisfactorily, Stephen believed that he still deserved praise as 'the ablest and most experienced political writer of his day'.[65] Moreover, his failure stemmed from the inadequate state of political knowledge in his time rather than from want of mental power.

Stephen proceeded to show that the work of Tocqueville explains facts which Burke merely observed. Burke correctly saw that France during the Old Regime was growing in prosperity and population. From this, he inferred that a revolution could have been averted. Tocqueville, on the contrary, concluded that the improving conditions in France led to rising expectations among the people which the Government was unable to satisfy, thereby making a revolution unavoidable. The old system of society and government was increasingly regarded as unjust and oppressive. Belated attempts at reform, culminating with the summoning of the Estates General in 1789, had the paradoxical effect of destroying rather than repairing the existing political structure. Grievances quietly tolerated for years suddenly become unbearable once the people realise that they are capable of redress. Stephen cited Tocqueville's well-known observation that 'experience shows that the most dangerous moment for a bad government is generally that when it begins to reform. . . . Evils which were suffered patiently as being inevitable, appear insupportable if the notion of being rid of them is conceived.'[66]

A significant contribution of Tocqueville's work was his demonstration that administrative centralisation began in France not with the Revolution, or with Napoleon, but as early as the age of Louis XIV. Stephen adverted to the fact that his father's *Lectures on the History of France*, written while he was Regius Professor of Modern History at Cambridge, reached the same conclusion, though Tocqueville's work benefited from a great deal more research in the primary sources. Fitzjames agreed that the strongly centralised administrative system in France helped to explain the success of Napoleon's despotic political system. After the failure of the Revolution, Napoleon inherited a ready-made bureaucracy: 'Men cannot make bricks without straw, and M. de Tocqueville's book shows that there was nothing vigorous left in France except the central administration.'[67]

VII

Stephen was also concerned with the important question of the relation between the State and religion. He viewed the Enlightenment and the French Revolution as a turning point in European history, which originated a secularism that threatened to dissolve the moral fabric of society. Before the revolution it was more or less assumed that Christianity was true, and that religion and morals ought to influence directly law and government. But the eighteenth century fostered the belief, encouraged by such men as Bentham and Voltaire,[68] that religion was false and that the State could be founded upon the basis of utility alone:

> The theories, which we so often hear described collectively as the principles of 1789, amount in a few words to the assertion that men can and do associate, and in France among other places actually have associated together for the purpose of conferring upon each other the elementary benefits of society – including all that is meant by the protection of person and property, at least, and tending, as every one can see, to include a great deal more – on the simple principle that they find such an association highly advantageous with a view to this present life alone, and independently of the question whether or not there is any other.[69]

The idea of a secular society left Stephen uneasy. He doubted whether such a society could sustain itself:

> Law proper will be founded upon simple temporal prudence, and government will have a growing tendency to become a mere affair of police, and to be separated from all moral control over the minds of men. Morals and religion, on the other hand, will suffer greatly, though in different ways. Morals will tend to become a mere sentiment or a mere speculation; and religion will tend to be merged in superstition.[70]

Stephen thus found that the religious liberalism which he supported and furthered sometimes bore bitter fruit. But he rejected categorically the idea that religion, if shown to be false, should nevertheless be retained simply because it is useful for social control:

> The question of the truth of a religion is at least as important as that of its utility, for truth is the highest form of utility, and grapes will grow on thorns, and figs on thistles, before all human life can be founded on a lie. . . . The question what is the truth, as far as we can grasp it, about God and the soul, is at least as important, as practical a question for every man as the question what is the nature of Democracy.[71]

Throughout his life, Stephen was increasingly engaged in exploring the relation of society to religion, morality and law. He recognised that such a task demanded great courage:

> Whatever the final result may be, it can hardly admit of a doubt, that none of those who have handled them [the ultimate questions] were so hopelessly wrong, as the writers and statesmen who thought that, because the discussion would be terribly dangerous, it either could or ought to be permanently avoided.[72]

As the articles on religion which he contributed to *Fraser's Magazine* testify, Stephen pursued the discussion unstintingly.

3 The Politics of Literature

I

Since Fitzjames Stephen identified the reconciliation of democracy with culture as the principal task of his age, he sought to combat what he regarded as a serious obstacle to its fulfilment. Early in the nineteenth century the English writer was liberated from the restraints of aristocratic patronage only to find himself subject to a new master – public opinion. Because the populace was largely undereducated, the writer was confronted with a dilemma: should he curry favour by appealing to the sentiments of the multitude, or should he attempt to elevate his audience to higher standards even at the risk of falling into disrepute? Stephen was concerned because many contemporary novelists had chosen the easy road to public acceptance. He knew that imagination and sentiment exercise a great influence upon popular opinion; but he deplored the fact that in his day important political and social issues were increasingly considered on the basis of emotion rather than of reason and utility. Stephen therefore assailed popular novelists for fostering a sentimental view of life and politics, inconsistent with true liberalism and culture. He did not wish to eliminate sentiment altogether, but he insisted that to be beneficial it must be regulated. He feared that, as a result of much current teaching, the newly-enfranchised classes would unjustifiably lose respect for England's most important institutions, and regard the vote as an instrument of vengeance upon their governors rather than as a sacred trust.

The Victorian age was the great period of the English novel. The tremendous growth in the reading public gave rise to the cheap press, the railway bookstall, the three-volume novel and the circulating library. Stephen acknowledged that fiction played a large part in the education of the young and inexperienced, for it is in novels that 'the springs of human actions are laid bare, and the laws of human society' are made known. Unfortunately, many novelists addressed themselves 'almost entirely to the imagination upon subjects which properly belong to the intellect', encouraging 'hasty generalizations and false conclusions' about life and society.[1] What Stephen resented most was the apotheosis of the working man in much of the popular literature of the day. The labouring classes had attracted a number of preachers who, taking full advantage of the ignorance of their audience, catered to public prejudices and encouraged dangerous sophistries. The 1840s and 1850s saw a number of propaganda novels (Stephen termed them 'party pamphlets')[2] – those of Benjamin Disraeli, Elizabeth Gaskell, Charles Kingsley and Charles Reade – that sought to answer the so-called 'Condition of England Question'. In a famous passage in *Sybil* (1845), Disraeli proclaimed that England was divided into 'two nations': the rich and the poor.

Stephen thought that the dangers of sentimental thinking were best exemplified in the novels of Charles Dickens, the most famous novelist of the age. Accordingly, he launched an attack upon Dickens and emerged as one of his most trenchant critics. The two principal articles which Stephen wrote were 'The License of Modern Novelists', for the *Edinburgh Review* in 1857;[3] and 'Mr. Dickens as a Politician', written the same year for the *Saturday Review*. Those who regard novels purely as works of art are likely to conclude that Stephen exaggerated the potential political effects of Dickens's novels and underestimated his genius. We find in Stephen's reviews little appreciation of Dickens's extraordinary gift of characterisation, his sparkling narrative, or his sense of humanity. Indeed, one writer has observed that Stephen's attack on Dickens 'reads like the indictment of a man guilty of sedition'.[4] But we must remember the perspective from which Stephen wrote: he was concerned mainly with the difficulty of reconciling democracy and culture at a time when the vast majority were poorly educated. We must also bear in mind that Stephen's intellectual background predisposed him to look unfavourably upon the novel. He never entirely relinquished the Evangelical distrust of imaginative literature, the fear that it might inordinately excite the passions and divert the faithful from doing the work of God. He also shared the Utilitarian preference for useful knowledge, and their conviction that one should not indulge in idle reading, but must always undertake it with some practical end in view.[5]

There was a more fundamental reason why Stephen opposed the increasing weight given to sentiment in his day. As a

Utilitarian, he believed that sentimentality was inconsistent with the solid bedrock of experience which should be the basis of politics. We have seen that John Stuart Mill's *System of Logic* taught Stephen that intuitionism was a fallacious and dangerous foundation for thought. Mill and the early Utilitarians considered sentimental all attempts to erect the State on abstract, *a priori* principles instead of on the empirical basis of utility. Mill pointed out that the Utilitarians found that virtually all their doctrines were attacked not on the grounds of experience, but by appeals to feeling alone:

> Utility was denounced as cold calculation; political economy as hard-hearted; anti-population doctrines as repulsive to the natural feelings of mankind. We retorted by the word 'sentimentality', which, along with 'declamation' and 'vague generalities', served us as common terms of opprobrium.[6]

II

Stephen's literary criticism assumed a close relation between literature and society. He was a staunch proponent of the realist conception of the novel. As early as 1855, he published a piece in *Cambridge Essays* called 'The Relation of Novels to Life', a remarkable and precocious effort which displays a great familiarity with English fiction.[7] Stephen maintained that the novel must portray life as accurately as possible. His greatest respect was reserved for eighteenth-century authors such as Defoe, Fielding and Swift. He made no mention of the 'sentimental' novelists of that time – Richardson, Sterne and Rousseau – but we can infer his disapproval. Stephen's ideal novel was *Robinson Crusoe*, unsurpassed, he thought, in its realism and in the correct handling of tender feeling.[8] In contrast, most of the English novels of his own century bore little relation to human experience and contributed little knowledge of the world. The suppression of all that is prosaic in order to sustain interest, the elaborately contrived plots to attain a dramatic effect, the undue prominence given to matters of love and marriage and the simplistic portrayal of character gave an inaccurate picture of life.

Few people today would consider Charles Dickens a radical. George Orwell correctly observed that he was essentially a moral critic who intended not the total reconstruction of society, but the adoption of needed but limited reforms.[9] In fact, most of the novels published in the Victorian age were pervaded by assumptions that were far from radical. Stephen never denied the abuses which Dickens attacked, but he feared that by exaggerating them Dickens exercised 'a very wide and pernicious political and social influence'.[10] Stephen carefully distinguished between the intentions of a novelist and the unforeseen consequences of his works. He lamented that, because the vast majority of Dickens's readers were 'intellectually weak' and 'incapable of sustained and systematic thought or inquiry', they were incapable of separating his caricatures from actual life.[11] Dickens exaggerated the evil aspects of English society while omitting much of the good. If only Dickens and his followers would look to 'broad general results', they would recognise that 'whatever defects exist in the administration of public affairs their general condition proves that much capacity and honesty is employed upon them'.[12] That Dickens and other popular novelists foster among their audience a false impression of English society and an unwarranted discontent with its institutions 'cannot but be a serious evil, and must often involve great moral delinquency'.[13]

The idea of subjecting the works of novelists such as Dickens to government censorship was unconscionable to Stephen. He cherished civil liberty too much to suggest such a drastic recourse. Yet he believed that, since these novels 'show strong sympathies for all that is most opposite to the very foundations of English life',[14] they should be subjected to responsible literary criticism.[15] The difficulty, as Stephen saw it, was that the novelist exercises a great political influence without correlative responsibility. When challenged on his rendition of the facts, he takes refuge in his art. Dickens 'exercises considerable political influence with hardly any political convictions. He introduces the gravest subjects in a manner which makes it impossible that he should do them justice. He scatters fire, and says, Am I not in sport?'[16]

Dickens used his novels to attack a variety of English institutions and their abuses. Imprisonment for debt was denounced in *Pickwick*, the Poor Law in *Oliver Twist*, the Court of Chancery in *Bleak House*, Utilitarianism in *Hard Times* and the entire administrative system in *Little Dorrit*. Virtually all of his novels attack some aspect of English society. Yet Stephen contends that Dickens epitomises the 'new school of politicians' that is interested in reform for its own sake:

In almost every department of public life, the task of obtaining results has been to a great extent superseded by that of inventing machinery. The world, we are all agreed, is out of joint, and it is touching to see how many doctors are anxious to reduce the dislocation. In politics, in law, and in twenty other walks of life, reforming has become a distinct branch of business.[17]

Dickens is singled out by Stephen as 'the most prominent and popular of the innumerable preachers of that flattering doctrine, that, by some means or other, the world has been turned topsy-turvy – so that all the folly and stupidity are found in the highest places, and all the good sense, moderation, and ability in the lowest'.[18] In fact, Dicken's constructive influence was minimal. Stephen makes the perceptive observation that most of the abuses which Dickens assails are dead issues, already corrected by more moderate reformers: 'He seems, as a general rule, to get his first notion of an abuse from the discussions which accompany its removal, and begins to open his trenches and mount his batteries as soon as the place to be attacked has surrendered.'[19] This was the case, Stephen adds, in the establishment of competitive Civil Service examinations, the reform of the Court of Chancery, and the abolition of imprisonment for debt.

Stephen was not an opponent of necessary reform. As a Utilitarian, it deserves stressing again, he supported most of the liberal reforms of the first half of the nineteenth century. He also agreed that many abuses remained in English society. But the essence of liberal Utilitarianism was moderate and gradual reform: the slow adaptation of institutions to meet the changing needs of a progressing society. What Stephen and the Utilitarians opposed was the attempt to reconstruct society summarily in accord with abstract principles. Reforms must be undertaken with due regard for history and tradition:

> If a man's house is not to his mind, he either builds a new one or repairs the old one; and whichever of the two operations may be the wisest, there can be no doubt that the English nation have in all constitutional reforms adopted the latter. There has never been at any period of our history a *tabula rasa*, like that which at the end of the last century existed for a time in France, on which homogeneous and consistent structures, either of law or government, could be raised. The consequence is, that our law is full of

fictions and our public offices full of intricacy. This is, no doubt, an evil to be remedied, but it is one which the present generation inherited, and which earlier generations considered a cheap price for the acquisition of political liberty.[20]

Stephen believed that the most flagrant faults of Dickens were displayed in *Little Dorrit*. George Bernard Shaw made the outlandish claim that a reading of this novel during his youth had converted him to socialism. He went so far as to declare that *Little Dorrit* is 'a more seditious book than *Das Kapital*'.[21] There is a grain of truth in Shaw's hyperbole; the novel's imaginative appeal was more effective than Marx's cold and systematic analysis of the capitalist system. In the first part, appropriately named 'Poverty', Arthur Clennam wishes to marry the impoverished Amy Dorrit, whose father is imprisoned for debt in the Marshalsea prison. In trying to aid the father, Clennam is continually frustrated by the inefficient bureaucracy of the Circumlocution Office, run by the Barnacle family. In due course, an unexpected legacy turns up, enabling the older Dorrit to go free. Dickens employed the 'Circumlocution Office' as a symbol for the entire English government. Its whole business lay in discovering 'How Not To Do It'. It should be noted that at that time, in the wake of the Crimean War, the operations of government in Britain were under severe criticism. Indeed, the Radical John Arthur Roebuck succeeded in having Parliament set up a special committee to investigate army and administrative mismanagement. The implications of *Little Dorrit*, in particular the portrayal of the Circumlocution Office, incensed Stephen.[22] As he saw it, the message of the novel was that 'the result of the British Constitution, of our boasted freedom, of parliamentary representation, and of all we possess is to give us the worst government on the face of the earth', staffed by fools, knaves, incompetents, and hypocrites.[23]

Stephen charged that Dickens was unqualified to attack English society because he lacked the requisite knowledge and experience. Although early in his life Dickens worked as a court reporter and also reported on the debates in the Commons, Stephen was unimpressed. The novelist's notions of the law 'are precisely those of an attorney's clerk'.[24] Dickens's qualifications, Stephen maintained, were inadequate compared with those of novelists such as Sir Walter Scott, who was a lawyer and an antiquarian, or Sir Edward Lytton, who distinguished himself in political life. No doubt, Stephen's anger made him unfair. But he was convinced that, if Dickens had his way, English liberty would succumb to despotism:

> He would have the pace of legislation quickened by the abolition of vain debates – he would have justice freed from the shackles of law – he would have public affairs conducted by officers of vast powers, unfettered by routine. He does not know his meaning. He does not see the consequences of his own teaching; and yet he is unconsciously tending to a result logically connected with the whole of it. Freedom, law, established rules, have their difficulties. They are possible only to men who will be patient, quiet, moderate, and tolerant of difference in opinion; and therefore their results are intolerable to a feminine, irritable, noisy mind, which is always clamouring and shrieking for protection and guidance. Mr. Dickens's government looks pretty at a distance, but we can tell him how his ideal would look if it were realized. It would result in the purest despotism.[25]

Stephen's most vicious assault appeared in a review of *A Tale of Two Cities*. The review greatly offended many of Dickens's admirers, and has been called 'the most infamous, perhaps, in the whole record of English criticism'.[26] Stephen's attack was so severe that a story circulated, fortunately apocryphal, that Dickens had suffered a fit and was confined to bed for months after being restored to his senses by the ministrations of 'a dozen physicians' and 'the constant application of warm flannels'.[27] Had it not been for the author's popularity, Stephen contends, the novel 'would in all probability have hardly met with a single reader'.[28] The plot is clumsy and disjointed, and illustrates the 'complete disregard for the rules of literary composition which have marked the whole of Mr. Dickens's career as an author'. It is also evident that he lacks sufficient understanding of his subject. Indeed, his knowledge of the French Revolution appears to have been derived from a single reading of Carlyle's popular *History*. Dickens's inadequate grasp of the facts leads to distortions. While it is true that there were great abuses in eighteenth-century English and French society, he grossly exaggerates them. Stephen refuses to acknowledge that Dickens's immense success rests upon reputable reasons: 'No portion of his popularity is due to intellectual excellence.'[29] Rather, it is owing to 'his power of working upon the feelings by the coarsest stimulants, and his power of setting common occurrences in a grotesque and unexpected light'.[30] Needless to say, Dickens survived Stephen's vehemence. He continues to be read, enjoyed and venerated. Yet Stephen's critical views were echoed by several contemporaries among the intellectual class. His brother Leslie, when asked to contribute an essay to a collection on Dickens, declined lest he 'strike a false note in a chorus of enthusiastic admirers'.[31] In his entry on Dickens in the *Dictionary of National Biography*, Leslie said that, 'if literary fame could be safely measured by popularity with the half-educated, Dickens must claim the highest position among English novelists'.[32] His political and social values 'imply a deliberate preference of spontaneous instinct to genuine reasoned conviction'.[33] Walter Bagehot saw Dickens as the major representative of a 'sentimental Radicalism' that arose during the first half of the nineteenth century.[34] Bagehot was most critical of the novelist's tone:

> Those who so address us may assume a tone of philanthropy, and forever exult that they are not so unfeeling as other men are; but the real tendency of their exhortations is to make men dissatisfied with their inevitable condition, and what is worse, to make them fancy that its irremediable evils can be remedied, and indulge in a succession of vague strivings and restless changes.[35]

George Henry Lewes, in his article 'Dickens in Relation to Criticism', went so far as to charge that 'thought is strangely absent from his works. I do not suppose a single thoughtful remark on life or character could be found throughout the twenty volumes.'[36] And Anthony Trollope bestowed on Dickens the epithet of 'Mr Popular Sentiment'. In an article for the *Spectator*, he charged that Dickens's 'teaching' is not really English, 'and tends to modify English family feeling in the direction of theatric tenderness and an impulsiveness wholly wanting in self-control'.[37]

The note that sounds clearest throughout the contemporary criticism of Dickens is that he encouraged a sentimental view of life. To Stephen, the excessive sentiment which Dickens poured into his novels was a paltry contrivance to attract a large audience. Stephen's views on sentimentality were adumbrated in his early essay 'The Relation of Novels to Life'. He could not tolerate the typical Dickens death-bed scene – those of Little Nell, Paul

Dombey and Dora Copperfield are some of the more famous. He was particularly disgusted by Dickens's account of the death of Little Nell – 'the scene over which so many foolish tears have been shed'.[38] This is an episode in *The Old Curiosity Shop* generally applauded by Dickens's contemporaries but considered excessive by today's standards. It has been greeted by extremes of both passion and cynicism. The Irish patriot Daniel O'Connell was supposed to have been so moved that he wept profusely and tossed the book out of the window. On the other hand, Oscar Wilde said that one must have a heart of stone to read the death of Little Nell without laughing.[39] Stephen denounced Dickens's maudlin sentimentality: 'He gloats over the girl's death as if it delighted him; he looks at it from four or five points of view; touches, tastes, smells, and handles it as if it was some savory dainty which could not be too fully appreciated.'[40]

Despite his assault upon Charles Dickens, Stephen made it a point to insist that the *Saturday Review* was not 'the enemy of popular literature'. What it opposed instead were 'the impertinent and unfounded assumptions of a particular clique of popular writers'.[41] One contemporary English novelist who won Stephen's praise was Thackeray. Stephen shared the opinion of most of the educated classes that his fiction was truer to life than that of Dickens. Yet Thackeray always remained second to Dickens in popularity. Soon after Thackeray's death in 1863, Stephen wrote an appraisal of his work for *Fraser's Magazine*. Thackeray's chief merit, he says, is that he wrote about the world he knew best. A critic of country gentry society, Thackeray confined himself to descriptions of human nature in its lighter occupations. He avoided what he did not understand: 'His memory has not to bear the disgrace of such ignorant and mischievous libels as the description of the Circumlocution Office, or the attack on the Court of Chancery in *Bleak House*.'[42] Yet Stephen finds fault with *Vanity Fair* for portraying only part of life. Though Thackeray deserves commendation for writing only about what he understood, Stephen wishes that he had understood more: the world of commerce and industry, 'the severer affairs of life'.

III

In conformity with the design announced in its prospectus, the *Saturday Review* also noticed foreign literature. Stephen naturally saw much to admire in the French school of realism, and he wrote favourably of Balzac's *La Comédie humaine*. The key to Balzac's greatness, Stephen alleges, is that he has 'a far higher conception of the objects and nature of his art' than can be found among contemporary English novelists.[43] Stephen is attracted most by Balzac's minute depiction of French society, a rich variety of scenes and characters from contemporary life drawn with extraordinary good faith. The result is 'a profound sense of reality':

> *La Comédie humaine* has, we think, greater merits, in some respects, than almost any other prose fiction whatever. Looking merely at the extent and variety of the scenes and characters which it represents, we know of no series of works which can be compared to it. It contains portraits from every rank and from almost all the important classes of French society, in Paris or the provinces. The power with which some of the characters are described is extraordinary, and the more so because their peculiarities are displayed without any of that minute dissection of motives which is so fashionable in this country, and yet without the melodramatic starts and fantastic tricks of expression which some of our most popular writers employ to cheat their readers into the impression that the animated puppets which crowd their canvas have real life and individuality.[44]

That Stephen found no objection to the portrayal of immorality in novels might at first seem surprising, but he did not share the prevalent Victorian prudery. Since immorality is part of life, he believed that it should be depicted, though never romanticised. He did not insist that immorality be condemned directly; the mere description of its evil effects should be enough to deter. Though the Abbé Prévost's *Manon Lescaut* deals with illicit love, Stephen maintained that it is not an immoral novel. The question of the morality of a novel depends not upon the subject matter, but upon how the work is executed. *Manon Lescaut* may be characterised as an 'eminently real' novel, since 'there is no idealizing vice, no confusing one kind of passion with another, no hesitation in painting the degradation of character that ensues'.[45] On one occasion, Stephen took issue with the critic David Masson, who had charged that the French realistic novels, treating vice in such detail, were visible signs of the pervasive corruption of French society. Stephen countered with a realist injunction: 'Art is but a version of life so contrived as to make a deep impression on the imagination. Unless, therefore, life is immoral, art can hardly be so.'[46]

But Stephen holds that Balzac sometimes departs from this admirable objectivity 'and needlessly dwells upon disgusting subjects for the sake of producing a dramatic effect, and sometimes, we fear, to gratify the pruriency of his readers'.[47] Some of his characters, in particular Rastignac, De Marsay and Delphine de Nucingen, are not true to life, because 'wickedness is not so dramatic as Balzac would have us believe; and needlessly to invest it with such a shape is in effect to give it a sort of sombre magnificence to which it is not entitled'.[48] Nevertheless, the immoral aspects of Balzac's novels 'are by no means their commonest or most prominent features'. Stephen praises *La Cousine Bette* and *Le Cousin Pons* as 'impressive illustrations of the hideousness of vice'.[49]

Gustave Flaubert's *Madame Bovary*, the story of an adulteress and her ultimate downfall, drew sharp criticism from Stephen. When it was published in 1857, Flaubert was tried for offending public morality, but was acquitted and immediately found himself famous. Only after 'considerable hesitation' did Stephen consent to review it, since 'it is not a work which we can recommend any man, no less any woman, to read'.[50] He finds the character of Emma Bovary, the adulteress, 'one of the most disgusting that we have ever happened to meet with', one which, if it ever became prevalent, 'could not for any length of time be compatible with the existence of society. The notion of duty or responsibility never seems to cross her mind.'[51] In sum, the novel is 'a disgusting performance'. Stephen acknowledges that even the Bible, *Paradise Lost* and *Othello* contain immoral passages. What is objectionable in Flaubert's novel is that, unlike these great works, it makes immorality attractive:

> It says emphatically . . . that adultery may very possibly end in the utter ruin and destruction of the sinning woman; but it does not seem to recognize the fact that in itself, and apart from the occasional and exceptional cases in which it may be so punished, it is vile, hateful, and treacherous.[52]

IV

No claim can be made for Fitzjames Stephen as a great literary critic. Concerned more with morals than art, his view of literature was unaesthetic. Whereas Matthew Arnold believed that literature should be a criticism of life, Stephen held that it should also accurately reflect life. Accordingly, he dismissed all literature which failed to conform to his standards of seriousness and realism. Nevertheless, while those who view literature primarily from an aesthetic point of view may find Stephen's criticism disappointing, they should understand his perspective. He saw much of the fiction of his day as the source of dangerous social panaceas and sentimental idealism, and as the basis for the new brand of politics which we have termed the new liberalism. He was convinced, moreover, that, when his countrymen fell prey to popular novelists, they did so at the expense of culture.

4 Towards a Science of Society

I

Fitzjames Stephen was one of many in his generation who were profoundly influenced by John Stuart Mill's *System of Logic*. Published in 1843, this work became an immediate and widespread success. Presenting in systematic form the underlying philosophy of Utilitarianism, it was long regarded by English liberal intellectuals as sacred scripture. Leslie Stephen has testified to its pervasive influence at Cambridge during the mid-nineteenth century.[1] And Mark Pattison wrote in his *Memoirs* that at Oxford the intense religiosity of the Tractarian Movement was superseded by the empiricism of Mill's *Logic*.[2] In its last book, 'On the Logic of the Moral Sciences', Mill postulated that since human affairs evince a regularity like that in the physical world, it was possible to construct a science of human nature and society analogous to the physical sciences.

What Mill referred to as 'the moral sciences', those dealing with man in society, are known today as the social or behavioural sciences. Collectively, they constitute the science of society. The idea of such a science originated during the eighteenth-century Enlightenment, when David Hume and other great thinkers attempted to apply the empirical method to moral subjects. But not until the nineteenth century were the methods and goals of the social sciences more clearly defined, first by Auguste Comte and then by Mill in his *Logic*. Many believed that within the near future virtually all the problems of man and society would be solved by the application of science. During a period of rapid and fundamental change, especially in nineteenth-century England, where a vast shift in political power seemed imminent with the growth of democracy, men are often induced to seek principles of social change and stability so that they may better direct and predict their fate. Fitzjames Stephen, converted to Mill's philosophy while he was a student at Cambridge, likewise saw promise in the application of the empirical method to society. Indeed, his *General View of the Criminal Law* (1863) was a bold and pioneering attempt to treat an important part of the law as a social science. He also wrote some articles, the subject of this chapter, which were a significant contribution to the method of such a science, and which helped dispel some popular misconceptions that hindered its development.

Stephen believed that a science of society must be placed upon a solid foundation by combining the analytical and historical methods. The analytical method consists of defining the constituent elements of a subject-matter. In the study of jurisprudence, for instance, it seeks to define such concepts as law, sovereignty, crime and sanction. The historical method studies the origins and development of each of the constituent elements and relates them to the political and social facts of their time. In his *General View*, Stephen successfully employed these two methods, complementing an historical presentation of the growth of the English criminal law and procedure with an analysis and classification of its elements. To Stephen, neither the analytical nor the historical method alone is sufficient: 'History and analysis, so far from being inimical, are complementary to each other, and neither can be safely dispensed with. History without analysis is at best a mere curiosity; and analysis without history is blind, though it may not be barren.'[3]

The benefits of this joint operation to law are illustrated by Stephen in an extensive article written for the *Edinburgh Review* in 1861, entitled 'English Jurisprudence'. It was a review of the second edition of John Austin's *Province of Jurisprudence Determined* and Henry Maine's recently published *Ancient Law*. Stephen first concentrates on Austin, the founder of analytical jurisprudence. The moral sciences, Stephen maintains, are severely handicapped by their lack of precise language. The exception is political economy, where Adam Smith and Ricardo formulated clear definitions of such concepts as rent, profit, wages and value. Stephen contends that the great achievement of Austin was that he precisely defined the fundamental elements of jurisprudence. He points particularly to Austin's definitions of law, liberty, right and sovereignty. Stephen believes that by adopting these definitions jurisprudence would be given the clarity necessary for a science.[4]

The Province of Jurisprudence was the product of a course of lectures delivered by Austin at the University of London between 1828 and 1832. They were studiously attended by John Stuart Mill, whose copious notes proved invaluable to later editors of Austin's work. As the title denotes, the object of the lectures was to determine the province of jurisprudence. Austin argued that its subject-matter is the positive law, defined as a command issued by a sovereign to a political subject and enforced by a sanction. This subsequently became known as the command theory of law. The influence of Hobbes upon Austin and the analytical jurists is clear. Austin defined the sovereign as a determinate person or group of persons possessing absolute power to make laws and limited only by the positive morality of society. Stephen conceded that this theory might appear to justify tyranny, but he insisted that in England the sovereign power was restrained by the rule of law.[5]

Like Bentham, Austin carefully distinguished between positive law, which is the province of jurisprudence, and morality, the province of legislation. Accordingly, jurisprudence is a descriptive rather than a normative discipline. Assuming that all law derives from the sovereign, the jurist analyses and classifies laws without regard to their morality, and leaves reforms to the legislator. Stephen believed that the distinction between the *is* and the *ought* provided by Austin's definitions would correct the sentimental thinking that muddled political discussion in his day:

> They entirely prevent the entanglement which is continually arising between an actual and ideal state of things; between the rights or powers protected by laws which do exist; and those which upon some principle or other ought to exist; and this confusion has given the tone to almost all the controversies upon such subjects which have agitated and still continue to agitate mankind.[6]

By the mid-nineteenth century, the Austinian conception of jurisprudence dominated English legal thinking. Though he acknowledged its obvious merits, Stephen saw a weakness in the exclusive devotion to the analytical method. The Austinian school was limited to an abstract examination of current legal systems, and neglected the historical study of the growth of English law and a comparative view of foreign law. But logical analysis alone is inadequate. As Stephen's contemporary Mr Justice Holmes proclaimed, 'The life of the law has not been logic: it has been experience.'[7] The rules by which a people are governed derive more from the necessities of the time than from the syllogism. The analytical jurists also failed to recognise that the sovereign is not the sole source of law, and that local customs often provide rules having legal force. Austin and his disciples erred by attributing to early stages of society legal conceptions which were in fact the product of a long historical evolution. These deficiencies, Stephen maintained, could be remedied only by combining the perceptions of the analytical method with historical study of the law.

According to Stephen, the application of the historical method to the study of law was a distinctive achievement of the nineteenth century. In an obituary article on Henry Hallam for the *Saturday Review*, which Stephen republished in his anonymous *Essays by a Barrister*, he praised Hallam as a pioneer of the English historical school. Hallam was the author of the popular *Constitutional History of England* (1827), a historical account of the development of the English Constitution from a Whig point of view. He was also well known for his work on the history of the Middle Ages. Though his reputation was eclipsed by that of Macaulay and S. R. Gardiner, Hallam's work was the first on modern England to achieve national and international importance.[8] Stephen found the principal writers on the English Constitution prior to Hallam seriously deficient. The great merit of Hallam's work, he declared, was that, more than any of his predecessors, he recognised that, in studying England, 'history is the *substantive*, and law ... is the *adjective*, and that without a deep acquaintance with both it is impossible to arrive at satisfactory conclusions about either'.[9] Coke's *Institutes* contain a great deal of constitutional and legal history, yet 'it never seems to occur to the writer that it makes the least difference whether an Act was passed in the thirteenth or in the sixteenth-century'.[10] As an introduction to a larger work that was never completed, Lord Hale's *History of the Common Law* suffers because it is a mere fragment. Moreover, it concentrates on the technical aspects of the law, ignoring the great questions of parliamentary power and royal prerogative.[11] Blackstone, author of the illustrious *Commentaries*, 'never appears to see the distinction between the reasons why an institution was founded, and the reasons which, after it has been founded, may be alleged in support of it'.[12] Even Bentham, who succeeded in overthrowing the blind reverence for the law fostered by the work of Blackstone, proceeded from a false view of English history and the Constitution. His exclusive devotion to analysis led him to infer that the Constitution, inasmuch as it is unwritten, did not exist.[13] The necessary corrective to these inadequate accounts of the English law and Constitution, Stephen urged, was to combine the ways of Bentham and Austin with those of Henry Hallam.

The best example of the historical method applied to law, Stephen contended, was Henry Maine's brilliant *Ancient Law* (1861). Stephen summarised the salient points of the work, in which Maine presented a history of the evolution of the law out of ancient custom, and the various devices by which laws are adapted to changes in society. Maine distinguished three stages in the development of primitive law. At first there was no law. This was the period of the Homeric 'Themistes', in which kings, allegedly under divine inspiration, made isolated judgements upon particular cases. With the decline in the sacred power of royalty and the rise of political aristocracies, the period of customary law ensued. Finally, there came the period of the written law or codes, exemplified by the Twelve Tables of Rome. This stage, Maine said, brought to a close the spontaneous development of the law. Further changes were effected by recourse to such external devices as fictions, equity and legislation in order to reconcile the codes with a changing society.

Maine also shed valuable light on the origins of the idea of natural law. He held that it grew out of the Roman conception of *jus gentium*, or law common to all nations. Through the influence of Greek philosophy this conception was gradually transformed from law common to all men to the moral conception of law binding on all men. The natural law, or *jus naturale*, was important because it provided a universal and immutable standard according to which legal systems could be judged. Stephen expressed high regard for Maine's chapters on the development of the laws of succession, property, contract and crime. He also praised the section in which Maine argued that society originated not with individual men, but with families or groups.[14] It was only gradually that the notion of the individual, as distinct from the family, developed. In primitive societies, everyone is born into a permanent status with fixed duties. The idea of contract, a free agreement between individuals, arose only in progressive societies after a long period of historical evolution. According to Maine's famous characterisation, 'the movement of the progressive societies has hitherto been a movement *from Status to Contract*'.[15]

Notwithstanding his praise for Maine's method, Stephen believed that his work is deficient because it neglects to subject the law to analysis. Maine was guilty of the genetic fallacy. His exclusively historical approach to jurisprudence led him to assume that, once he surveyed the origin and history of an institution or opinion, it was unnecessary to relate it to any standard of truth or utility. But legal studies should not be a mere antiquarianism. One cannot, for instance, refute a doctrine such as natural rights just by describing its genesis and development over time. Without a standard of truth, the historical method becomes a mere apology for the existing condition. Thus, Stephen concluded:

> Maine is debarred by what he calls his 'method' from attempting to alter what exists. The only relation in which he can consistently view opinions is that of their succession to one another; and if he does not derive tests of truth and utility from some other system, he will get none from his own.[16]

Here again we have evidence of Stephen's liberalism. The narrow devotion to history at the expense of theory impedes necessary alterations in the realms of speculation and society.

Stephen was confident that by combining the analytical and historical methods, the social sciences might enjoy a promising future. Because of Austin, most of the analysis had been completed; what remained was a great deal of historical investigation along the lines developed by Maine:

> It is not impossible that by a wise combination of analysis and history . . . jurisprudence and morals may come to be studied amongst us with a scientific and practical completeness unknown elsewhere. The most important part of the analysis has been already completed; and though much remains to be done in the direction indicated by Mr. Austin, his labours, and those of Bentham, have prepared the way for a vast amount of historical investigation. The combination necessary to make such investigations fruitful is a very rare one. They require not merely learning but those powers of seeing what is essential and

what is not; of entering into the modes of thought and feeling of past ages; of compressing masses of detail into broad and connected statements; and of presenting unfamiliar thoughts in a perspicuous and interesting shape, which nothing can give except careful training, varied knowledge, both of books and men, and a mind equally skilled in investigating details and principles. Every page of Mr. Maine's book contains proof of these qualities, and the manner in which he has executed the task which he has undertaken proves that he is fully capable of doing as much for one element of English jurisprudence as Mr. Austin did for the other.[17]

Given the possibility of a science of jurisprudence, what service might it render? An answer may be found in Stephen's *General View*. Like Austin, he held that jurisprudence deals with the concepts and distinctions common to every system of positive law. It is properly concerned not with the law as it ought to be, which is the province of legislation, but with classifying and describing the relations with which the law must deal, and the limitations placed upon it by the nature of human affairs.

To Stephen, an effective system of criminal law depends upon both the science of jurisprudence and the art of legislation. For the criminal law is not merely a trade but 'an art founded on a science, the art of making wise laws, the science of understanding and correctly classifying large departments of human conduct'.[18] The jurist, by applying the science of jurisprudence, may advise the legislator of certain practical considerations which limit his power. Parliament, for example, is legally omnipotent, but it cannot bind its successors. For, if the succeeding Parliament were bound by the laws of the former, it would not really be sovereign. Stephen explained that laws passed during the reign of George III remain laws only by virtue of the fact that they have been maintained by Parliament under Queen Victoria.[19] Stephen believed that, notwithstanding the sovereignty of Parliament, all laws must be in harmony with human nature. Indeed, human nature is antecedent to, and, in large degree, independent of law. This, he maintained, is the correct interpretation of the law of nature or natural law.[20] Laws are natural only when they are in accord with the actual relations existing in human nature. Classical political theory may be divided into two principal schools: those, including Machiavelli, Hobbes, Hume and the English Utilitarians, who believed that politics must be founded on human nature; and those, such as Locke and Rousseau, who believed that politics must be founded on universal, eternal, and immutable standards of justice. Clearly, Stephen belongs to the former school.

II

Stephen's principal contribution towards a science of society lay in his efforts to dispel some popular misconceptions which hindered its development. In his day, the question of whether history was capable of being made into a science attracted great attention. Though Stephen's writings on social science refer almost exclusively to law and history, they may be logically extended to all the social sciences. He entered the controversy touched off by Henry Thomas Buckle's *History of the Civilization of England* (2 vols, 1857–61), which was the first attempt in England to treat history as a science. Buckle projected a multi-volume work dealing with the comparative history of European civilisations, but he lived to complete only the first two volumes. Nevertheless, the work was a great success and expressed the prevalent Victorian faith in progress. Following Mill, Buckle alleged that, since human affairs manifest a regularity like that of the physical world, it was possible to discover laws which regulate human society. Human actions, he contended, are the consequence of physical, moral and intellectual antecedents, the knowledge of which would enable us to predict human behaviour not only in the aggregate, but also in the particular.

Despite its great success, Buckle's work aroused considerable opposition. Many feared that science, having assaulted the foundations of Christianity, was now being enlisted to disprove that man was a moral being. The Professors of Modern History at Oxford and Cambridge, Goldwin Smith and Charles Kingsley respectively, published lectures in which they argued that a science of history, postulating the regularity of human affairs and apparently in conflict with freedom of the will, was detrimental to morality.[21] The historian James Anthony Froude's fear of the moral effect of a scientific history led him to adopt a position of scepticism and relativism concerning man's knowledge of the past.[22] The controversy was taken up in the periodicals, as two anonymous articles were published in the *Westminster Review* attacking the positions of Smith and Kingsley.[23] Stephen entered the debate with three extensive articles: two were written for the *Edinburgh Review* on Buckle's *History;* another, entitled 'The Study of History', was published in two parts in the *Cornhill Magazine*. These articles demonstrate Stephen's vigorous sense of logic, his grasp of subtle distinctions, and his common sense. Indeed, John Stuart Mill, in a chapter added to the fifth edition of his *Logic* in 1862, applauded Stephen's *Cornhill* articles on the science of history as 'the soundest and most philosophical productions which the recent controversies on this subject have called forth'.[24]

Regardless of whether Buckle succeeded in establishing a science of history, Stephen contended that it would in no way conflict with morals. Like Mill, he saw that, without free will, science would be useless as a guide for social planning and political action. Many of the apostles of a scientific history implied in their writings that human actions are not free. Indeed, Buckle held that, since human actions are governed by fixed laws, free will is an unverifiable metaphysical idea. Stephen acknowledged the unhappy consequence of such a view; for if human actions are not free, man incurs no responsibility for them. Yet he praised Buckle for his intellectual and moral courage:

> Most writers are so nervous about the tendencies of their books, and the social penalties of unorthodox opinion are so severe, and are exacted in so unsparing a manner, that philosophy, criticism, and science itself too often speak amongst us in ambiguous whispers that ought to be proclaimed from the house tops.[25]

Stephen believed that, viewed correctly, a science of history, or any social science, is irrelevant to morality. Unfortunately, both the proponents and the adversaries of scientific history had misapprehended the principal issue of the controversy as being between freedom and necessity. But a correct understanding of Austin's definition of law would dispel any fears that a science of history would be detrimental to morals. Austin distinguished between laws proper and metaphorical laws. We have already noted that he defined a law as a command from a political sovereign enjoining a course of conduct and backed by a sanction. The notion of law applied to the physical world is purely metaphorical, a description of the regularity of nature. A law proper is normative or prescriptive; a physical law is descriptive. Stephen offered the example of parliamentary laws as opposed to physical laws. In the former, the law governs the facts; in the latter, the facts make the law.[26] Thus, when we speak of man and society as being subject to laws, we do not imply any necessity; we are merely recording the course of human actions. Buckle is therefore incorrect when he writes of conduct as 'obeying' certain laws. The social sciences do not govern human conduct. 'A science stands to its subject-matter exactly in the relation which a map stands to the country which it represents', and 'it has no more tendency to govern the conduct to which it refers than the Nautical Almanac has to govern the tides'.[27] Science demonstrates not that men are without freedom, but that they tend to exercise their freedom in a regular manner.

A clear understanding of the nature of scientific knowledge would also obviate much controversy. Stephen contended that knowledge derived from science is not absolute, but limited and conditional. Science can only claim a 'negative certainty', and scientists must be willing to revise their conclusions upon further evidence. Stephen also pointed out that general scientific laws do not enable us to predict individual events. Even if we knew all of the antecedents of human behaviour, we should still be unable to predict the actions of particular persons.

> Historical science would [like the law of gravity] have no assignable relation to any particular state of facts. It would form a mere skeleton, giving nothing but hypothetical conclusions, and always leaving unclassified a vast mass of circumstances which the historical philosopher would be able to consider in no other light than that of disturbing causes.[28]

For this reason, Stephen concluded that although history, like law, would benefit from the application of the empirical method, Buckle had gone too far in his claims for a science of history. Like Mill, Stephen believed that because the social sciences must deal with variable and indefinite facts, they will never provide the accurate and individual predictions of the physical sciences:

> The laws which govern the material world, and the causes of physical phenomena, are more or less discoverable by the human mind, because the tendency of analysis, and of its results, is to render the apprehension of those causes and laws more simple and direct. But the course of inquiry directed to human actions, or to that aggregate of human actions which is called history, is

totally opposite to the course of inquiry of physical science. The moral relations of mankind, the motions of the mind determining certain actions, and the combination of particular causes in the general result, are by their nature infinite, and the further they are traced the more intricate does their connexion become.[29]

III

In the final book of the *Logic*, Mill said that a science of society must be founded upon a science of individual man. Before we can predict the actions of men in society, we must have a knowledge of individual men. Mill also introduced a new science of the formation of individual character, called 'ethology'. This science was to be based upon the deductive principles of psychology.[30] While psychology is the science of the elementary laws of the human mind, ethology attempts to determine the character produced in accord with those laws. The idea that a science of society must be founded upon human nature or psychology originated not with Mill, but with David Hume, who wrote, back in the eighteenth century, that 'the science of man is the only solid foundation for the other sciences'.[31] The psychology which Hume and Mill assumed was that of the empirical associationist school, of which the foremost exponents had been Locke, David Hartley and James Mill.

In search of the proper method for the moral or social sciences, John Stuart Mill rejected both pure induction and pure deduction as inadequate for dealing with the complexities of human affairs. He charged that the inductive method, that of Baconians such as Macaulay, failed to perceive that simple induction cannot be applied to collective behaviour.[32] The deductive method, utilised by Hobbes and Bentham, was deficient because it attempted to deduce all human behaviour and social phenomena from a single aspect of human nature.[33] According to Hobbes, for instance, all government is founded on fear; according to Bentham on individual self-interest. Mill concluded that the best method for studying the social sciences was what he called the 'inverse deductive, or historical method', by which general laws are derived from a study of the facts of history, and their truth is then determined by comparing them with the general principles of human nature.[34] No historical generalisation is acceptable unless it corresponds with what we know about human nature.

Stephen agreed with Mill that the social sciences must be based ultimately upon history and psychology. Accordingly, he attacked Buckle for failing to found his putative science of history upon human psychology. Buckle proceeded on the assumption that all men possess a uniform character, and that variations are solely the product of external circumstances. Instead of placing his history on the solid ground afforded by a science of 'the functions and the constitution of the mind', Buckle denied the value of psychology, choosing instead to base his work upon statistics. Stephen countered that the social sciences must act on premises which Buckle failed to appreciate:

> We utterly disbelieve that without a scientific acquaintance with the functions and the constitution of the mind, gathered from the observation of individual minds, it will ever be possible to construct a real science of history. To attempt to draw metaphysical or psychological conclusions from statistical data is no more than an elaborate way of inquiring into the distance between one o'clock and London Bridge.[35]

Another source of dispute between the proponents and the opponents of a science of history was the role of the individual in history. While the proponents tended to minimise the importance of individuals, the opponents often exaggerated their role. Buckle believed that man was at the mercy of general laws. Though great men adorn the pages of history, they are mere creatures of their age. It was this view that induced Mill to add to a later edition of his *Logic* a chapter defending the role of individuals in history and praising Stephen's contribution to the debate.[36] Stephen recognised that both a proper estimation of the place of individuals and due regard for the importance of general causes are necessary for a scientific treatment of history. Clearly, he believed that the hero-worship embodied in Carlyle's famous dictum that 'the history of the world is but the biography of great men' was excessive. Individuals, no matter how great, must satisfy the needs of the age. Yet the importance of individuals is still considerable:

> If Napoleon Bonaparte and Louis XVI had changed places, there might still have been a French Revolution, but it would have been comparatively bloodless. No one can doubt for a moment that the Roman republic would have subsided into a

military despotism if Julius Caesar had never lived; but is it at all clear that in that case Gaul would ever have formed a province of the empire? . . . The Norman conquest, in the same way, was as much the act of a single man as the writing of a newspaper article.[37]

IV

Fitzjames Stephen, then, was convinced that a science of society, if attained, would not conflict with human freedom, religion or morals. If properly employed, it would guide rather than subvert freedom. He also believed that the advocates of a science of society must understand that, because the social sciences were still in a nascent stage, a general theory of social action was not yet possible. A great deal of historical investigation remained to be done, supplemented by the definitions and concepts which the analytical method would yield. One must therefore accept for the time being limited and provisional results – what sociologists today term theories of the middle range. Most important, Stephen was certain that to succeed the social sciences must strive to develop a science of psychology; for only when we have a more precise knowledge of human character can we claim to be on the way towards a science of society.

5 The Criminal Law

I

Had he written nothing else on the law, Fitzjames Stephen would have been assured a place of prominence among English legal writers by his *General View of the Criminal Law of England*. Published in 1863, it was the first survey of the growth of the English criminal law which successfully combined the analytical and the historical methods of jurisprudence. We know from his brother that Fitzjames conceived the work at least as early as 1858,[1] as an amplification of a germinal essay he had contributed to the *Cambridge Essays* the year before, 'The Characteristics of English Criminal Law'.[2] In 1861 he was diligently preparing his brief on behalf of Rowland Williams, who was on trial for heresy. Nevertheless, the successful completion of his labours for the Education Commission during that year, and the temporary rift among the staff of the *Saturday Review*, afforded Stephen the leisure to complete an extensive work on the criminal law.

To lay the groundwork for a science of jurisprudence, Stephen sought to illuminate the general principles upon which the English criminal law was founded, and to suggest ways in which it might be improved. His methods were history and analysis: history furnished the bedrock of experience and showed the evolution of the law through the ages; analysis revealed the basic components of a legal system and provided sound principles of judgement. Stephen's immediate purpose was to unveil the essence of the English criminal law. In this he was eminently successful; the *General View* displays a mind of exceptional power and originality. The book has withstood the criticism of posterity. The noted legal historian Sir William Holdsworth, reviewing the legal literature published between the Reform Act of 1832 and 1875, called Stephen's work 'the most original of all books on the criminal law'.[3] Sir Frederick Pollock praised it as 'the first attempt that had been made since Blackstone to explain the principles of English law and justice in a literary form'.[4] More recently, Sir Leon Radzinowicz hailed it as 'the first scholarly and literary introduction to the subject'.[5] Stephen would later publish a remarkable three-volume *History of the Criminal Law of England*, which remains a valuable source for scholars. We shall concentrate on the *General View*, because it established Stephen's reputation as a legal writer and constitutes the first mature and comprehensive statement of his legal thought.

Stephen had an even more fundamental reason for writing. In a period that witnesed the growth of democracy and the passing away of the old order, it was important to have a clear notion of the criminal law as the cement which helped hold society together. Believing that the criminal law was invested with the ultimate sanction of the sovereign, Stephen undertook to explain and justify such authority as could legitimately be exercised over the people. He was conscious of the difficulty which has beset political and social theorists since time immemorial: the delicate balance that must be struck between the law and public morality, between the demands of the State and the demands of the people, between the power of the State to command and the right of the people to be free. He expressed the immediate purpose of his work succinctly: it is to serve neither as a practical reference work nor as a guide to professional legal study, but to present in an intelligible and interesting manner

> an account of the general scope, tendency, and design of an important part of our institutions, of which surely none can have a greater moral significance, or be more closely connected with broad principles of morality and politics, than those by which men rightfully, deliberately, and in cold blood, kill, enslave, and otherwise torment their fellow-creatures.[6]

Stephen begins by setting down the premises upon which the criminal law is founded.[7] Like Bentham and the analytical jurists, he believes that the science of jurisprudence depends upon clear and precise definitions of the law and its various elements. He therefore espouses the Austinian conception of law. Austin defined a law as a command or injunction from the sovereign to the subject to do or forebear to do some act under pain of punishment. A crime is simply the disobedience to a law. It follows, Stephen observes, that all laws are in the strict sense criminal, for they are by definition commands which might be disobeyed, and that the phrase 'criminal law' is really a tautology. The public usually reserves to the realm of criminal law only morally heinous acts such as murder, rape and burglary; for in the popular understanding a crime is not merely the infraction of a law, but an act revolting to the moral sentiments of society. Nevertheless, Stephen contends that the criminal law cannot be restricted to only those acts which the public considers criminal, for the law must be applied irrespective of morality.

At the same time, Stephen realises that the Austinian definition of law is too inclusive to be practical. For the sake of convenience, he distinguishes between a crime and a tort.[8] A crime is an act forbidden by law under pain of punishment imposed for the public safety. A tort is an act forbidden by law in which penalties are exacted for the sake of private individuals. It is clear that Stephen adopts Blackstone's distinction between a crime or public wrong and a private or civil wrong: a crime is an injury to the whole community considered as a community; a private wrong is an infringement of the rights of individuals considered merely as individuals. Stephen acknowledges that in practice it is often difficult to distinguish between a public and a private wrong; indeed, many violations of the law are breaches of both public and private rights. Nevertheless, he maintains that the different methods pursued in remedying the wrong constitute a substantial distinction.

Every system of criminal law, Stephen points out, is composed of two fundamental parts:[9] the substantive, or 'laws forbidding specified acts under specified punishments'; and the adjectival, or 'laws by which these general provisions may be applied to particular cases'. The first part may be termed the law of crimes and punishments, and includes the general principles of criminality, the definitions of crimes, and the allotment of punishments; the second may be termed the law of criminal procedure, and includes the prescribed modes of trial and its preliminaries, the rules of evidence, and the infliction of punishment.

Having established the province and the natural classification of criminal law, the bulk of the *General View* is devoted to a history of the construction of English criminal law; an examination of the general principles of criminality; the definitions of particular crimes; the rules of criminal procedure, and a comparison between the English and French procedural systems; the principles and rules of evidence; a criticism of the unsystematic character of the English criminal law, and suggested remedies. It concludes with detailed and instructive accounts of four English and three French criminal trials, to illustrate the differences between their respective systems of criminal procedure. Throughout the work, comprising nearly 500 pages, Stephen displays a singular mastery of the English law and its history, and a firm grasp of its relation to philosophical principles.

The English criminal law derives from three sources: the common law – a loose set of definitions and descriptions of crimes based upon general customs and existing from time immemorial; Acts of Parliament, or statutory law, intended to supplement the common law; and case law, or the decisions of judges in the courts. The common law served as the foundation for the entire system, and through the centuries has received abundant praise in the writings of Bracton, Coke, Sir Matthew Hale, Blackstone, and others. Statutory enactments and judicial decisions arose out of the discretionary application of legal principles in accordance with the infinite variety of circumstances and the inadequacy of the common law to meet them. The great increase in prosperity during the Industrial Revolution led to a spate of statutes in the eighteenth century designed to meet the many new offences that either escaped with impunity or were inadequately punished. Moreover, the systematic reporting of cases since the beginning of the nineteenth century produced many additions to the law. The result was that the English criminal law in Stephen's day comprised a vague and inadequate common law, supporting an unsystematic superstructure of statutes and an intricate mass of judicial interpretations embodied in case law. Denunciations by Jeremy Bentham, 'unsparing though not unjust',[10] in Stephen's view, and the example of several foreign countries whose law had been successfully codified, induced the English to attempt to reduce their law to order. Three different sets of Consolidation Acts were passed, the last in 1861, revising, though not codifying, the criminal statutes by collecting them into single statutes and repealing those that had fallen into desuetude.

II

After a chapter giving an historical sketch of the English criminal law, Stephen returns to theory by discussing the principles of criminality. Anglo-American law has always recognised certain subjective or mental elements as necessary for an action to constitute a crime. The common law maxim 'Actus non facit reum, nisi mens sit rea' means that in order to constitute a crime an act must be accompanied by a guilty mind or *mens rea*, criminal intent. This concept of *mens rea* has long been a source of dispute among jurists, since to some it implies that immorality is an essential ingredient of a crime. There are, Stephen asserts, two fundamental requirements for criminal responsibility.[11] The person must commit an act, which is composed of intellect and will; that is, he must act knowingly and willingly. The act must also be accompanied by an intent or purpose specifically forbidden by the law.[12] One does not necessarily have to intend to violate the law which one actually violates, but one has to intend to do the act which the law forbids. The absence of any one of these constituent mental elements – intellect, will and criminal intent – refutes the allegation that a crime has been committed.

Stephen then considers, in what is perhaps the most important part of the book, the difficult and paramount question of the relation of law to morals. His position is in substantial agreement with that of the analytical jurists. A scientific study of the law necessitated that a distinction be made between the law as it is – the province of jurisprudence – and the law as it ought to be – the province of legislation. Nevertheless, since the maintenance of a system of criminal law depends upon its general concordance with public morals, the legislator must be careful to harmonise law and morals whenever possible.

Lawyers, Stephen affirms, have always felt 'great and reasonable reluctance' to permit moral distinctions in the law, because they recognise the inexact state of moral terms. Yet, imprecise and unscientific as these terms are, it is absolutely necessary that legal definitions of crimes take into account morals, since 'the administration of criminal justice is based on morality. It is rendered possible by its general correspondence with the moral sentiments of the nation in which it exists, and if it habitually violated those sentiments in any considerable degree, it would not be endured.'[13] It was obvious to Stephen that any system of criminal law which failed to punish such morally heinous acts as murder and rape could not subsist. In Utilitarian fashion, he nevertheless insists that the law does not concern itself with whether or not a particular system of morals is true.

It has nothing whatever to do with the truth. It is an exclusively practical system, invented and maintained for the purposes of an actually existing state of society. But though the law is entirely independent of all moral speculation, and though the judges who administer it are and ought to be deaf to all arguments drawn from such a source, it constantly refers to, and for practical purposes notices the moral sentiments which as a matter of fact, are generally entertained in the nation in which it is established.[14]

Though the criminal law and morals must be in substantial harmony, they are not co-extensive. Blackstone drew the important distinction in his classic *Commentaries* between crimes *mala in se*, acts wrong in themselves and patently immoral; and crimes *mala prohibita*, acts that are not immoral but are crimes only because they are prohibited by law. In essence, there can be legal guilt without moral guilt. But Stephen found that the boundary between law and morals is often difficult to maintain. At first he was willing to tolerate the term 'malice' in the definitions of crimes, as implying that the criminal act was done in anticipation of certain evil consequences forbidden by the law.[15] In later years he would argue that both 'malice' and the concept of *mens rea* should be dropped, because they connote that moral culpability is necessary for a criminal act.[16] To equate morals with the law is to confuse motive and intent. Motive belongs to the moral realm and is not a constituent element of a crime. The most laudable motive has no bearing upon whether a crime has been committed. The test of criminality is intention.

The relation between the law and morals, in Stephen's judgement, is that they are often in harmony, but they might also be entirely independent, or even conflict. They are in accord, he tells us, in cases of gross violations of public morals, such as murder, rape and burglary.[17] Here law and morals support one another and, though the definitions of crimes do not refer to motives, they must satisfy as much as possible the moral indignation which the crime excites. Law and morals are unrelated in cases such as laws prohibiting smuggling, and laws requiring that marriage be celebrated at a certain time and place. In these cases the acts derive their moral significance exclusively from the fact that they are condemned by the law.[18] Finally, law and morals may conflict, as in certain attacks upon the authority of the State. The nobles, for instance, who invited William III to England and precipitated the Glorious Revolution of 1688 were legally traitors, though the moral opinion of a large portion of the nation at that time regarded their deed as an example of the highest patriotism.[19]

The aim of the jurist and the legislator should be to harmonise the law and morals as far as possible. This is accomplished by framing legal definitions of particular crimes that are in close agreement with the moral character of the act defined. In Stephen's view, legal definitions should fulfil three important functions: they ought to distinguish each crime from all other crimes; they should express fully and clearly the legislator's intent; and they should conform as much as possible with public morals. Legal definitions must therefore take into account popular sentiment wherever possible, so that the law may recognise circumstances which aggravate, extenuate or eliminate moral guilt. In cases where law and morals are independent, or in which they conflict, the legislator ought to frame his definitions so as to compromise public morals as little as possible.

When legal definitions incorporate public morals, they do so not in regard to motive, but in regard to intent. The law, to Stephen's mind, should closely parallel moral feelings by distinguishing different intentions congruent with the gradations of criminality generally accepted by the community. Thus a specific intent must be proved in order for an act to constitute a crime. The distinction, based upon intent, between murder and manslaughter, corresponds to the fact that popular morality recognises varying degrees of responsibility.[20] Stephen concedes that the law can never completely satisfy the moral indignation which a crime provokes, for legal definitions refer necessarily to intent, and demand a precision that is wanting in the realm of morals.

III

In cases of flagrant violations of public moral sentiment, the criminal law supplies a great punitive benefit. As a child of English Utilitarianism, Stephen inherited from Bentham the deterrent view of punishment: the aim of punishment is to prevent crime. Stephen worked from the assumption that the function of the law is to preserve order. Yet he believed that deterrence only partially explained the importance of the criminal law. He refused to go as far as Bentham, who said that, if the fine of a shilling were enough to deter men from committing murder, that would be proper punishment. Stephen held that the criminal law also legitimately satisfies the passion of revenge which crime arouses in the public. The law is the agent of public moral retribution; it provides for the legitimate and regulated, as opposed to private and potentially excessive, expression of an emotion that is an integral part of human nature. Before Freud, Stephen perceived that the repression of instinctual drives is the price we pay for civilisation. He put this notion in a memorable epigram: 'The criminal law stands to the passion of revenge in much the same relation as marriage to the sexual appetite.'[21] Later, in the *History of the Criminal Law of England*, he elaborated upon this theme:

> The sentence of the law is to the moral sentiment of the public in relation to any offences what a seal is to hot wax. It converts into a permanent final judgment what might otherwise be a transient sentiment.... In short, the infliction of punishment by law gives definite expression and a solemn ratification and justification to the hatred which is excited by the commission of the offence and which constitutes the moral or popular as distinct from the conscientious, sanction of that part of morality which is also sanctioned by the criminal law.[22]

Stephen thus takes his place with the retributionist theorists, including Kant and Hegel, who believed that justice requires that a criminal be punished whether or not the punishment benefits either himself or those whom he injured. According to the deterrent theory, punishment is justified by its consequences; according to the retributive theory, the justification lies in the wrongness of an act. Stephen maintained that the popular indignation which a serious crime arouses should not be ignored:

> I think it highly desirable that criminals should be hated, that punishments inflicted upon them should be so contrived as to give expression to that hatred, and to justify it so far as the public provision of means for expressing and gratifying a healthy natural sentiment can justify and encourage it.[23]

Passages such as this – and others could be cited – might be singled out by Stephen's opponents in an effort to show that he advocated a repressive society. His writings have frequently been contrasted with those of John Stuart Mill: Mill depicted as a great liberal, Stephen as an authoritarian conservative. But Stephen insisted that the law must be founded ultimately not upon idealism, but upon human nature. His prevailing thought was that true liberalism must accord with experience.

The retributive theory played a large role in Stephen's advocacy of capital punishment. By the early nineteenth century there were some 200 crimes punishable by death in England. Though in the great majority of cases capital punishment was not enforced, the law was clearly in need of reform. Beginning with the Acts of Sir Robert Peel, the number of capital offences was gradually reduced, until by 1861 the death penalty had been abolished for all but four crimes. This gave rise to a movement to eliminate capital punishment altogether.[24] A Royal Commission was appointed in 1864 to investigate the possibility of reducing the number of crimes classified as murder. Stephen's arguments on the death penalty were set forth in detail in three appearances as a witness before the Commission and in two articles for *Fraser's Magazine*.[25]

Stephen supported the legal reforms of the past half-century, and did not wish to see the death penalty reinstated for crimes in which it would be too severe to enforce. But he insisted that for crimes dangerous to the State, such as treason, and gross violations of public morality, such as murder and rape, capital punishment should be retained for its deterrent and retributive value. He acknowledged that it might be possible to reform a criminal. But the only effective means which even the best administered prison can apply to this end are discipline and forced labour. Though prison may instil some good habits, it rarely changes hearts. The State must recognise that there are certain extremely wicked and incorrigible criminals whose lives should not be spared.[26] Yet, as one writer has observed, if Stephen's proposals for the redefinition of the felony of murder and for the broadening of the M'Naghten rules had been adopted in his day, the result would have been a substantial reduction in the exercise of capital punishment.[27]

Stephen's conception of punishment as a means of expressing collective vengeance illustrates his deep knowledge of social psychology. Walter Bagehot, Stephen's contemporary and in many ways a kindred spirit, contributes to our understanding of the psychological role of certain 'theatrical' elements of the English Constitution – namely, the Monarchy and the House of Lords –

for the maintenance of a cohesive State. Likewise, Stephen contributes to our understanding of the psychological importance of the criminal law: the criminal law preserves the social order by providing acceptable and controlled channels for the expression of public moral sentiments. Stephen's vision is even broader, for he points out a reciprocal relation between law and morals. Not only has the law throughout the centuries kept pace with changing moral sentiments, but it has also significantly shaped morality. The mere fact that a law denounces a certain act is enough to induce people to regard it with horror. While some persons abstain from murder because they are terrified of capital punishment, thousands more abstain merely because the law condemns it and 'murderers are hung with the hearty approbation of all reasonable men'.[28] Furthermore, Stephen submits:

> Even indifferent or virtuous acts will come to be condemned by the moral sentiment of particular times and places, if the law condemns them. . . . Wicked acts often pass unreproved where the law permits them. . . . It is this secondary effect of criminal law which makes it important that law and morals should harmonize as far as possible, so that the one should gratify the sentiments which the other excites.[29]

IV

It was perhaps on the criminal liability of the insane that Stephen was most advanced for his time. During the mid-nineteenth century, and indeed until very recently, the legal definition of insanity in the British Commonwealth and in virtually all the United States was derived from the famous M'Naghten rules of 1843. In that year Daniel M'Naghten, allegedly under the delusion that the Prime Minister, Sir Robert Peel, meant him personal harm, mistook Peel's secretary, a Mr Drummond, for the Prime Minister, and fatally shot him. M'Naghten was tried and acquitted on the ground of insanity.[30] The decision aroused considerable debate, and the House of Lords resorted to the extraordinary measure of soliciting from the judges certain opinions on the question of mental illness so as to explain the acquittal. The result was a legal definition of insanity which provided an intellectual criterion. The most important of the M'Naghten rules stipulated that to establish a defence on the ground of insanity, it must be clearly proved that, at the time of the committing of the act, the party accused was labouring under such a defect of reason, from disease of the mind, as not to know the nature and quality of the act he was doing; or, if he did know it, that he did not know what he was doing was wrong.[31]

An age sympathetic to the intellectualism of Mill's *System of Logic* had little difficulty in accepting so rational a criterion for mental stability.

Stephen was in substantial agreement with the M'Naghten rules. He was moved by his profound respect for civil liberties to defend the rights of those whose illegal acts were the result of a deranged mind. He doubted the utility of punishing men for acts which they either could not help or could not know to be wrong.[32] Moreover, the harmony which must be fostered between law and public morals dictated that extenuating circumstances be weighed in determining criminal liability. The question of madness and responsibility occupied Stephen's interest throughout his life. As early as 1855, he defended the law regarding insanity in an essay read before the Juridical Society in London, and in a paper delivered at the 1864 annual meeting of the National Association for the Promotion of Social Science he did likewise.[33] Yet it is important to note that on these occasions, and especially in his *General View*, Stephen construed the additional element of an irresistible impulse, one which destroys the will, to fall within the M'Naghten criterion. In his view:

> The only question which the existence of such impulses can raise in the administration of criminal justice is, whether the particular impulse in question was irresistible as well as unresisted. If it were irresistible a person accused is entitled to be acquitted because the act was not voluntary and was not properly his act. If the impulse was resistible, the fact that it proceeded from disease is no excuse at all.[34]

By assuming the notion of an irresistible impulse to fall within the definition of insanity, Stephen was broadening and supplementing the prevailing interpretation of the M'Naghten formulation, thus affording wider immunity. Many within the legal community believed that insanity was solely a disease of the intellect. They assumed that in cases of an uncontrollable impulse, unless the person was also suffering an intellectual impairment, he was entirely responsible for his acts. Stephen discerned that insanity often destroyed either or both of the constituent elements – intellect and will – requisite for a crime. He possessed a knowledge of human personality that was far more sophisticated than that of most of his contemporaries. He understood that the personality is an integrated whole, comprising intellect, will and emotions, and that these faculties were so closely related that the impairment of one must necessarily disturb the others. He believed that, in cases of an irresistible impulse, the urge to commit a crime may be so powerful as to preclude the knowledge of right and wrong. Since such actions could hardly be said to follow upon sufficient deliberation and knowledge, he considered them to fall within the M'Naghten rules.

Because it was not generally understood to have been originally included, Stephen eventually decided that it was necessary to add an explicit statement of the doctrine of irresistible impulse to the present law. After his unsuccessful attempt to incorporate the doctrine in his Draft Criminal Code of 1878, he returned to the question in a chapter of his *History of the Criminal Law*. There he embarked upon an extensive discussion of madness and responsibility based upon thorough research into a variety of medical texts and displaying an impressive knowledge of forensic psychiatry.[35] He insisted that the law of insanity was in need of supplementation: ignorance of the wrongness of an act owing to mental illness should not be the sole basis for a plea of insanity. With something as complex as the human personality it was simplistic to claim that a mental disease affecting the will has no influence upon the intellect. He summarised his position:

> All that I have said is reducible to this short form: knowledge and power are the constituent elements of all voluntary action, and if either is seriously impaired the other is disabled. It is as true that a man who cannot control himself does not know the nature of his acts as that a man who does not know the nature of his acts is incapable of self control.[36]

Not until the twentieth century would Anglo-American law accept the notion of an irresistible impulse as grounds for a plea of insanity.

V

Stephen was as much concerned with the law of criminal procedure as he was with the substantive criminal law. For the administration of justice, by means of procedure, was an important guardian of English liberties and essential to the proper functioning of English law. He had necessarily begun his *General View* with an examination of the substantive criminal law. As he explained, the current procedural law had developed over centuries, while the substantive law was largely the product of more recent statutes. Though the law of procedure had developed prior to that of substance, he believed that a more logical arrangement for a book treating the criminal law would be to begin with the substantive law, and follow with the procedures by which it was implemented.[37] Part of his discussion of criminal procedure includes drawing an illuminating comparison between the English and the French systems, one he had originally made in his essay 'The Characteristics of the English Criminal Law'. By employing the comparative method, Stephen made a salient contribution to the field of comparative law. Like his long-time friend and fellow legal historian Sir Henry Maine, he believed that the comparative method was an important complement to the historical point of view.

We have defined criminal procedure as that part of the law which regulates the way in which general provisions are applied to particular cases; it is the method by which individual persons may be prosecuted for committing crimes. Stephen distinguishes two basic types of criminal procedure:[38] the 'litigious' – that which regards the criminal trial as a private dispute between the plaintiff and the defendant presided over by a judge, and decided by a jury; and the 'inquisitorial' – that which regards the criminal trial as a public inquiry the object of which is to obtain the truth in the public interest. Conceding that no system of criminal procedure conforms perfectly to either of these types, Stephen characterises the English system as essentially litigious, and the French as essentially inquisitorial.

Of the two systems, Stephen believes that the French is the more efficient in detecting crime and prosecuting criminals. For in the inquisitorial method these functions belong to the government, which provides for an elaborate and efficient pre-trial collection of the evidence by various State officers. The egregious disadvantage, from a liberal point of view, is that, while crimes are most effectively detected and prosecuted, the verdict is virtually reached prior to the trial, rendering the jury 'an anomalous excrescence'.[39] The trial is merely the culmination of a long process of detection in which the verdict is a foregone conclusion. There is, moreover, little respect for the civil liberties of the accused. He is not allowed to manage his own defence, he is placed in solitary confinement, and torture is often employed to secure his confession. He is, in effect, guilty until proved innocent.

In sharp contrast, the English litigious system affords far greater respect for individual rights. The detection and prosecution of crime are not placed in the hands of the State, but depend upon the initiative of private individuals. The accused may retain his own counsel and employ witnesses; and the evidence is prepared by attorneys acting on behalf of the prosecution and the defence instead of by public officers. Such is the adversary system. In England, Stephen observes, trial by jury is a reality, a litigation between the plaintiff and the defendant. The jury is 'the cardinal point in English criminal law', and is regarded by many as 'the most important of English liberties'.[40] It also helps to convince the public that the criminal law is equitably executed, an important function inasmuch as 'the administration of criminal justice is the commonest, the most striking, and the most interesting shape, in which the sovereign power of the state manifests itself to the great bulk of its subjects'.[41] Stephen views the trial as a kind of drama in which the public moral code is ratified and popular moral indignation visibly satisfied. Trial by jury also assists the general concordance between law and morals by providing the incidental benefit of a 'safety valve for public feeling', since in cases where adherence to the strict letter of the law would produce great hardship, the jury may modify its verdict to conform with public sympathy. Though this benefit should not be directly intended by a legislator, when it does exist it should not be 'despised or lightly forfeited'.[42]

Stephen acknowledged the defects of the English system; obviously, any system which manifested such solicitude for individual rights must inevitably allow many crimes to go undetected. But he believed that the advantages of the French procedural system could not be introduced in England without undermining the entire administration of justice. In an article for the *Cornhill* in 1860, he maintained that the inefficiencies of the English criminal procedure were a fair price to pay for liberty.⁴³ But, in the interest of the rights of the accused, he did suggest an important reform in the English procedure. He advised that a special court of appeal for criminal cases be instituted to provide the accused with an opportunity for appeal when, in the judgement of the Government, new evidence appears after a trial and sheds doubt on the verdict.⁴⁴ This reform was not, in fact, effected in England until the Criminal Appeal Act of 1907.

Despite its defects, then, Stephen believes that the English administration of justice is an extraordinary blessing. It is 'a generous, humane, and high-minded system eminently favourable to individuals'. Though its 'noble and generous temper frequently defeats itself', and sometimes 'produces the very hardships which it ought to prevent', its inadequacies 'should be remedied with a careful hand, and with the greatest solicitude to preserve unimpaired its essentially free and noble character'. Moreover, the English criminal procedure is 'a great practical school of truth, morality, and compassion'. Stephen elaborates on this important pedagogic function:

> No spectacle can be better fitted to satisfy the bulk of the population, to teach them to regard the government as their friend, and to read them lessons of truth, gentleness, moderation, and respect for the rights of others, especially the rights of the weak and the wicked, than the manner in which criminal justice is generally administered in this country.⁴⁵

Stephen singles out the English bench for special praise as the agent of profound compassion and magnanimity:

> No one can fail to be touched when he sees a judge, who has reached the bench by an unusual combination of power, industry and good fortune, bending the whole force of his mind to understand the confused, bewildered, wearisome, and half-articulate mixture of question and statement which some wretched clown pours out in the agony of his terror and confusion.⁴⁶

VI

Many pages of the *General View* are devoted to discussion of the rules of evidence. They are important, Stephen maintains, to ensure that jury trials reach judgements on a sound basis; and they are indispensable for the proper administration of justice. The English rules of evidence, he informs us, developed as late as the eighteenth century, and are composed for the most part of judicial decisions. Indeed, they constitute a striking illustration of judge-made law:

> The construction of a whole department of law, of such intricacy, such extent, and such vast importance, in little more than a century, is the most remarkable instance which the law affords of the importance of the legislative powers which judges possess in virtue of their right to declare with authority what the law is.[47]

Stephen includes an entire chapter on a philosophical discussion of the principles upon which rules of evidence should be founded. As he understood it, they were inextricably connected to the laws of the mind. The subject was important to him for a more general reason: the rules of evidence were also applicable to the religious, philosophical and scientific questions that deeply interested him. Indeed, on more than one occasion he expressed the desire to write a book on the rules of evidence governing these questions.

In his philosophical exposition on these rules, Stephen's mentor was obviously John Stuart Mill, whose *Logic* had proclaimed the virtues of empiricism and the scientific method. In later years, Stephen prided himself on the fact that he was probably the first to show the relation between Mill's logical theory and the law of evidence.[48] Like Mill, Stephen starts from the assumption of a fixed order in the universe:

> All the facts with which we are acquainted, visible or invisible, internal or external, are connected together in a vast series of sequences which we call cause and effect, and the constitution of things is such that men are able to infer from one fact the existence, either past or future, of other facts.[49]

Stephen defines evidence as any fact or facts that can be used to infer the existence of another fact. The inferences drawn from evidence are governed by the rules of logic. He charges that English lawyers have often confused the meaning of the word 'evidence' by overlooking the important distinction between the relevancy of facts and the method of proving the facts. 'On all common occasions', he says, 'the evidence itself, and the inference that the evidence is true, are both described as evidence.'[50] He gainsays the difference alleged to exist between direct and circumstantial evidence as a distinction without a difference, since in practice no line can be accurately drawn between the principal and the subsidiary facts in a case. He also undertakes a brief psychological discussion of the nature of belief.[51] What is the reason for believing evidence? Here he borrows from Bentham's *Rationale of Evidence* when he indicates that we believe what is true according to logic and the testimony of practical experience. Truth, for Stephen, is inseparable from utility. We believe what is true because it is necessary for successful action; the everyday intercourse of life could not continue unless people were disposed to believe. Nevertheless, Stephen concludes that evidence can lead only to a degree of probability, for even in the physical sciences absolute certainty is unattainable.

Stephen resumed his treatment of the philosophy of evidence in the important introduction to his *Indian Evidence Act* (1872), entitled 'Principles of Judicial Evidence', published shortly after he returned home from India. As in his *General View*, he felt constrained to analyse the theory upon which the law of evidence rested. He submitted that, because evidence employed the laws of induction and deduction, it could become a science analogous to the physical sciences. The law of evidence, he explained, is a matter of relevancy or logic. Admissible evidence is composed of facts in issue, and all facts which are relevant. Those facts are relevant which either affect the probability of the facts that are in issue, or which serve as a basis for inferences concerning them. Relevant facts relate to facts in issue either as cause or effect.

Stephen has been criticised, most notably by such legal scholars as Thayer and Wigmore, for equating admissibility with relevancy, for assuming that the sole test which facts must undergo in order to be admitted as evidence is to be related either as cause or effect to the facts in issue.[52] But relevancy alone, Stephen's critics claim, is too narrow a basis for admissibility. On this count they are undoubtedly correct. There are tests of admissibility other than logical relevancy. Relevant facts may even be excluded as evidence. Besides, according to law, facts must pass some auxiliary and extrinsic tests. Certain facts may be relevant but be excluded because they bear only a remote connection to those at issue; others may be excluded because they might be prejudicial, or

The Criminal Law

illegally obtained. Clearly, Stephen exaggerated the role of logic in evidence. His effort to incorporate Mill's teaching on the syllogism into the law of evidence led him to underestimate the fact that evidence is not only a matter of logic, but also a matter of law.

In his defence we might refer to Henry Maine, who wrote in the *Fortnightly Review* that Stephen's introduction to the Indian Evidence Act 'seems to me more nearly correct than any hitherto given to the world by a lawyer'.[53] Maine accurately perceived Stephen's end. The English law of evidence, primarily the product of scores of judicial decisions, particularly since the eighteenth century, had developed historically as a series of exclusionary or negative rules. The result was that a text describing the law would begin by presenting the negative rules, such as the inadmissibility of hearsay, and follow with the rules of admissibility as numerous exceptions to the primary exclusionary rules. The English law of evidence, in other words, had developed in a negative form. What Stephen accomplished, and Maine applauded, was to set forth the evidential rules positively instead of negatively. Stephen believed that the law of evidence could be better understood and more systematically arranged by proceeding according to the order of thought rather than the order of time. He realised that, if codified, the evidence law must be stated positively, because negative rules, what is not evidence, do not constitute evidence.

Following these premises, Stephen's Indian Evidence Act set down all the positive rules of relevancy. Thus, all facts in issue, and relevant to the issue, are admissible evidence. This arrangement had the advantage of making explicit what had been the unexpressed principle of the negative rules, and rendered the law of evidence more comprehensible to both the student and the layman; and this, we might add, is after all the purpose of any Code or Digest. We have the testimony of Stephen himself:

> The object of drawing the Act in this manner was that the general ground on which facts are relevant might be stated in as many and as popular forms as possible, so that if a fact is relevant its relevancy may be easily ascertained. These sections are by far the most important, as they are the most original part of the Evidence Act, as they affirm positively what facts may be proved, whereas the English law assumes this to be known, and merely declares negatively that certain facts shall not be proved.[54]

After treating the general principles of evidence in relation to the criminal law, Stephen spends a chapter of his *General View* on the particular English rules. He discusses those pertaining to both the admissibility of evidence and the competency of witnesses. Evidence, he says, must be confined to the points in issue; the best evidence must be given; hearsay is not evidence; confessions are not evidence under certain circumstances; and the burden of proof is on the prosecution. Taking his lead from Bentham, Stephen holds that there are only a few objections to the competency of witnesses.[55] He agrees with the existing rule that, for want of understanding, children under the age of reason should be excluded. But those persons suffering from mental illness ought to be ineligible only if the nature of their malady is such that it precludes their understanding the nature of an oath and the character of the proceeding in which they are engaged. Regarding the competency of husbands and wives, he believes that they should be permitted to summon their spouse as a witness. Most importantly, Stephen opposes the ineligibility of an atheist as a witness. The supposition that an oath is without binding effect upon a person who has no fear of eternal damnation arises from a simplistic conception of human nature. For religion is not the only assurance of truthfulness; men may feel compelled to tell the truth for reasons such as habit, the fear of exposure, or a sense of duty. In any event, Stephen is confident that the greatest guarantee that the jury will be presented with the truth rests not so much in the competency of witnesses as in the nature of the judicial process itself, 'the fact that the great security against judicial errors lies in the power of exposing or contradicting false evidence, not in preventing false evidence from being given'.[56]

VII

No subject engaged Stephen's legal talents as much as codification; nor was any subject as much a source of personal frustration and disillusionment. In the later years of his life it became almost an obsession with him. It might be said that the *General View* was written ultimately in preparation of a criminal code, and that his labour in India was undertaken to prove to his countrymen that a code of the English law was feasible. Stephen was convinced that, although the common law, the statute law and the judicial decisions constituted an unarranged, unsystematic and often inscrutable legal system, they nevertheless 'hold in suspension an admirable criminal code well adapted to the wants and feelings of the nation, and framed upon practical experience of them'.[57]

The ideal of a complete code of the English criminal law was one that Stephen inherited from Bentham, Austin and the Utilitarians, as a means to a lucid and systematic body of law and a prerequisite to the scientific treatment of jurisprudence. In a series of articles for the *Saturday* in 1856, Stephen defended the idea of a code but conceded that the present time was inauspicious for such an ambitious venture.[58] He knew of the ingrained opposition of the English to codification. He knew also that the industry of three successive royal commissions had failed to produce a criminal code. It was inconceivable, he said, that Parliament would delegate legislative power of such magnitude to private hands. Even if Parliament itself were to undertake to codify the law, the debates in committee would preclude the unity of purpose and execution necessary for a code, and destroy its comprehensiveness. Though he believed that codification was not to be expected at that time, he did insist that it was possible to prepare sufficiently for its future accomplishment. The expurgation and consolidation of the statutory law, reform in the system of case-reporting, and an improved system of legal education were essential for eventual codification.

We must distinguish clearly between consolidation and codification of the law. Sir Courtenay Ilbert, a successor to Stephen as Legal Member of the Governor-General's Council in India, defined consolidation as applied to the statute law as 'the combination in a single measure of the enactments relating to the same subject-matter, but scattered over different Acts'.[59] It entails a complete rewriting, since obsolete statutes must be deleted. Codification, as defined by Ilbert, is 'an orderly and authoritative statement of the leading rules of law on a given subject, whether those rules are to be found in statute law or in common law'.[60] In his *General View*, Stephen was willing to postpone the goal of codification in favour of the more modest project of reforming the Consolidation Acts of 1861. He conceded that these Acts formed a criminal code complete enough for practical purposes.[61] But he insisted that, together with the common law, they were capable of improvement, and might be adapted to 'the gradual changes of society, and the gradual growth of experience'.[62] As they stood, they were replete with unnecessary intricacies and unnecessary technicalities. The remedying of these defects would produce 'a clear and wise penal code'.[63]

Stephen therefore proposed the improvement of the Consolidation Acts by a combination of parliamentary and judicial legislation: parliamentary statutes to formulate new definitions of crimes, and judges to apply these definitions to specific circumstances. By imputing such legislative power to the judiciary, he was implicitly dissenting from Bentham and Austin, who had cast aspersions upon judge-made law. Indeed, Stephen contended that judges are 'one of the best subordinate legislators in the world';[64] under the guise of merely declaring the law, the judge actually makes it. Others have shared Stephen's high regard for the judiciary. Blackstone praised the English judge as 'the living oracle of the law'; and, in our own century, the distinguished jurist Benjamin Cardozo, in acknowledgement of the important role of the judge, saw fit to dedicate a now famous series of lectures to the principles of judicial interpretation.[65] The work, Stephen declared, of successive generations of 'admirably qualified' judges, with an 'immense amount of experience and of shrewd practical acquaintance' with the law, has produced a case law containing 'an immense store of true principles, and strong common sense, applied to the facts with consummate practical skill', marred only by the fact that they are unsystematic and unorganised, and 'so much mixed up with special circumstances that it is infinitely less useful than it might be made'.[66] The legislative powers of the judge, then, are 'absolutely essential to the public good, and it would be desirable not to destroy or restrain, but to recognize and extend them'.[67] The judge is a guardian of civil liberty and the rule of law.

For the co-ordination of the legislative powers of Parliament and the judiciary, Stephen suggested the institution of a new and independent agency of government, the Department of Legislation and Justice, or the Ministry of Justice, to be headed by the Lord Chancellor.[68] The idea for a body to mediate between the courts and Parliament was not new to the English-speaking world. Bentham had urged such a ministry in his draft of a Constitutional Code.[69] Stephen's contemporary Lord Westbury also saw its value; and, in the twentieth century, Cardozo and Pound have renewed the suggestion.[70] The Ministry of Justice, Stephen explained, would superintend all criminal legislation, whether parliamentary or case law. It would draft all parliamentary criminal statutes;

control the system of reporting cases; be empowered to summon judges to clarify particular points of law; it might also extract rules and principles from decisions dealing with particular branches of the law, and derive a set of rules independent of the particular circumstances of the cases decided. Stephen insisted that these reforms could not be carried out by private hands, but must be the product of a concerted effort; for the suggestions of individuals would either be put aside or adopted unsystematically. Only a permanent office, organised specifically for the purpose of reforming the criminal law, could be successful. Interestingly enough, in later years, after his extraordinary success in drafting codes of the Indian law, and faced with parliamentary indifference, Stephen would undertake the task of codifying the criminal law as a private venture. But, in the 1860s he was hopeful that progress in the area of law reform could be made in lieu of a complete criminal code. The benefits would be glorious; the responsibility awesome:

> There is every reason to believe that by patient and systematic study the law of England might be made a system as complete and not less influential than that of Rome. When we consider the prodigious effects which Roman law produced upon the whole history of modern Europe, and when we bear in mind the fact that the law of England will in another century be the law of immense populations in North America and in the Indian Empire, the importance of making it as good as it can be made cannot be overrated.[71]

VIII

Fitzjames Stephen's *General View of the Criminal Law of England* was highly regarded in his day. Though it did not increase the number of his legal briefs, and thus failed to put an end to the financial insecurity which nagged him throughout his career, the book established his reputation as a legal writer. The fame that Stephen achieved in his lifetime rests primarily on his efforts as a codifier and as a writer on the criminal law. Justice Willes, a distinguished contemporary of Stephen, believed that the *General View* was a 'grand book', and frequently consulted it in chambers.[72] A review in the *Law Magazine and Review* recommended it as a work 'calculated to foster and encourage upright conduct and honourable feelings'.[73] The reviewer for *Fraser's* applauded 'that sound practical spirit which animates and gives value to the whole of his work', and praised Stephen for 'the success which he has achieved in his attempt to make the general principles of criminal law intelligible to all classes, and to indicate the various points in which it is still capable of improvement'.[74] In 1895, the year after Stephen's death, the *Law Journal* characterised it as 'preeminently the most readable English lawbook of the century'.[75]

The *General View* sheds light upon a distinctive characteristic of Stephen's mind. Perhaps in no other thinker of the age were the various aspects of thought so consciously related. To Stephen, law, religion, morality and politics composed a seamless web. In an era that was witnessing the breakdown of many old certainties of Victorian thought – the waning of religion and the growth of democracy – he could look to the ideal of a well-administered, just and scientific criminal law as the ultimate sanction for what he cherished most in society. His book laid the groundwork for the treatment of the law as a social science, and the subsequent development of the English criminal law has proved him one of its most perceptive and sagacious commentators. Stephen continued his legal speculations in later years, expanding the *General View* into the *History of the Criminal Law of England*, and devoting his time and energies to the cause of codification.

6 India

I

India. For years the word evoked the deepest sentiments in countless Englishmen. They considered it their mission to bestow upon a lawless and barbaric sub-continent the imperishable legacy of Western civilisation. As a boy Fitzjames Stephen had been fascinated by Macaulay's *Essays*, especially those on Clive and Hastings, founders of British India.[1] And throughout his life he retained fond memories of his father's achievements on behalf of the Empire as Under-Secretary of State for the Colonies. In 1862 his friend Henry Maine was appointed Legal Member of the Viceroy's Council in India. Macaulay had been the first to hold the office, from 1834 to 1838, and he had distinguished himself by reforming the Indian legal and educational systems. In 1868 Maine suggested that Stephen succeed him as Legal Member. After much deliberation, Stephen wrote to the Under-Secretary, Grant Duff, accepting the position, and he was formally appointed on 2 July 1869.

The decision had been difficult. Stephen was concerned for the welfare of his family (by this time he had seven children), which he would have to leave behind during an anticipated five-year tenure of office. Moreover, he was now forty years old and worried about his professional prospects. His law practice, which never provided the financial security he desired, might be even less fruitful after a long absence. For a short time, Stephen was beset by melancholy:

> I am thoroughly and grievously out of spirits about these plans of ours. On the whole I incline towards them, but they not infrequently seem to me cruel to Mary, cruel to the children, undutiful to my mother, quixotic and rash and impatient as regards myself and my prospects. . . . I have not had a really cheerful and easy day for weeks past, and I have got to feel at last almost beaten by it.[2]

Yet there were circumstances which favoured Stephen's accepting the position. His brother-in-law, Henry Cunningham, was appointed public prosecutor for the Punjab in 1868. Henry's sister, Emily Cunningham, with whom Stephen corresponded for several years expressing to her his deepest convictions, had gone to India to join her brother. This assured Stephen that he would have close friends in India. But the most encouraging fact was that his wife, whom he deeply loved, would be able to visit him. She would make two protracted visits during his tenure of office, accompanied on each occasion by their daughter Rosamond. In 1871 Stephen rejoiced when another child, Dorothea, was born in India. Stephen's married life was a source of great comfort to him. Though his double profession of journalism and the bar often kept him from home, Mary Stephen remained greatly devoted to her husband. When late in life Fitzjames undertook to write his autobiography, he stressed their happy marriage and confessed that Mary was 'the supreme blessing of my life'.[3]

Another important influence on Stephen's decision was that he saw India as an opportunity to give his legal talents free rein. India had always been a place of interest to the English Utilitarians, who saw it as a sort of social laboratory in which they could put their theories to the test of experience. Stephen inherited from the Utilitarians the passion for efficient and benevolent government. From his Evangelical forbears he inherited the religious fervour with which he would devote himself to his new legal tasks. He was fascinated by India. 'Legally, morally, politically, and religiously, it appears to me, on the whole, nearly the most curious thing in the world.'[4] He admitted that he had 'an almost missionary feeling about the country and the office'.[5] Stephen's work in India would confirm in his mind thoughts that had been maturing for years and which he would bring to his famous conflict with John Stuart Mill.

Stephen set sail in November and reached Calcutta on 12 December 1869. During the voyage he used his time well. Between the day he left England and his arrival at Bombay he wrote twenty articles for the *Pall Mall Gazette*, and he continued to contribute to the newspaper during his India stay. As usual, his appetite for work was insatiable. 'If I were in solitary confinement,' he confessed, 'I should have to scratch newspaper articles on the wall with a nail.'[6] Needless to say, he looked upon his legal work in India with lively anticipation.

One must bear in mind the philosophical assumptions with

which Stephen undertook his work.⁷ There was a liberal side to Benthamite Utilitarianism, but there was also an authoritarian side. The stress upon the connection between utility and liberty in early nineteenth-century England was the product more of historical circumstances than of logic. For no necessary connection exists between utility and either liberty or authority. Circumstances alone decreed that the authoritarian element in Utilitarianism should find fertile soil in India and should become the philosophical basis of British imperialism.

The Utilitarians adopted certain elements of the political philosophy of Hobbes, chiefly his ideas of sovereignty and the rule of law. Hobbes's reputation, it will be recalled, had suffered since the seventeenth century because he supported the losing side in the struggle over sovereignty between King and Parliament. But during the early nineteenth century the Benthamites found in him a valuable source of support for their programme of reforms. Like Hobbes, Bentham and his followers preached law as the instrument for improvement. Later in the century, Sir Alfred Lyall, after many years of distinguished service in India, wrote that government there came closest to the ideal set forth in Hobbes's *Leviathan*, 'that mortal god to whom we owe, under the immortal God, our peace and defence'.⁸ While the Utilitarians supported liberty at home, they worked toward a benevolent despotism in India. Whenever utility demands, they argued, benevolent government is more important than free government. Even Mill, in his essay *On Liberty* (1859), advocated despotism for what he termed 'backward states of society'. The liberal and the authoritarian elements in Utilitarian thought were never successfully reconciled. In their conflict one can discern the root of Stephen's disenchantment with Gladstone's modern popular liberalism, as well as the ultimate origins of the split in the Liberal Party over Home Rule in 1886.

II

The work of Fitzjames Stephen in India as the Legal Member of the Governor-General's Council forms a principal contribution to the monumental achievement of Anglo-Indian legislation.⁹ Throughout the first half of the nineteenth century, India was ruled by the East India Company under the supervision of a Board of Control in London. For purposes of administration, India was divided into the three presidencies of Bengal, Madras and Bombay. The Governor-General in Council, later called the Viceroy, legislated for Bengal, while governors in council legislated for Madras and Bombay. The Company's charter had been renewed by the Charter Act of 1833, which, in addition to creating the post of Legal Member of the Governor's Council, also empowered the Governor-General to legislate for all India, thereby rescinding the legislative authority of the other presidencies. In order to provide British India with a comprehensive and definite system of law, the Act provided that the Governor-General appoint the first resident Indian Law Commission.[10] All this coincided with an era of Benthamite reform in England, where the Reform Act had been passed in 1832 and Whig principles were in the ascendant.

The salient product of the Law Commission's efforts was Macaulay's brilliant draft of a penal code, which, though completed by the time he left India in 1838, was not adopted until years later. Stephen later expressed great admiration for the Code:

> The Penal Code has triumphantly supported the test of experience for upwards of twenty-one years during which time it has met with a degree of success which can hardly be ascribed to any other statute or anything approaching to the same dimension. It is, moreover, the work of a man who, though nominally a barrister, had hardly ever (if ever) held a brief, and whose time and thoughts had been devoted entirely to politics and literature.[11]

It is clear that Stephen believed Macaulay to have fulfilled the designs of codification: 'The Indian Penal Code may be described as the criminal law of England freed from all technicalities and superfluities, systematically arranged and modified in some few particulars (they are surprisingly few) to suit the circumstances of British India.'[12] In essence, Macaulay had bequeathed to India a masterly distillation of the English criminal law.

With Macaulay's return to England, after almost four years of extraordinary labour, the Commission lost much of its initial vigour, lingered on for some years, and ultimately dissolved. After the defeat of the Sikhs in 1849, the Punjab was annexed to the British Empire and the problem arose of providing the new territory with an effective government. Realising that the complex

Regulations of Bengal were not applicable to the Punjab frontier, the Governor-General, Lord Dalhousie, delegated its rule to a lieutenant-governor, Lord Lawrence. This was the origin of the Non-Regulation system, in which absolute power, uniting the executive and legislative functions, was vested in vigorous men to legislate for the newly-acquired lands. The law-reform impetus was partially revived with the appointment of a second Indian Law Commission in 1853, this time sitting in London. The Legal Member, Sir Barnes Peacock, revised parts of Macaulay's Penal Code, which was finally enacted in 1860. Stephen contended that the long delay had the beneficial result of establishing a model code, an amalgam of Macaulay's intellectual prowess and Peacock's technical skill and practical knowledge. 'An ideal code', Stephen declared, 'ought to be drawn by a Bacon and settled by a Coke.'[13] Moreover, the Commission produced the Codes of Civil and Criminal Procedure, which became law in 1859 and 1861 respectively. Thus by 1861 British India possessed a substantive penal code and codes of criminal and civil procedure.

The tragic Indian Mutiny of 1857, more a protest against encroaching Westernisation than a rebellion against foreign rule, demonstrated to the British the need for an improved administration, and inaugurated a period of increased legislation.[14] The government of India was transferred from the East India Company to the Crown in 1858, and the office of Secretary of State for India was instituted. The Indian Councils Act of 1861 further complicated the existing corpus of Anglo-Indian law by restoring the legislative power to the presidencies. In the same year a third Indian Law Commission was created in London. It produced drafts of the Contract and Evidence Bills, which did not become law during its lifetime, and it drafted the Succession Act, which was passed in 1865. All three bills had been introduced by Henry Maine. The Commission resigned in 1870 after a quarrel with the Governor's Council over the draft of the Contract Bill.

When Stephen succeeded Maine as Legal Member in 1869, the Indian law had grown extremely complex and unsystematic. There were the Regulations of the Governor-General and those of the legislative bodies of the presidencies. There were the laws governing the so-called Non-Regulation provinces (the Punjab, Oudh, the Central Provinces and Burma). In conjunction with the Anglo-Indian law, there was also a mass of customary Hindu and Muslim law relating to the family. The result was a body of law plagued by intricacy and uncertainty. As Stephen said, 'all the faults of the English system are rapidly reproducing themselves in India'.[15] But he believed that it was possible to reduce the Indian law to compact and intelligible form. This end, he thought, was particularly urgent, law in India being of great importance as the basis for the vigorous operation of the British administration, and the maintenance of peace and order in the vast sub-continent.

One could not expect that, as in England, the inadequacies of the law would be redeemed by a proficient bar and judiciary. Cases not provided for in the written law were decided by Indian judges according to 'justice, equity, and good conscience'.[16] But these civilian judges were not lawyers and they were handicapped by an imperfect understanding of the intricacies of the law. The English judges of the Supreme and High Courts of India had never risen to professional eminence. In Stephen's view:

> The practical result of throwing the reins, so to speak, on the neck of the judges, has been to introduce a vague, uncertain, feeble system, which, as is generally the case with systems administered by unprofessional judges, who nevertheless consider themselves bound to administer law, combines the defects of a weak grasp of principle with a great deal of occasional subservience to technicality.[17]

English professional lawyers are capable of arriving at general principles of law by means of induction from precedents, sometimes sifting through a mass of incomplete and often conflicting material. But 'the unprofessional judge seldom gets beyond a certain number of illustrations and rules, more or less imperfectly understood'.[18]

As a remedy, Stephen advocated the twin devices of codification and consolidation. By the former, he meant 'the reduction for the first time, to a definite written form, of law, which had previously been unwritten, or written only in an unauthoritative form, such as that of textbooks and reported cases'. And by the latter he understood 'the reduction to a single Act of all the written law upon any given subject'.[19] He pointed to the admirable example of the Punjab codes as evidence that codification was practicable in India: finding the province impossible to administer without law, Lord Lawrence and a Board of Administration had enacted a penal code and codes of civil and criminal procedure, which, though subject to a number of objections and eventually superseded, at least provided for fair and efficient rule.

India

Stephen's tenure as Legal Member was marked by extraordinary legislative activity. An indefatigable worker, his performance evokes the memory of his father's incredible feat of drafting, in the space of a weekend, the bill of 1833 abolishing the slave trade in the British Empire. Fitzjames revised the Code of Criminal Procedure, and codified the Evidence and Contract Acts, all of which were passed into law in 1872. In addition, he consolidated and amended large sections of the Indian Statute Book, added new sections to the Penal Code, furnished a legal foundation for the administrative regulations of the Punjab, and aided in the construction of a system of interstate law. He also wrote an extraordinary minute on the Indian judicial system, drew up twelve comprehensive Acts and assisted in the preparation of eight others. All this was accomplished within two and a half years, Stephen's term being interrupted by a combination of financial and family concerns. He resigned his post after holding it for only half of the usual five years.

With his characteristic sensitivity to the realities of power, Stephen summarised what the Anglo-Indian Codes had enabled the British to accomplish in India:

> If it is asked how the system works in practice, I can only say that it enables a handful of unsympathetic foreigners (I am far from thinking that if they were more sympathetic they would be more efficient) to rule justly and firmly about 200,000,000 persons, of many races, languages, and creeds, and, in many parts of the country bold, sturdy, and warlike.... The Penal Code, the Code of Criminal Procedure, and the institutions which they regulate, are somewhat grim presents for one people to make to another, and are little calculated to excite affection; but they are eminently well calculated to protect peaceable men and to beat down wrong-doers, extort respect, and to enforce obedience.[20]

As a whole, the Anglo-Indian codes have been judged extraordinary. Sir M. E. Grant Duff, Under-Secretary for India while Stephen was in office, thought that, next to the repression of internecine warfare, the codes were the greatest monuments of British beneficence:

> The Indian codes are not complete, and what exists of them is not perfect, but with reference to the large portions of law of

which they treat there are no better codes in the world, and if they are compared with the hideous chaos which we call law at home, which no layman understands and no lawyer can practice without having a library at his elbow, they are as light to darkness.[21]

Sir William Holdsworth, the great historian of the English law, wrote that they were 'one of the most remarkable, and will perhaps be the most lasting of all the achievements of British rule in India'.[22]

Stephen's prodigious contribution to these codes, accomplished with such speed, was inevitably marred by some faults. James Bryce travelled in India during 1888 and canvassed the opinions of competent individuals on the codes. He concluded that the two procedural codes were generally applauded as bringing order to a chaos of intricate statutes. But the Evidence Act, in which Stephen attempted to apply the principles of John Stuart Mill's *Logic* to the rules of evidence, was criticised as being too metaphysical. The Contract Act was found to be poorly constructed, nebulous in language, and superfluous in most of its provisions. Moreover, by enforcing the Western idea of the sanctity of contracts, a liberal dogma Stephen espoused, it greatly increased the power of creditors over debtors. 'Stephen's capacity', Bryce concluded, 'for the work of drafting was deemed not equal to his fondness for it. He did not shine either in fineness of discrimination or in delicacy of expression.'[23]

Recently, Sir Leon Radzinowicz has mitigated Bryce's censure:

> Such criticism was justified, but in no way does it invalidate the final judgment that Stephen was one of the greatest architects to bridge the gap between the Western World and India in the legal sphere. He played a large part in forging a bond between the two countries that has survived the bitter stresses from which a relationship based on conquest cannot help but suffer.[24]

Sir Frederick Pollock, himself a notable codifier, said that the Indian Contract Act was the product of three distinct stages, and that the introductory definitions added by Stephen during the final stage were 'not altogether in harmony with the body of the work'. Yet the end result, though certainly not a model code, was 'a generally sound and useful one'.²⁵ Pollock also observed that, had Stephen's aim been to produce codes absolutely beyond criticism, they might never have been produced. Moreover, he warned that any critical estimate of Stephen's codifying efforts must consider that for him codification was an ongoing process, requiring periodic revision and correction.²⁶ Sir Courtenay Ilbert, a successor to Stephen as Legal Member, marvelled at his productivity, but conceded that some might have reservations concerning the quality and durability of the codes: 'Fitzjames Stephen was a Cyclopean builder. He hurled together huge blocks of rough hewn law. It is undeniable that he left behind him some hasty work in the Indian Statute Book, some defective courses of masonry which his successors had to remove and replace.' Yet Ilbert also noted that for Stephen codification implied no finality, and that his codes generally satisfied the purpose they were designed to meet: to serve the unprofessional judge or magistrate as a guide to the Anglo-Indian law.²⁷

Despite these reservations, by the time Fitzjames Stephen set sail for home he could take pride in the fact that he had played a large part in the creation of an Indian legal system which was more clear and systematic than that of England itself.

III

Fitzjames Stephen had the opportunity to state in detail his views on India in a chapter which he contributed to W. W. Hunter's *Life of the Earl of Mayo* (1875). Mayo had been Viceroy during Stephen's term as Legal Member, and was assassinated in 1872. Stephen held him in high regard, and believed that they were in substantial agreement as to the principles of Anglo-Indian legislation. Essentially, the chapter is an explication and defence of those principles. India possessed a separate Legislative Department to superintend the enactment and the reform of the laws. Its functions were purely legislative, as the Indian Councils Act in 1861 carefully separated legislative from executive powers. The Legislative Department was also restricted: it could not initiate legislation, but had to await proposals from the other branches of government. Nevertheless, India had the advantage of continuous legislation. Whereas in England bills introduced and debated in separate legislative sessions were usually consigned to oblivion when they failed to pass, the continuity of the Indian system permitted the undertaking of legislative schemes of considerable magnitude. This opportunity, along with the relatively fixed tenure of the higher Indian government officials, served to 'give a degree of vigour and system to Indian legislation unlike anything known in England'.[28] Increasingly after his Indian service, Stephen set up the Indian legislative system as a foil to what he believed to be the relative inefficiency of British parliamentary government.

Despite its merits, the Anglo-Indian legislation was subjected to a considerable degree of hostile criticism in Stephen's day. The Charter Act of 1833, in accord with the design to create in India a centralised and uniform system of law, had vested all legislative power in the Governor-General in Council. The laws which this Legislative Council promulgated, known as the Acts of the Government of India, gradually supplanted the elaborate system of 'Regulations' and were applicable to the entire country. Critics charged that the British had overlegislated, and that they had followed principles unsuitable to the Indian way of life. Many contended, or at least implied, that India should be ruled not by law, but at the discretion of the district officers. Since laws serve to limit the executive, India should not be governed by law. In the more recently acquired provinces, a paternalistic regime, known as the Non-Regulation system, had been instituted, by which all power – executive, magisterial and judicial – was united in the hands of a district officer. The critics of Indian legislation assumed that, if the rule of law were introduced in these Non-Regulation provinces, the government would necessarily be inefficient. Stephen sought to defend the Indian legislation, and his arguments are best understood in the light of his Hobbesian views of the nature of sovereignty and the necessity of the rule of law.

What the opponents of rule by law failed to perceive was that their principle, if acted upon, would subvert British rule in India. The main distinction, Stephen contended, between the Anglo-Indian government and that which it supplanted, was that the British established the rule of law in place of despotic government at the discretion of the native rulers. Peace and tranquillity replaced anarchy. To Stephen, the advantages of British rule were patent, for 'the moral and general results of a government by law admit of no comparison at all with those of despotism'.[29] He pointed to the fact that his countrymen were responsible for bringing to India a vigorous system of administration and a coherent body of law. The British, he asserted, were not interested merely in replacing one despotic system by another, but in bringing civilisation to a primitive land. Like his Utilitarian and Evangelical forbears, Stephen understood the British mission in India to be the introduction of Western values, including private property and the inviolability of contract. Only by the rule of law are men secure in life and property, and is society capable of growing in wealth. Once these advantages are admitted, the opponents of Indian legislation must also concede that it is 'impossible to stop short of a complete system of law providing for all the common exigencies both of daily life and of government'.[30]

The first condition of benevolent government, Stephen submitted, is rule by law rather than the arbitrary determination of a ruler.

> To suppose that law and despotic power can subsist side by side, is to show complete ignorance of the very nature of law. The essence of a system by which person and property are secured, lies in the general principle that no man is to suffer harm either in person or in property, except according to law. Despotic power or personal government, which is the same thing, is nothing but a power to compel people in general to obey the orders of the ruler, whatever those orders may be; but this compulsion can be effected only by inflicting, or by threatening to inflict, harm either on their persons or their property in case of disobedience, which cannot be if they are not to be so harmed except by law.[31]

Stephen observed that equality before the law was a reality in India. For the principle that the government is liable to be sued in the courts was firmly established. The most impecunious peasant could obtain redress for grievances against the Indian Government much more simply and effectively than the richest and most influential man could against the British Parliament.

The benefit of the rule of law is illustrated, Stephen insisted, by its providing for the growth of private rights in India, especially the right to landed property. To him, the value of private property was axiomatic. A fundamental doctrine of classical liberalism was that property was an essential safeguard of liberty. The individual must have something of his own that is secure from arbitrary infringement by government. For centuries, Stephen says, private property was foreign to India. Society was 'worn to the bone',[32] for the country consisted of an aggregate of village communities, each a self-contained unit with its own sovereignty and ruled according to custom. A Hobbesian state of nature existed, as blood-feuds and boundary disputes abounded and were settled by force. But with the coming of English law the village communities began to decline and disappear. To Stephen the reason was that they were inconsistent with the principles of British rule:

> Loose customs, village communities, and violence in order to settle disputes between man and man or village and village, are as inevitably connected together on the one hand, as are strict law, an organized government, and the rigid administration of justice on the other. The reason why village communities and other forms of joint property break up under our rule, is simply that the law permits no violence and ultimately no coercive authority, except its own. But in order that this may be done at all, it is absolutely necessary to have laws in the full sense of the word. If Government does not allow a man to assemble his friends, arm them with bludgeons and axes, and march out against a set of neighbouring villagers who have interfered with his pasture or his watercourse, it must determine whether he or his antagonist is in the right; and it must be made distinct for the purpose of getting to a decision: and this is law. In a word, peace and law go together, just as elastic custom and violence go together.[33]

Stephen acknowledged a recent historical interest in the Indian villages. In his *Ancient Law* (1861), Henry Maine brilliantly demonstrated that the notion of private property was a relatively late evolution; for centuries vast portions of the human race had lived with the conception of communal ownership. In his Rede Lecture 'The Effects of Observation of India on Modern European Thought',[34] delivered at Cambridge in 1875, Maine expressed confidence that a knowledge of Indian society would greatly contribute to social science and illuminate various aspects of the development of human society. Forgetting that the present is the development of seeds sown in the past, 'we are perhaps too apt to consider ourselves as exclusively children of the age of free-trade and scientific discovery'.[35] In his *Village-Communities in the East and West*, first published in 1871, Maine applied the complementary historical and comparative methods to the study of Indian and Teutonic villages in order to throw light upon such questions as the growth of feudalism and the origins of private property. While Maine was able to view the Indian villages functionally, in relation to their time, Stephen did not share his scholarly detachment. He looked at the present utility of the village communities and found them wanting. With a contempt for traditional Indian society reminiscent of James Mill's *History of British India* (1817), he issued the following admonition:

> I think that there is some danger lest these inquiries should be perverted so as to support inferences which I know would be entirely repudiated by their author. The historical interest of these institutions and their durability speak for themselves; but the merits of an institution are not to be measured either by its durability or by its historical interest. The fact that the institutions of a village community throw light on the institutions of modern Europe, and the fact that village communities have altered but little for many centuries prove only that society in India has remained for a great number of centuries in a stagnant condition, unfavourable to the growth of wealth, intelligence, political experience, and the moral and intellectual changes which are implied in these processes. The condition of India for centuries past shows what the village communities are worth. Nothing that deserves the name of a political institution at all can be ruder or less satisfactory in its results. They are, in fact, a crude form of socialism, paralysing the growth of individual energy and all its consequences. The continuation of such a state of society is radically inconsistent with the fundamental principles of our rule both in theory and in practice.[36]

For Maine, the ideal was scientific objectivity: 'It is not the business of the scientific historical enquirer to assert good or evil of any particular institution. He deals with its existence, not with expediency.'[37] In contrast, Stephen stressed the fact that the Indian village communities had simply failed to bring advanced civilisation to the country. He thought that Maine's writings were enlightening, but he was more concerned with the present foundations of sovereignty in India than with the remote objectivity required of scholarship. The differing approaches of the two men were remarked upon in a letter Stephen wrote to Lord Lytton:

> Maine always appears to me to have a mind as powerful as it is transparently clear and ingenious. I wish his powers ran in a more human channel than the odd one he has dug out for himself in the study of ancient law and early institutions. He and I have the queerest friendly battles on the subject of the proper method of theorizing about law. He always appears to me to be satisfied when he understands as a matter of historical fact how the law came to be what it is on a certain point. The work I care about is ascertaining specifically what the law on a given subject actually is, and then throwing it into as plain and systematic a form as I can. However, I admit that you can never really understand what the law is unless you know its history, and as he admits that the principal practical value of his pursuits is to lay the foundation for mine, we get on admirably together.[38]

IV

In addition to his substantive work, Stephen composed a *Minute on the Administration of Justice in British India*. This sizable work admirably exhibits his analytical mind and his powers of compression. Written originally in 1870, it was revised the following year and published just before he left India, in 1872. Leslie Stephen called it 'one of Fitzjames's most remarkable pieces of work'.[39] Sir Frederick Pollock believed that it contained 'some of Stephen's best and most characteristic work', and that it merited being published in England, inasmuch as 'many parts of it are of general interest to students of legislation and judicial systems'.[40] A series of questions had been presented to the local governments upon the subject of the administration of justice in India, and the *Minute* is an extensive discussion of the various issues raised by their replies. There is no need to go into Stephen's more technical arguments and his various suggestions for reforming specific defects in the judicial administration, but it is instructive to see how the *Minute* amplifies some of his arguments in support of the Anglo-Indian legislation.

Stephen believed that the aim of his countrymen should be 'to obtain as good a system for the administration of justice as is consistent with the maintenance of the British power in India'.[41] He conceded that, because the British owed their position in India to conquest, the Indian judicial system in certain respects fell short of that in England. Indian justice must be administered by foreigners who speak a different language and have been raised in a different culture from that of the natives. India has, moreover, not been blessed with the checks which the press and the legal profession are capable of exerting in England. Finally, Stephen alleged, justice is being administered among a people who have not been taught a scrupulous concern for the truth. Nevertheless, he was generally satisfied with the systems of law and administration that the British had established in India:

> In the first place there is hardly any nonsense at all in the system. It is a system carefully and laboriously constructed; superintended with extraordinary watchfulness and care, and worked by men who are paid for it and give their whole attention to it. It is not a heap of institutions, resting on no principle, formed upon no system and incapable of being understood except by a long course of historical study. . . . Whatever may have been the defects of Indian government, want of interest in the work done, want of vigilance in superintending the manner in which it was done, want of energy and enterprise in improving the manner of doing it, are not amongst them.[42]

Stephen favoured the extension of the Regulation system to the Non-Regulation provinces whenever these reached the point where government could no longer be handled efficiently by one ruler. Against the advocates of personal rule, Stephen argued that it was erroneous to assume that the provinces had previously been governed without law. In fact they were often ruled by a system of law more simple and coherent than that in the Regulation provinces. He adverted to Lord Lawrence's brilliant administration in the Punjab, where, it will be recalled, his regime had set up penal and civil codes, and codes of criminal and civil procedure. 'The notion that there is an opposition in the nature of things between law and executive vigour, rests on a fundamental confusion of ideas and on traditions which are superannuated and ought to be forgotten.'[43] Stephen did not propose abolishing the executive functions of the local officers. 'The maintenance of the position of the District Officers is absolutely essential to the maintenance of British rule in India.'⁴⁴ But he did advocate a degree of separation between their powers. He would reserve the administration of the criminal law to the executive, while the civil law would be left in the hands of the judiciary. This arrangement would correspond with the nature of sovereign power:

> In a few words, the administration of criminal justice is the indispensable condition of all government, and the means by which it is in the last resort carried on. But the District Officers are the local governors of the country, therefore the District Officers ought to administer criminal justice.⁴⁵

The opponents of Anglo-Indian legislation, according to Stephen, based their arguments upon another fallacy: it was incorrect to assume that the Regulation and the Non-Regulation systems represented two conflicting theories of government. As a Hobbesian he believed that the distinction between government by law and government without law was meaningless. Without law, government is impossible. Every province, whether Regulation or Non-Regulation, was really governed by law. 'The question, therefore, is between one kind of law and legal administration and another, not between government by law and government without law. The question, indeed, lies much more between different forms of administration than different forms of law.'⁴⁶

V

Having established that India must be governed by law, Stephen directed his attention to 'one of the cardinal questions of Indian government':⁴⁷ whether the British ought to rule through native agencies and upon native principles.⁴⁸ Like all questions of government, he thought that it should be answered by reference to the principle of utility. One view that had found favour among many was that the British should establish native rulers throughout India, supported by British organisation. Stephen believed that this proposal was defective in both theory and practice.

> Whenever a history of the Indian Empire worthy of the subject is written, a large part of it will be occupied with a specification

of the numerous attempts which have been made to give practical effect to the theory that India ought to be governed by, or at least through, the natives of India according to Indian ideas.[49]

The pages of such a history, Stephen proclaimed, would be replete with reports of failure. Indian ideas of government had been refuted by centuries of calamity and anarchy. If the British were to govern through native agencies, the whole of India would be plagued by personal intrigue, 'the curse of every despotic State', and live under the perpetual threat of revolt and civil war.[50] To rule through native agents it would also be necessary to maintain a large native army, subjecting the Government to the persistent danger of mutiny. Stephen suggested that the Mutiny of 1857 ought to be interpreted as 'the break-down and explosion of the policy which so many persons are anxious, for different reasons, to revive under a variety of forms'.[51]

Stephen concluded by rejecting government by natives according to native principles on theoretical grounds. The Indian population is composed of Hindus and Mohammedans. Since every government has 'a moral and social standard which gives colour to its legislation and to its institutions', the British must, if they are to govern according to native principles, choose to govern by either those of the Hindus or the Mohammedans.[52] But to govern according to one faith would conflict with the fundamental beliefs of the other. The Government of India must therefore be founded upon Western principles, those 'which have been shown by the experience of Europe to be essential to the attainment of peace, order, wealth, and progress in the arts and sciences'.[53]

In later years, Stephen found his assumptions challenged by the radical John Bright. In a speech at Manchester in December 1877, Bright alleged that British power in India was founded on ambition, crime, and conquest. He suggested that the British should make amends for their infamous deeds by preparing the Indians for self-government as soon as possible. He also advocated that the Indian Empire should be divided into five or six independent political units, free from control by London. Stephen had been following Indian affairs closely since his return to England in 1872, and was an intimate friend and correspondent of Lord Lytton, Viceroy from 1876 to 1880. Indeed, he was a staunch supporter of Lytton's policy of intervention in Afghanistan to check Russian expansion. In response to Bright's accusation, and indirectly in defence of Lytton's rule, Stephen wrote a lengthy letter to *The Times* praising the British achievement and singling out the true basis of the Indian Empire – justice founded on force:

> If I thought that our power in India had originated in crime and was maintained by brute force, it would have no interest for me. In that case I should turn my attention to other matters and leave a hopeless system to reach its natural end by its own road. I feel, however, that such a view is utterly false, and that we, the English nation, can hardly degrade ourselves more deeply than by repudiating the achievements of our ancestors, apologizing for acts which we ought to feel as proud as the inheritors of great names and splendid titles must feel of the deeds by which they were won, and evading like cowards and sluggards the arduous responsibilities which have devolved upon us. . . . I deny that ambition and conquest are crimes; I say that ambition is the great incentive to every manly virtue, and that conquest is the process by which every great State in the world (the United States excepted) has been built up. . . . The British Power in India is like a vast bridge over which an enormous multitude of human beings are passing, and will (I trust) for ages to come continue to pass, from a dreary land, in which brute violence in its roughest form had worked its will for centuries – a land of cruel wars, ghastly superstitions, wasting plague and famine – on their way to a country of which, not being a prophet, I will not try to draw a picture, but which is at least orderly, peaceful, and industrious, and which for aught we know to the contrary, may be the cradle of changes comparable to those which have formed the imperishable legacy to mankind of the Roman Empire. The bridge was not built without desperate struggles and costly sacrifices. Strike away either of its piers and it will fall, and what are they? One of its piers is military power: the other is justice; by which I mean a firm and constant determination on the part of the English to promote impartially and by all lawful means, what they (the English) regard as the lasting good of the natives of India. Neither force nor justice will suffice by itself. Force without justice is the old scourge of India, wielded by stronger hand than of old. Justice without force is a weak aspiration after an unattainable end. But so long as the masterful will, the stout heart, the active brain, the calm nerves and the strong body which make up military force are directed

to the object which I have defined as constituting justice, I should have no fear, for even if we fail after doing our best, we fail with honour, and if we succeed we shall have performed the greatest feat of strength, skill, and courage in the whole history of the world.[54]

Another test of Stephen's principles came about in 1883, when Sir Courtenay Ilbert, Legal Member of the Viceroy's Council under the Marquis of Ripon, introduced a bill, subsequently known as the Ilbert Bill, that would permit the trial of British subjects by judges of the Indian race. This was during the period of Gladstone's Second Ministry (1880–85), when many entertained the idea of instituting representative institutions in India with an eye towards its eventual self-government. The Bill aroused an unexpected outburst of controversy, and was finally settled by a compromise. For a long time, Britons had enjoyed the privilege of a trial only by a session judge or justice of the peace of their own race. In accord with the Code of Criminal Procedure which Stephen had revised in 1872, there existed two sets of courts in India: one to administer the criminal law to Indian subjects, another to administer the criminal law to British subjects. Since 1877, Indian judges had criminal jurisdiction over Europeans in the presidencies (Bengal, Madras and Bombay), but Ilbert's Bill was designed to extend that jurisdiction to the outlying regions.

Stephen strongly opposed the Bill and sent some angry letters to *The Times* stating his position.[55] He protested what he considered 'the policy of shifting the foundations on which the British Government of India rests':

It has been observed in many articles, some published in *The Times*, that if the Government of India have decided on removing all anomalies from India, they ought to remove themselves and their countrymen. Whether or not that mode of expression can be fully justified, there can, I think, be no doubt that it is impossible to imagine any policy more fearfully dangerous and more certain, in case of failure, to lead to results to which the Mutiny would be child's play, than the policy of shifting the foundations on which the British Government of India rests. It is essentially an absolute government, founded not on consent, but on conquest. It does not represent the native principles of life or of government, and it can never do so until it represents heathenism and barbarism. It represents a belligerent civilization, and no anomaly can be so striking or so dangerous as its administration by men who, being at the head of a Government founded upon conquest, implying at every point the superiority of the conquering race, or their ideas, their institutions, their opinions, and their principles, and having no justification for its existence except that superiority, shrink from the open, uncompromising, straightforward assertion of it, seek to apologize for their position, and refuse, from whatever cause, to uphold and support it.[56]

At a time when many regarded the growth of democracy and the agitation for Irish Home Rule as a serious threat to the existence of the Indian Empire, such sentiments were not uncommon. They were echoed by Stephen's friend Sir John Strachey, who had served ably in India under three viceroys in various official capacities. Stephen chose to dedicate his *Liberty, Equality, Fraternity* to him; and Strachey reciprocated by dedicating his own work *India* to Stephen.[57]

Stephen proceeded to develop his ideas on the subject of governing in accord with native principles in his article 'Foundations of the Government of India'.[58] It seems that the harsh tone of his letters to *The Times* on the Ilbert Bill had offended some readers, particularly his successor as Legal Member, Sir Arthur Hobhouse. Stephen conceded that he may have erred by expressing his views in 'a needlessly trenchant and unpopular style'.[59] He took pains, therefore, to assure his readers that he did not understand the British conquest of India to have been in a rapacious sense. His staple arguments about the British bringing order to chaos, light to darkness, and benevolent government to a primitive despotism were repeated. He suggested that we view the matter practically: 'The history of Europe down to our own days is such that if titles resting upon conquest were regarded as iniquitous, universal anarchy would ensue, even if a prescription of say a century, were to be regarded as sufficient to establish the rights of occupiers.'[60]

From the fact that the British owed their rule in India to conquest rather than consent, Stephen drew an inference which he regarded as inevitable. The government of India must be absolute. It must proceed in accord with the ideas of the governors, not those of the governed. Representative institutions are therefore out of the question, unless one is prepared to accept the dissolution of the Empire and the failure of the British mission in India. Stephen rejected the notion that absolute government is inherently inferior to parliamentary government. The manner of governing a country must be decided not on the basis of abstract natural rights, but on the basis of utility. Like John Stuart Mill, Stephen believed that what was good for England was not necessarily good for India. Lacking a tradition of self-government, India was consequently unfit for representative institutions. Though the natives might be permitted to serve within the lower echelons of the government, the reins of power must remain firmly in British hands. Stephen attacked what he characterised as 'the doctrine of the Divine Right of Representative Institutions or of the Sovereignty of the People', and those who held that 'the exercise of absolute power can never be justified except as a temporary expedient used for the purpose of superseding itself, and as a means of educating those whom it affects into a fitness for parliamentary institutions'.[61] The British have no moral obligation to prepare the Indians for self-government. Indeed, Stephen thought that it was doubtful whether, in certain respects, Britain's own government was superior to that which it had imposed on India. By this time Stephen – in large measure owing to the frustration of his codification schemes at home, his experience in India, and domestic political developments – had grown extremely pessimistic as to the effectiveness of the British parliamentary system. He was convinced that in India benevolent and efficient government were more important than free government.

Despite his belief in the superiority of Western civilisation, Stephen insisted that the native customs and religions should be interfered with as little as possible. The old Utilitarian goal of an extensive political and social reconstruction of India along European principles was impracticable. 'No one can feel more distinctly than I the madness of the smallest unnecessary interference with the social habits or religious opinions of the country. I would not touch a single one of them except in cases of extreme necessity.'[62]

Legislation should be strictly limited, dictated solely by utility. It was justifiable only to sustain British rule and the administration of the Indian Government. All laws that exceeded this end were 'mischievous and dangerous. . . . No law should be made till it is distinctly perceived and felt to be necessary. No one can admit more fully or feel more strongly than I the evils and dangers of mere speculative legislation in India.'⁶³ In his *Liberty, Equality, Fraternity* Stephen contended that all government must have a moral basis. In order to maintain the foundations of their government in India, the British must rule according to their own moral principles, and on the assumption that no native religion is true. Nevertheless, he insisted that only in cases of flagrant violations of Western morals had the British interfered with the Indian religions by means of legislation. Some gross forms of barbarism and intolerance had therefore been extirpated. The practice known as suttee, or the immolation of native widows upon their husbands' funeral pyres, was abolished in 1828 during the governor-generalship of Lord Bentinck. Along the same lines, female infanticide and personal slavery had also been abolished. Laws were passed to allow Hindu widows to remarry, to enable native converts to Christianity to obtain divorces, and to permit persons of no religion to marry.

Stephen thought that by means of a benevolent government which showed the necessary concern for native society, the British would produce a profound social revolution in India, the ultimate consequences of which were incalculable. British interference need only be indirect to bring about the decay of the old social order. The village communities had begun to disappear only because the rule of law had been imposed upon a customary society. The mere introduction of law and order, the sanctity of contract, and education 'will produce a social revolution throughout every part of India, modifying every part of the daily life of the natives, and changing every article of all their creeds'.⁶⁴ Stephen conceived the British role in India to be primarily that of teachers whose mission was to impart their law, 'the gospel of the English'. The greatest effect would be moral:

> The establishment of a system of law which regulates the most important part of the daily life of the people, constitutes in itself a moral conquest more striking, more durable, and far more solid, than the physical conquest which renders it possible. It exercises an influence over the minds of the people in many ways comparable to that of a new religion.⁶⁵

Again we find Stephen insisting upon the pervasive moral influence of the law. Nowhere was the connection between law and morals more acknowledged than in India; from time immemorial, he observed, the Hindus and Mohammedans were accustomed to viewing law and religion as different aspects of the same thing.

The British, then, had been entrusted with the mission of being midwives in the birth of a modern India. The success of this maieutic function depended, of course, upon the maintenance of British rule. Their duty was to ensure that the social revolution was directed towards a beneficial result. Just what India would ultimately be like, Stephen could not say, but he speculated that it would probably not reproduce Europe in politics, morals or religion.[66] Within the framework of English law, it would develop doctrines, customs, and institutions of its own. What Stephen did not foresee was that the revolution he envisaged would ultimately give birth to the Indian nationalist movement.

VI

Fitzjames Stephen relished his work in India, and considered it the most important accomplishment of his life. The Indian Empire was one of 'the very boldest and most successful enterprises ever tried by mortal man'.[67] And Stephen was proud to have participated in that enterprise. As he confided to Lord Lytton, 'I am no poet as you are, but Delhi made my soul burn within me, and I never heard "God save the Queen" or saw the Union Jack flying in the heart of India without feeling the tears in my eyes, which are not much used to tears.'[68] In his departing speech before the Legislative Council, Stephen conveyed a feeling of deep admiration for those who had devoted themselves to serving British India: 'I have seen much of the most energetic nation in the world; but I never saw anything to equal the general level of zeal, intelligence, public spirit and vigour maintained by the public service of this country.'[69]

During a period that has been characterised as the heyday of British rule in India, Stephen played a major part in reforming the Indian law along English lines. He wrote to his good friend and long-time colleague on the staff of the *Saturday Review*, G. S. Venables, that he considered his role in India to be that of a 'Benthamee Lycurgus'.[70] The metaphor was well chosen; considering his pessimism concerning English politics, one is not surprised to find him comparing himself with the Spartan Lycurgus rather than Solon, the founder of Athenian democracy. Shortly after his return to London in 1872, Stephen attended the annual dinner of the Cambridge Apostles. During the preliminary amenities, he suggested a toast to its chairman, Sir Henry Maine, who had returned from India in 1869. He proposed, one suspects only partly in jest, that the legislation passed during their service there would henceforth be known as 'the Acts of the Apostles'.[71]

India exerted a profound influence upon Stephen's thought. As he wrote in 1872, 'India has been a sort of second university course to me. . . . There is hardly a subject on which it has not given me a whole crowd of new ideas.'[72] Though his views had been substantially formed before he went there, he was finally able to test them according to experience. The chance to observe at first hand the British achievement in India demonstrated to him the advantages of enlightened and efficient government. During his India years, Stephen continued to ponder philosophical questions. But he had a new perspective: 'I am for one thing perpetually thinking about India. Indian politics, Indian laws, and the light thrown by India on all great questions of government, morals, and religion, which after all are the only things in the world worth much thinking about.'[73] His correspondence reveals that, in addition to a project for a book on British India, he eventually planned to write a work on politics, morals and religion which, he later claimed, were merely 'one subject under different heads'.[74]

More than thirty years earlier than Stephen, Macaulay had left India confident that he had helped launch a legal and educational system that would lead to the Westernisation and eventual self-government of India. He returned to write his majestic *History*, a celebration of the virtues and triumphs of Whig liberalism. His fervent hope was that India would someday emulate the British form of government. Stephen could not share Macaulay's optimism. During his absence, he had closely followed British politics and become apprehensive of Gladstone's popular liberalism. The Liberal leader had won much support from the urban working classes as a result of the Reform Act of 1867 and democracy was on the march. The political writings of John Stuart Mill that Stephen had read and accepted as a young man now seemed radically wrong in the light of Indian experience. Stephen left India convinced that he had participated in a government in many ways more efficient than its British counterpart. He returned home to write his *Liberty, Equality, Fraternity*, an expression of concern over the recent course of British liberalism, and a powerful attack upon its fundamental assumptions.

7 Liberty, Equality, Fraternity

I

While sailing homeward to England on the Red Sea in the spring of 1872, and fresh with the experience of India, Fitzjames Stephen began firing 'broadsides' at John Stuart Mill.[1] The result was a series of brilliant and penetrating articles written for the *Pall Mall Gazette*, later collected and published in March 1873 as *Liberty, Equality, Fraternity*.[2] The book is the most comprehensive statement of his thought, illustrating the relationships he understood to exist between politics, law, religion and morality. Leslie Stephen considered it an 'apologia' or manifesto of his brother's deepest convictions.[3] Fitzjames later said, somewhat unjustly to himself, that it was 'little more than the turning of an Indian lantern on European problems'.[4] India was where many of the ideas which he had been expounding for more than a decade were fully developed and put to the test of experience. As he noted in the Preface to the first edition, his Indian labours had 'strongly confirmed the reflections which the book contains, and which had been taking shape gradually in my mind for many years'.[5]

The object of the book is a critical examination of the doctrines implied by the popular phrase 'Liberty, Equality, Fraternity'. In particular, it is a refutation of the writings of John Stuart Mill. For Mill, liberty, equality, and fraternity are logically linked as means for achieving the Utilitarian goal of the greatest happiness for the greatest number. Liberty is the means to individual development and social improvement; equal opportunity is necessary to remove the artificial and unjust barriers to these ends; and fraternity is the sentiment necessary to foster among men a concern for the common good.

'Liberty, Equality, Fraternity' had been a worldwide republican slogan during the French Revolution and later served as the creed of the Religion of Humanity – a secular religion best known in the form of Positivism. Originating in France during the first part of the nineteenth century with Auguste Comte, Positivism spread to England and had a significant influence upon such intellectuals as John Stuart Mill, Thomas Henry Buckle, George Eliot, John Morley and Frederic Harrison. In England, Mill was its most distinguished exponent. We have seen that when Mill's essay *On Liberty* first appeared in 1859, Stephen reviewed it with general approval, expressing only minor reservations.[6] But after his Indian experience he felt constrained to write to Mill that he hoped 'to set forth certain qualifications to your essay on Liberty, which it [India] has led me to believe in'.[7] To Stephen, the mere fact that a phrase had become popular furnished a presumption that it was distorted or misdirected. His objection to 'Liberty, Equality, Fraternity' was that the words had come to be regarded as denoting absolutes, irrespective of reason, history and utility. In the years following the Reform Act of 1867, the fear increased that the working classes would adopt the Religion of Humanity in its absolute form and overturn the entire social order. Stephen therefore returned to his concern with reconciling culture and democracy.

Stephen directed his attack specifically against the later works of Mill. Actually, the two men agreed more than they differed. What Stephen feared was not so much the ideas of Mill as the implications and tendencies of the absolute form in which he expressed them. In criticising liberty, equality and fraternity, Stephen did not intend to support slavery, restrictive caste and hatred. As in so many doctrinal disputes, the disagreement was over principles and assumptions, not ends. In his correspondence, Stephen was careful to remark that the difference between himself and his opponents was 'rather a difference of colour than of substance. I think I am quite as humane and public spirited as my neighbours.' To this he was careful to add the significant qualification that 'my public spirit is rooted in India'.[8] Stephen chose to attack Mill because he was the only contemporary English writer who had expressed himself competently and systematically on the Religion of Humanity. He believed, moreover, that Mill was the only writer on the subject with whom he agreed sufficiently to disagree with profitably.[9] Some of his arguments against Mill's *On Liberty* were anticipated by earlier critics in the reviews that appeared shortly after its publication,[10] but none of these reviews offer a critique as powerful or comprehensive as that of Stephen; John Morley, Mill's intellectual disciple, recollected that it was Fitzjames Stephen who 'led the first effective attack on Mill's pontifical authority'.[11]

Stephen insisted that he did not wish to launch a captious attack upon the writings of a man to whom he was so greatly indebted intellectually. Though he was proud to call himself a disciple of Mill's earlier works, he believed that his later essays – *On Liberty*, *Utilitarianism* and *The Subjection of Women* – epitomised the popular notion of the Religion of Humanity. He contended that in these works Mill had departed radically from the Benthamite Utilitarian principles, infusing his thought with a dangerous sentimentality, and exposing 'a side of his teaching which is as repugnant as the rest of it is attractive to me'.[12] Stephen thus found himself, as he confided to his sister-in-law, 'falling foul' of Mill in his 'sentimental mood', which he regarded as a desertion of 'the proper principles of rigidity and ferocity' upon which Mill had been reared.[13] Stephen never anticipated that he would one day be expressing such profound objections to the thought of a man who was the foremost exponent of English Utilitariansim. He reflected:

> It is curious that after being, so to speak, a devoted disciple and partisan of his [Mill] up to a certain point, I should have found it at last impossible to go on with him. But his politics and his morals are not mine at all, though I believe in and admire his logic [*A System of Logic*] and his general notions of philosophy.[14]

For Stephen, it deserves stressing again, liberalism must be founded upon human nature, history and utility. Because Mill neglected these empirical bases, Stephen charged, the consequences and inconsistencies of his liberalism must be shown.

Written within a relatively short span of time as a series of newspaper articles, *Liberty, Equality, Fraternity* suffers somewhat in organisation. Since it was not published initially as one piece, Stephen, fearing that his readers might have forgotten an important point made in a previous issue, sometimes felt constrained to repeat an argument. Had he been afforded more time, he later confessed, he would have preferred to write a more direct expression of his views independently of Mill's works.[15] He would have begun with a discussion of human nature, followed by a treatment of its influence upon law, morality and religion. Instead, circumstances compelled him to present a systematic refutation which closely adhered to the sequence of Mill's thought. But this procedure had a decided advantage: rather than offering merely a different philosophy, it enabled Stephen to attempt to demonstrate specifically the fundamental weaknesses of Mill's thinking. Regardless of whether he succeeded in refuting Mill, Stephen produced a work compelling and provocative in its arguments, and which compares admirably with the highest exemplars of Victorian prose.

Some readers are liable to be repelled by Stephen's blunt manner of expression, his penchant for stating his views in the most forthright and critical fashion. During his youth he had been known as 'the Gruffian' and 'the Giant Grim'; and as a member of the Cambridge Apostles his powerful oratory and relish for polemics earned him the sobriquet 'the British Lion'.[16] His contemporaries often compared him with Dr Johnson; for both men engaged in a relentless war upon sentimental dreamers and popular commonplaces. In his polemical writings Stephen was often merciless and always hard-hitting in his arguments; he was devoid of the finesse of such a man as Matthew Arnold. While Arnold's weapon was the rapier, Stephen's was the bludgeon. Style is the mirror of the mind, and Stephen's mind was consummately legal. He wrote to convince and to refute. He had an instinct for the jugular and always drove his arguments with a hammer. But one seldom hammers on difficult matters with delicacy.

Stephen's physical appearance was as formidable as his prose. He stood over six feet tall, weighed more than 200 pounds (over fourteen stone), and gave a stern impression. Only those who knew him well were able to discern the kindness beneath the somewhat coarse exterior. Stephen's sometimes brutal frankness stemmed not from insensitivity but from an excessive honesty. He shunned the euphemism. When writing on the criminal law, for instance, he insisted that men must recognise that when they imprison they enslave, and when they hang they kill. When he wrote on India, he said that as foreigners who rule by conquest, the English must expect to be hated. The point is that men must be prepared to face courageously the facts and their consequences. Nevertheless, anyone who would call the mass of mankind ignorant, indifferent and selfish, anyone who would deny the equality of men, and declare that force rather than discussion ruled the world, was unlikely to endear himself to his readers. But Stephen was convinced that if we ignore such unpalatable truths we do so at our peril.

II

John Stuart Mill, we have seen, believed that a more formidable and insidious form of tyranny attended the growth of democracy than that which his countrymen might fear from an oppressive ruler. For the danger in a democracy lies in a 'tyranny of the majority', by which society imposes, through law or public opinion, its will upon the conduct and ideas of the individual. To safeguard against this danger Mill submits, in the introductory chapter to his essay *On Liberty*, 'one very simple principle ... to govern absolutely' all relations between society and the individual. It has become the classic statement of the liberal point of view:

> The object of this essay is to assert one very simple principle, as entitled to govern absolutely the dealings of society with the individual in the way of compulsion or control, whether the means used be physical force in the form of legal penalties, or the moral coercion of public opinion. That principle is that the sole end for which mankind are warranted individually or collectively in interfering with the liberty of action of any of their numbers is self-protection; that the only purpose for which power can be rightfully exercised over any member of a civilized community against his will is to prevent harm to others. His own good, either physical or moral, is not a sufficient warrant. He cannot rightfully be compelled to do or forbear because it will be better for him to do so, because it will make him happier, because in the opinions of others to do so would be wise or even right. These are good reasons for remonstrating with him, or reasoning with him, or persuading him, or entreating him, but not for compelling him, or visiting him with any evil in case he do otherwise. To justify that, the conduct from which it is desired to deter him must be calculated to produce evil to someone else. The only part of the conduct of any one for which he is amenable to society is that which concerns others. In the part which merely concerns himself his independence is of right, absolute. Over himself, over his own body and mind, the individual is sovereign.[17]

Mill concludes by specifying the realm of human liberty:

> It comprises, first, the inward domain of consciousness; demanding liberty of conscience in the most comprehensive sense; liberty of thought and feeling; absolute freedom of opinion and sentiment on all subjects, practical or speculative, scientific, moral, or theological. The liberty of expressing and publishing opinions may seem to fall under a different principle, since it belongs to that part of the conduct of an individual which concerns other people, but being almost of as much importance as the liberty of thought itself, and resting in great part on the same reasons, is practically inseparable from it. Secondly, the principle requires liberty of tastes and pursuits, of framing the plan of our life to suit our own character, of doing as we like, subject to such consequences as may follow, without impediment from our fellow-creatures, so long as what we do does not harm them, even though they should think our conduct foolish, perverse or wrong. Thirdly, from this liberty of each individual follows the liberty within the same limits of combination among individuals.[18]

Mill's principle appears logical enough: it asserts that there is a sphere of human activity, the self-regarding acts, in which compulsion cannot be applied, either by law or public opinion. As a principle it has great moral appeal, for who would dare deny that human liberty ought to be protected and extended? Nevertheless, Stephen undertook to demonstrate that the 'one very simple principle' is specious, and that it is actually contrary to the doctrine of utility upon which Mill claims it to be established.

As classical liberals – in the tradition of Locke – Mill and Stephen agreed that liberty is the absence of restraint. It is the silence of the law; liberty and law stand in inverse relation to each other. Where Mill and Stephen disagree lies in the value they place upon liberty. In order to understand their debate it is important to bear this in mind. As a Hobbesian and a Benthamite, Stephen valued efficient and benevolent government more than liberty. He believed that law, in conjunction with the additional sanctions provided by morality and religion, was the instrument for the attainment of the common good. Liberty, subject as it is to the principle of utility, has only contingent value. It is, moreover, dependent upon law. Because the interests of men in society do not automatically harmonise, liberty must be limited to insure its viability. 'It is only under the protection of a powerful, well-organized, and intelligent government that any liberty can exist at all.'[19] For without law men would revert to the state of nature, where no one would be secure.

> Law, in many cases, means not only a command, but a beneficial command. Liberty means not the bare absence of restraint, but the absence of injurious restraint. Justice means not mere impartiality in applying general rules to particular cases, but impartiality in applying beneficent general rules to particular cases.[20]

Stephen was not opposed to liberty as such, and in the course of this chapter it will become clear what limits he placed upon government interference with the individual. But he thought that liberty is only one of several complementary values, among them culture, tradition, morality and community, that are necessary for a good society.

Mill, on the other hand, had an affirmative conception of liberty. He believed that the only safeguard against the tyranny of the majority in a democracy lay in stressing liberty as a positive value. He thought that to preserve individual freedom there must be a sacrosanct area of human life exempt from societal and State interference. Liberty is the means to human improvement and should be extended as far as possible consistent with his principle. Government is entrusted with no positive functions, its purpose being merely to protect. Only if the individual is free to reach his own perfection without interference can there be the full and diverse development of human character necessary to counteract the oppressive aspects of majority rule. Moreover, the only means to truth on most of the great speculative questions that concern mankind lies in affording the greatest possible freedom to thought and discussion.

Stephen, as we know, belonged to the school of thought, including Arnold and Walter Bagehot, which held that democracy must be reconciled with culture. He insisted that Mill's 'one very simple principle' would bring on the tyranny it was intended to prevent. If allowed 'to govern absolutely', in Mill's words, all relations between society and the individual, the principle would, Stephen argued, supply a justification for the undereducated multitude to run roughshod over all institutions, and destroy the good along with the bad. He believed that in an age of democratisation, authority and order need to be safeguarded more than liberty. As a liberal in the classical sense, Stephen concurred with Mill that the individual should be free from arbitrary government. Though unwilling to go as far as Mill, he also believed that religion and morals should be openly discussed without fear of legal restraint. Yet he thought that Mill undervalued the role of the law in preserving liberty, and he objected to the categorical manner in which Mill expressed his views.

Stephen begins his refutation by expounding a theory of human action to which he is confident Mill would subscribe.[21] All voluntary actions, he submits, are the result of motives, which may be either hope and pleasure, or fear and pain. A voluntary act that springs from hope or pleasure is regarded as free; a voluntary act that springs from fear or pain is regarded as done under compulsion. According to this theory, he alleges, Mill's principle is tantamount to denying that one is ever justified in trying to affect anyone's conduct by appealing to fear or pain, except for the sake of protection.

Mill's principle, Stephen contends, would subvert all religion and morality, which are forms of compulsion that appeal to fear independently of protection. Indeed, they exercise a degree of compulsion more extensive and profound than the law.

> Criminal legislation proper may be regarded as an engine of prohibition unimportant in comparison with morals and the forms of morality sanctioned by theology. For one act from which one person is restrained by the fear of the law of the land, many persons are restrained from innumerable acts by fear of the disapprobation of their neighbours which is the moral sanction; or by fear of punishment in a future state of existence, which is the religious sanction; or by the fear of their own disapprobation, which may be called the conscientious sanction, and may be regarded as a compound case of the other two.[22]

For Stephen, then, the social order depended upon much more than the law. Mill's principle, he adds, would defeat the purpose of all religion and morality by condoning all kinds of indulgence so long as people refrain from harming others. One would be justified in saying on the Day of Judgement, 'I pleased myself and hurt nobody else.'[23] But religion and morality necessarily impose upon mankind, for reasons beyond protection, standards of conduct to which few persons would adhere if left to their own devices. History shows, moreover, that religious and moral systems have been established, spread, and maintained only by means of coercion by law and public opinion, regardless of individual choice.

Mill's principle is also contradicted by the necessary methods employed for the maintenance of political and social institutions. It would prohibit, for instance, all forms of taxation to which people refused to consent unless the revenue was intended for the military, the police or the administration of justice. 'To force an unwilling person to contribute to the support of the British Museum is as distinct a violation of Mr. Mill's principle as religious persecution.'[24] Coercion is also the principal means by which political and social institutions have been reformed. Stephen is certain that Mill and his disciples would not deny that the political and social changes since the sixteenth century have been on the whole beneficial to mankind. Yet they were brought about by force which had nothing to do with protecting the State or the individual. 'It would surely be as absurd to say that the Reformation or the French Revolution was brought about freely and not by coercion as to say that Charles I walked freely to the block.'[25]

Mill conceded that there were certain social 'inconveniences which are strictly inseparable from the unfavourable judgement of others',[26] and inflicted for reasons other than the general welfare, discomforts to which a person may be subjected in that portion of his acts regarding only himself. But Stephen argues that Mill shows an unwarranted bias against the law when he draws such an arbitrary distinction between these social penalties and the legal. Stephen cannot understand why Mill would accept social inconveniences, which may easily become excessive and unjust, and reject similar ones that are organised, well-defined, and systematically inflicted by the criminal law.

> This organization, definition, and procedure make all the difference between the restraints which Mr. Mill would permit and the restraints to which he objects. I cannot see on what the distinction rests. I cannot understand why it must always be wrong to punish habitual drunkenness by fine, imprisonment, or deprivation of civil rights, and always be right to punish it by

the infliction of those consequences which are 'strictly inseparable from the unfavourable judgement of others'.[27]

Here we have a disagreement between Mill and Stephen which stems from their differing conceptions of the threat posed by democracy in their day. Because Mill believed that liberty was most endangered, he held that the province of law ought to be limited as much as possible. Because Stephen believed law and order to be in greater danger, he stressed that they were more important to society. He also insisted that the liberty which Mill valued was dependent upon the rule of law. In view of the fact that the criminal law concretises and regulates popular vengeance, which would otherwise be capricious and unduly severe, he believed that the penal consequences of social disapprobation should never be underrated or ignored.

Stephen strikes a telling blow against Mill's principle when he argues that the distinction between self-regarding and other-regarding acts upon which it is founded is untenable. Although this distinction has originated much controversy, it retains its appeal today because it seems to provide a clear and absolute limit to governmental interference with the individual. Mill assumed that in most cases it may be clearly ascertained which actions affect the individual alone, and those which affect society as well. Stephen maintains that the distinction is fallacious, for the most important part of our conduct affects both ourselves and others. Hence Mill's principle is futile in practice, since 'it assumes the existence of an ideal state of things in which everyone has precisely the position which, with a view to the general happiness of the world, he ought to hold'.[28]

Mill's principle is also undermined by the exceptions he allows. Mill qualified his rule when he said that it ought to apply only to those persons who have attained maturity of their faculties. This would exclude children, and 'those backward states of society in which the race itself may be considered as in its nonage'. Stephen replies that maturity and civilisation are matters of degree, and that as yet there are no valid tests for them. Benevolent despotism, Mill argues, is a legitimate form of government for barbarians, since 'liberty as a principle has no application to any state of things anterior to the time when mankind have become capable of being improved by free and equal discussion'.[29] Stephen fails to find this helpful because, depending upon how it is construed, it could imply that compulsion is always or never justifiable.

Mill was convinced that once mankind had become capable of being improved by free discussion, compulsion must be sharply limited. Indeed, he assumed that the progress of civilisation is marked by a reduction in the role of compulsion in favour of persuasion. But this argument, Stephen retorts, fails to take into account human nature. Since few people are in fact capable of improvement by free discussion, Mill's principle would always apply to only a small minority:

> Estimate the proportion of men and women who are selfish, sensual, frivolous, idle, absolutely commonplace and wrapped up in the smallest of petty routines, and consider how far the freest of free discussion is likely to improve them. The only way by which it is practically possible to act upon them at all is by compulsion or restraint.[30]

Mill's argument is also contradicted by the facts of history:

> If we look at the conduct of bodies of men as expressed in their laws and institutions, we shall find that, though compulsion and persuasion go hand in hand, from the most immature and the roughest ages and societies up to the most civilised, the lion's share of the results obtained is due to compulsion, and that discussion is at most an appeal to the motives by which the strong man is likely to be actuated in using his strength. Look at our own time and country, and mention any single great change which has been effected by mere discussion. Can a single case be mentioned in which the passions of men were interested where the change was not carried by force – that is to say, ultimately by the fear of revolution?[31]

As a disciple of Hobbes, Stephen recognised that force lies at the root of all government. Issues before Parliament are decided not by discussion but by power:

> Such questions as the admission of Jews into Parliament and the legislation of marriage between brothers and sisters-in-law drag on and on after the argument has been exhausted, till in the course of time those who take one view or the other grow into a

'Liberty, Equality, Fraternity'

decided majority, and settle the matter their own way. Parliamentary government is simply a mild and disguised form of compulsion. We agree to try strength by counting heads instead of breaking heads, but the principle is exactly the same.

There is no sense in fooling ourselves,

> it is not the wisest side which wins, but the one which for the time being shows its superior strength (of which no doubt wisdom is one element) by enlisting the largest amount of active sympathy in its support. The minority gives way not because it is convinced that it is wrong, but because it is convinced it is a minority.[32]

Though we cannot eliminate force from the State, we can regulate its form. The function of politics, in Stephen's view, is the proper employment and restraint of power:

> To direct that power aright is, I think, the principal object of political argument. The difference between a rough and a civilised society is not that force is used in the one case and persuasion in the other, but that force is (or ought to be) guided with greater care in the second case than in the first. President Lincoln attained his objects by the use of a degree of force which would have crushed Charlemagne and his paladins and peers like so many eggshells.[33]

III

Having shown that Mill's principle is destructive and based upon an illusory distinction, Stephen proceeds to a critical examination of Mill's second chapter, on the liberty of thought and discussion. Here too he dissents not so much from Mill's ideas as from the extent to which he attempts to take them. He agrees with Mill that questions of religion and morals should be discussed openly and without legal restraint. But he believes that in order to establish this right Mill 'has stated a theory which is very far indeed from the truth, and which, if generally accepted, might hereafter become a serious embarrassment to rational legislation'.[34] Mill provided a summary of his position which deserves to be quoted in its entirety:

> We have now recognized the necessity to the mental well-being of mankind (on which all their other well-being depends) of

freedom of opinion and freedom of the expression of opinion on four distinct grounds.

First, if any opinion is compelled to silence, that opinion may, for aught we can certainly know, be true. To deny this is to assume our own infallibility.

Secondly, though the silenced opinion be an error, it may, and very commonly does, contain a portion of truth; and since the general or prevailing opinion is rarely or never the whole truth, it is only by the collision of adverse opinions that the remainder of the truth has any chance of being supplied.

Thirdly, even if the received opinion be not only true, but the whole truth, unless it is suffered to be and actually is vigorously and earnestly contested, it will by most of those who receive it be held in the manner of a prejudice, with little comprehension or feeling of its rational grounds.

Fourthly, the meaning of the doctrine itself will be in danger of being lost or enfeebled and deprived of its vital effect on the character and conduct; the dogma becoming a mere formal profession inefficacious for good, but cumbering the ground, and preventing the growth of any real and heartfelt conviction from reason or personal experience.[35]

To this day, Mill's arguments in favour of virtually absolute freedom of thought and discussion appear axiomatic. Yet Stephen subjects them to cogent criticism, attacking, as always, Mill's fundamental assumptions. Mill contends that no one can have a rational assurance of the truth of a proposition unless there is absolute freedom to contradict it, and that to deny such freedom is to assume infallibility. Stephen responds that this argument defies sense experience: 'There are plenty of reasons for not forbidding people to deny the existence of London Bridge and the river Thames, but the fear that the proof of these propositions would be weakened or that the person making the law would claim infallibility is not among the number.'[36] Moreover, an opinion may be suppressed without necessarily asserting its falsehood or claiming infallibility. It may be suppressed because it is true, or because it is doubtful, or because it is dangerous. When Henry VIII and Queen Elizabeth restricted the religious expression of Catholics and Puritans, they did not assume their own infallibility. 'What they thought – and it is by no means clear that they were wrong – was that unless religious controversy was kept within bounds there would be a civil war, and they muzzled the disputants accordingly.'[37]

Mill argues that a silenced opinion may be partially true, and that this partial truth can be revealed only by free discussion. But this argument, Stephen contends, applies only to a minority:

> The incalculable majority of mankind form their opinions in quite a different way, and are attached to them because they suit their temper and meet their wishes, and not because and in so far as they think themselves warranted by evidence in believing them to be true.[38]

Mill maintains that the full appreciation of the rational grounds of a truth depends upon whether people are free vigorously to contradict it. Stephen retorts that, rather than establishing a rational foundation for opinions, 'the notorious result of unlimited freedom of thought and discussion is to produce general scepticism on many subjects in the vast majority of minds'.[39] Finally, Mill asserts that a truth comes to be held without conviction unless it is discussed. Stephen alleges that men learn more from experience than discussion: 'I should say that doctrines come home to people in general, not if and in so far as they are free to discuss all their applications, but if and in so far as they happen to interest them and appear to illustrate and interpret their own experience.'[40]

In his third chapter, Mill asserted that the object of his principle was to create the conditions requisite for the full development of individuality. He invoked the words of Wilhelm von Humboldt that 'the end of man . . . is the highest and most harmonious development of his powers to a complete and consistent whole'. Mill believed that the free development of individuality was essential for social progress, and for the maintenance of a politically involved intellectual elite. Mill, it will be recalled, was no lover of democracy. In a revelatory passage, he expressed his fear that the decline of individuality which accompanied democracy endangered the influence which an enlightened few should exercise upon government. He was convinced that no government can transcend mediocrity 'except in so far as the sovereign Many have let themselves be guided . . . by the counsels and influence of a more highly gifted and instructed One or Few'.[41] John Morley, referring to these words, maintained that *On Liberty* was 'one of the most aristocratic books ever written'.[42] Just as Mill had argued that the attainment of truth depends upon virtually absolute freedom of thought and discussion, he now argued that the full development of originality and individuality depends upon the greatest possible freedom of conduct. Accordingly, he advocated that 'different experiments of liberty' and 'varieties of character' should be tolerated so long as they do no harm to other people. In this way only might the talented few escape the tyranny of the majority.

In Mill's view, the great impediment to the development of individuality in England was the indifference fostered by a pervasive Calvinist conception of human nature. During the late eighteenth and early nineteenth centuries Calvinism exerted an influence upon Evangelicalism, a reform movement within the Anglican Church. Mill scornfully described Calvinism's 'narrow theory of life' and 'the pinched and hidebound type of human character which it patronises'. He summed up the Calvinist view of man:

> The one great offence of man is self-will. All the good of which humanity is capable is comprised in obedience. ... Human nature being radically corrupt, there is no redemption for any one until human nature is killed within him. To one holding this theory of life, crushing out any of the human faculties, capacities, and susceptibilities, is no evil: man needs no capacity, but that of surrendering himself to the will of God.[43]

Interestingly enough, while Mill charged the Calvinist philosophy with stifling individuality, Matthew Arnold, calling it 'Hebraism', attacked it for overstressing the individual.[44] He thought that it fostered among the English a tendency to value action for its own sake, and a dangerous attitude of 'doing as one likes' without regard for reason, authority and culture.

Mill's attack upon Calvinism underscores another important difference between himself and Stephen, one which first surfaced in Stephen's early reviews of *On Liberty*.[45] It is now a commonplace that political thought is founded ultimately upon a conception of man. All of Stephen's thought is coloured by a negative view of human nature. To the end of his life he maintained that the majority of men are either wicked, selfish or indifferent. This view sheds light upon his authoritarianism: because many men are bad, they must be restrained; because many are indifferent, they must be ruled. Contrasting his estimate with Mill's, Stephen alleges that 'the great defect of Mr. Mill's later writings seems to me that he has formed too favourable an estimate of human nature'.[46]

Because Mill refused to face the facts, because he insisted that men could be entrusted with the greatest possible degree of freedom, Stephen declared him a sentimentalist. We have seen that Stephen was reared in an atmosphere of Evangelical piety. Though he managed over the years to shed its theology, he never divested himself of its view of man.

With Mill's denigrating words in mind, Stephen defends the Calvinist conception of human nature as being more in accord with facts and history than Mill's sentimental idealism. Mill assumed that the removal of restraints tends to encourage the growth of individuality. On the contrary, Stephen replies, 'restraint and coercion in one form or another is the great stimulus to exertion. . . . A life made up of danger, vicissitude, and exposure is the sort of life which produces originality and resource.'[47] Thus restrictions properly applied by religion may be more conducive to the development of individuality than absolute liberty.

Stephen believed that England's greatness was due in large part to the influence of the Evangelical ethos. Generations of Englishmen had been reared to cherish the Evangelical values of diligence, individuality, respectability and earnestness. He charges that, in making individuality an end in itself, Mill has merely made a case for eccentricity. Mill confounded the proposition that goodness is various with the proposition that variety is good. 'Eccentricity is far more often a mark of weakness than a mark of strength. Weakness wishes, as a rule, to attract attention by trifling distinctions, and strength wishes to avoid it. Originality consists in thinking for yourself, not in thinking differently from other people.'[48] Stephen concludes by translating Calvinism into modern language:

> Speak or fail to speak of God as you think right, but the fact that men are deeply moved by ideas about power, wisdom, and goodness, on a superhuman scale which they rather apprehend than comprehend, is certain. Speak of original sin or not as you please, but the fact that all men are in some respects and at some times both weak and wicked, that they do the ill they would not do, and shun the good they would pursue, is no less certain. To describe this state of things as a 'miserable bondage' is, to say the least, an intelligible way of speaking. Calvin's theory was that in order to escape from this bondage men must be true to the better part of their nature, keep in proper subjection its

baser elements, and look up to God as the source of the only valuable kind of freedom – freedom to be good and wise.[49]

This passage helps clarify Stephen's conception of liberalism. When he asserts that the only worthwhile kind of liberty is the 'freedom to be good and wise', he is merely saying in another way that true liberalism must be consistent with tradition, authority and culture. In order to achieve this proper balance, men must transcend the baser elements of human nature in the interest of the common good. This view of liberalism closely parallels that put forth by Matthew Arnold under the name of culture. 'I am a Liberal,' Arnold insisted, 'yet I am a Liberal tempered by experience, reflection and renouncement, and I am, above all, a believer in culture.'[50]

IV

We have seen that for Stephen liberty had merely contingent value: it was good or bad depending on the time, place and circumstances. Moreover, it was incomprehensible to him except as a negation. It is significant that not until halfway through his refutation of Mill does Stephen embark upon a definition of liberty. In Hobbesian fashion, he defines it negatively as the absence of restraint:

> Discussions about liberty are in truth discussions about a negation. Attempts to solve the problems of government and society by such discussions are like attempts to discover the nature of light and heat by inquiries into darkness and cold. The phenomenon which requires and will repay study is the direction and nature of the various forces, individual and collective, which in their combination or collision with each other and with the outer world make up human life. If we want to know what ought to be the size and position of a hole in a water pipe, we must consider the nature of water, the nature of pipes, and the objects for which the water is wanted; but we shall learn very little by studying the nature of holes. Their shape is simply the shape of whatever bounds them. Their nature is merely to let the water pass, and it seems to me that enthusiasm about them is altogether thrown away.[51]

While Stephen opposed the exaltation of absolute liberty, he also objected to – and this is extremely important to remember – the exaltation of order as an end in itself. Like liberty, order is subject to utility. Just as liberty, regarded as an absolute, leads to anarchy, so authority, when considered an end in itself, leads to despotism. Those who choose to eulogise such words as 'order' and 'society' should be prepared to answer the following question: 'What order and what sort of society it is to which their praises refer?'[52] Stephen's political thought transcends the perennial battles between liberals and conservatives. He saw profound truth in the paradox that stability and change are equally necessary, though diametrically opposed. Society depends upon the tempering influence of each upon the other:

> It is quite true that since the seventeenth century – to go no further back – the Puritan, the Whig, and the Radical have been more successful than the Cavalier, the Tory, and the Conservative; but the existing state of society is the result of each set of forces, not of either set by itself, and certainly not the result of the forward effort by itself. . . . It appears to me that the *erreur mére*, so to speak, of most modern speculation on political subjects lies in the fact that nearly every writer is an advocate of one out of many forces, which, as they act in different directions, must and do come into collision and produce a resultant according to the direction of which life is prosperous or otherwise.[53]

This comprehensive view of politics, recognising the mutual necessity of liberty and order, would enable the English to promote yet restrain change – in short, to reconcile culture and democracy.

Having defined liberty negatively, Stephen expounds three criteria, consistent with the principle of utility, for determining when compulsion is inexpedient: 'Compulsion is bad: (1) when the object aimed at is bad; (2) when the object aimed at is good but the compulsion employed is not calculated to obtain it; (3) when the object aimed at is good, and the compulsion employed is calculated to obtain it, but at too great expense.'[54] He then applies these criteria to the question of liberty of thought and discussion. All forms of compulsion in favour of opinions which are not 'so probable that a reasonable man would act upon the supposition of their truth' are forbidden. Moreover, he summarily rejects 'all the coarser forms of persecution'. Thus he condemns the legal persecution of thought, and coercion which might result in 'the extermination or general paralysis of the thinking powers in order to be effective'.⁵⁵ In the first case the end is unattained; in the second it is attained at inordinate expense.

Yet, unlike Mill, Stephen believes that there are instances in which compulsion may rightfully be applied to thought and discussion. He asserts that the legal establishment of various forms of religious, moral and political opinion is justified to the extent that it fulfils the criteria he sets for the just employment of compulsion. 'Governments ought to take the responsibility of acting upon such principles, religious, political, and moral, as they may from time to time regard as most likely to be true, and this they cannot do without exercising a very considerable degree of coercion.'⁵⁶ Like Edmund Burke, Stephen believed that government is founded ultimately upon religion:

> All government has and must of necessity have a moral basis, and . . . the connection between morals and religion is so intimate that this implies a religious basis as well. I do not mean by a religious basis a complete agreement in religious opinion among either the governors or the persons governed, but such an amount of agreement as is sufficient to determine the attitude towards religion.⁵⁷

Stephen is not advocating that Parliament establish a religious creed and enforce it with legal penalties. To do so would abolish the freedom of conscience necessary to a free society. But he insists upon recognition of the fact that, since society is dependent upon a community of ideas, including assumptions as to what is true in religion and morals, the State cannot ignore moral and religious matters.

The danger of Mill's attempt to separate Church and State, Stephen tells us, is that 'it tends to emasculate both Church and State. It cuts human life in two. It cuts off religion from active life, and it reduces the State to a matter of police.'⁵⁸ Adherence to Mill's view would deprive the State of its necessary spiritual basis. Stephen contends that the temporal and spiritual powers are identical in sphere, and differ only in their sanctions. The sacred and the secular interpenetrate; they are two aspects of the same thing. For example, the laws of marriage, education, and ecclesiastical property belong to both the temporal and the spiritual spheres. 'The attempt to distinguish between temporal and spiritual, between Church and State, is like the attempt to distinguish between substance and form.'⁵⁹ Here we see Stephen, rather than Mill, departing from old Liberal principles. Liberal thought had always assumed that the separation of the sacred and the secular powers was fundamental to the preservation of freedom.

Yet Stephen believed that, practically speaking, a government cannot avoid deciding upon moral and religious matters. The British in India, he observes, had forced the Indian religions to tolerate one another. Though the British did not persecute or specifically outlaw the native religions, they nevertheless instituted an educational system that assumed their falsehood. Moreover, certain religious practices, such as human sacrifices, were punished as crimes because they clearly violated European standards of morality. In short, the English quickly realised that they could not govern India except on the principle that the native religions were false:

> They found, as everyone who has to do with legislation must find, that laws must be obeyed upon principles, and that it is impossible to lay down any principles of legislation at all unless you are prepared to say, I am right, and you are wrong, and your view shall give way to mine, quietly, gradually, and peaceably, but one of us two must rule, and the others must obey, and I mean to rule.[60]

In an important passage of the essay *On Liberty*, Mill defended the right to express freely opinions upon such fundamental religious dogmas as the existence of God and a future state. Views on these matters, he said, should be free from legal or public sanctions. Stephen found himself in only partial agreement. He rejects outright the legal prosecution of dissident religious opinions except in those rare instances in which they constitute an immediate threat to the social order. Leslie Stephen has testified to his brother's aversion to all forms of oppression, particularly to religious oppression.[61] But Fitzjames does accept social intolerance, or the coercion employed by public opinion. A person who believes in God and a future state may disapprove of those who do not. He may even try by the frank expression of that disapproval to deter the publication and adoption of dissident religious views. Stephen contends that, since morals are necessary for the maintenance of society, and since morals are dependent upon religion, there are instances in which social intolerance of dissenting religious opinions is justified. 'If, then, virtue is good, it seems to me clear that to promote the belief of the fundamental doctrines of religion is good also, for I am convinced that in Europe at least the two must stand or fall together.'[62] The essential thing is that religion, morality and political opinion are of such vital importance that they should not be open to idle speculation:

> It seems to me that to publish opinions upon morals, politics, and religion is an act as important as any which any man can possibly do; that to attack opinions on which the framework of society rests is a proceeding which both is and ought to be dangerous. I do not say that it ought not to be done in many cases, but it should be done sword in hand, and a man who does it has no more right to be surprised at being fiercely resisted than a soldier who attacks the breach.[63]

Not only is complete toleration inconsistent with the foundations of society, but it is also contradicted by experience. Stephen holds that there are necessary and inevitable struggles between moral and religious systems, just as there are struggles between nations and classes, in so far as men are actuated by different interests and views. The ideal, then, should be not absolute tolerance, but to convince men of the necessity of moderating unavoidable conflicts.[64]

Stephen was well aware that social intolerance in religious matters is liable to great abuse. He suggests, therefore, a principle which, if followed, 'would leave little room for moral intolerance in most cases'. He maintains that the ground for moral tolerance lies not in Mill's principle, but in the recognition 'that people should not talk about what they do not understand. No one has a right to be morally intolerant of doctrines which he has not carefully studied.' Yet he insists that 'men who really study these matters should feel themselves at liberty not merely to dissent from but to disapprove of opinions which appear to them to require it, and should express that disapprobation'.[65]

Stephen then compares the consequences of the application of his and Mill's views on toleration. Mill would condemn Pontius Pilate for crucifying Christ on the grounds that Pilate interfered with liberty of thought and discussion otherwise than for social protection. Stephen replies that Pilate was justified, regardless of the value of Christ's teaching, because his paramount duty was the preservation of peace and order in Palestine. Religious intolerance was justified in this instance because the very existence of the State was judged to be at stake. Pilate might have erred in his judgement, but we cannot expect him to have acted otherwise. Had he followed Mill's principle, he would have risked 'setting the whole province ablaze'.⁶⁶ The same reasoning would apply, Stephen argues, if a religious reformer appeared in British India whose preaching was likely to disturb the public order. In this instance a British officer would be justified in executing him as a rebel.

Stephen's bluntness on these matters earned him enemies. Yet, in Hobbesian fashion, he was only insisting that, irrespective of the merit of the persecuted opinions, no sovereign State can be expected to tolerate its own dissolution. When compelled to choose between liberty and order, a State must choose order. It is important to recognise that Stephen's views on toleration do not constitute a departure from the English liberal tradition. Classical liberals such as John Milton and John Locke wrote works on toleration which are highly regarded today. Yet each carefully limited the scope of toleration: Locke would not have the State tolerate atheism, and Milton advocated intolerance towards both atheism and Popery.⁶⁷

Stephen also discusses the application of Mill's principle to moral behaviour. The legal enforcement of morals raises a number of difficult questions which must be considered by every society, and which are still vigorously debated today. Recently in England, the arguments of Stephen and Mill have been eloquently restated by Lord Devlin and H. L. A. Hart.⁶⁸ The controversy between Lord Devlin and Hart is concerned chiefly with matters relating to sexual morality, and was touched off by the publication in 1957 of the Wolfenden Report, which recommended that homosexual behaviour between consenting adults should no longer be considered a crime. With some minor reservations, Hart, in support of the Wolfenden Report, takes Mill's position on the relation of law and morals; and Lord Devlin argues along lines analogous to those of Stephen. Indeed, Hart has pointed out, and Lord Devlin has duly acknowledged, that many of the latter's arguments, and even his tone, were anticipated by Fitzjames Stephen.⁶⁹

Mill's principle would prohibit compulsion, either by law or by public opinion, from being applied to private vices. Society has no right to interfere with those actions which concern only the individual. Hence the State, in the interest of individual liberty, ought to tolerate such behaviour as fornication, gambling, prostitution and alcoholism. At one point Mill attempted to view objectively the question of whether a person should be permitted to keep a gambling house or indulge in prostitution. Stephen was outraged: 'How can the State or the public be competent to decide that gross vice is a bad thing? I do not think the State ought to stand bandying compliments with pimps.' Here is how he would handle the matter:

> My feeling is that if society gets its grip on the collar of such a fellow it should say to him. 'You dirty rascal, it may be a question whether you should be suffered to remain in your native filth untouched, or whether my opinion about you should be printed by the lash on your bare back. That question will be determined without the smallest reference to your wishes or feelings; but as to the nature of my opinion about you, there can be no question at all.'[70]

Stephen's point is that it is virtually impossible to distinguish vices regarding the individual alone from those affecting society at large. Mill himself perceived the serious objections to his sharp distinction between self-regarding and other-regarding acts. Consequently, he devoted a later section of *On Liberty* to a significant abridgement of his principle. He conceded that a person may be punished for an act ordinarily considered self-regarding if the act involves the violation of 'a distinct and assignable obligation' to another person or persons: if a man, owing to intemperance or extravagance, is unable to support his family or pay his debts, his vice is no longer self-regarding and is liable to punishment. Stephen thought that Mill's qualification did little to improve his prinicple.[71] He admits that as far as legal coercion is concerned, it might be possible to draw a line between private vices injurious to others and those which are truly self-regarding. But he contends that the distinction is futile when applied to public coercion.

It is true that, practically speaking, a legal indictment can be drawn against the person only when there is a distinctly assignable injury. It is also true that the criminal law, 'an extremely rough engine', should be employed with great caution.[72] But Stephen holds that the compulsion of public opinion may rightfully be exercised even in instances where the injury to society is not clear and specific. He adduces the example of a group of nobles, the pillars of society, who indulge in the grossest forms of private vice. In Stephen's opinion such people are far more injurious to society by their example than the petty thief, yet Mill's principle would prohibit public disapproval unless the harm done be assignable to specific persons.[73] Thus Stephen insists that for purposes other than social protection the moral coercion of public opinion may be employed to support morals and condemn vice.

This leads to the question of whether Parliament should enforce morals. Stephen believes that the State may employ legislation to promote virtue and prevent vice. In accord with his utilitarian criteria for the exertion of compulsion, he concludes that the object is good because society depends upon a moral foundation, and mankind has reached a consensus on what is good and evil in many areas of life. Moreover, the means, the criminal law, has been proved effective. And the expense is not excessive in so far as the moral basis of society is protected. The criminal law is the most powerful instrument which society has at its disposal for the prevention of vice. Yet it is limited by practical circumstances. Before an act may be punished as a crime it must be capable of distinct definition and specific proof. Lesser vices, such as ingratitude or perfidy, are ordinarily beyond the purview of the law, and are left to the moral compulsion of public opinion. It is the 'excessive harshness' of the criminal law which limits its application to the grosser forms of vice, to those acts, such as murder, rape and robbery, which endanger the moral foundation of society. The criminal law 'is the *ratio ultima* of the majority against persons whom its application assumes to have renounced the common bonds which connect men together'.[74]

Though unwilling to go as far as Mill, Stephen was careful to set definite limits, dictated by utility, to the interference with morals by law and public opinion. Neither legislation nor public opinion ought to meddle with things of little consequence. And they ought not to proceed upon insufficient evidence. One risks inflicting a grave injustice by condemning a person one does not know or a book one has not read. Moreover, the law must be in substantial accord with existing moral standards. It cannot punish what public opinion does not also condemn. Most importantly, legislation and public opinion must scrupulously avoid invasions of privacy.

> To try to regulate the internal affairs of a family, the relations of love or friendship, or many other things of the same sort, by law or by the coercion of public opinion, is like trying to pull an

eyelash out of a man's eye with a pair of tongs. They may put out the eye, but they will never get hold of the eyelash.[75]

V

The first four chapters of *Liberty, Equality, Fraternity* are devoted to a searching critique of Mill's essay *On Liberty*. In the remaining three chapters, again concentrating on certain writings of Mill, Stephen broadens his attack to include the other elements of the new democratic creed: equality and fraternity.

Stephen had no more respect for popular notions of equality — the second article of the democratic creed — than he did for those of liberty. Indeed, he declared that equality was 'by far the most ignoble and mischievous of all the popular feelings of the age'.[76] He directed his attack specifically at the egalitarian theory propounded by Mill in his essays *Utilitarianism* (1861) and *The Subjection of Women* (1869). Stephen thought that Mill's idea of equality, like his doctrine of liberty, would intensify rather than prevent the evils of democracy. *On Liberty* had been written to propose a principle to guard against the dangers to individual liberty inherent in a democracy. Yet Stephen believed that the equality which Mill presumed to exist among persons actually endangered individual freedom. In fact, he contended that the two cardinal doctrines of democracy — liberty and equality — are contradictory.

According to traditional liberal theory, liberty — most importantly the liberty to acquire private property — leads to inequality. 'All private property springs from labour for the benefit of the labourer; and private property is the very essence of inequality.'[77] Stephen believed that, if people are given the largest possible liberty to exercise their natural abilities in their own interest, 'the result will not be equality but inequality reproducing itself in a geometric ratio'.[78] The unequal conditions that exist in society are therefore inevitable. Private property is essential to liberty, inasmuch as it secures for the individual a realm of private autonomy, free from arbitrary infringement by the State. Equality, Stephen maintained, would abolish private property, and hence liberty. He believed that in a democracy equality would take the form of an equal distribution of property. Such a measure might promote equality and fraternity, but it would be fatal to individual liberty:

Assume that every man has a right to be on an equality with every other man because all are so closely connected together that the results of their labour should be thrown into a common stock out of which they are all to be maintained, and you certainly give a very distinct sense to Equality and Fraternity, but you must absolutely exclude Liberty. Experience has proved that this is not merely a theoretical but also a practical difficulty. It is the standing and insuperable obstacle to all socialist schemes, and it explains their failure.[79]

To Stephen, and to a great number of his contemporaries among the middle and upper classes, democracy meant socialism. After many of the working class were enfranchised by the Reform Act of 1867, he feared that the workers would use their new power to enlist the government to establish equality by radically interfering with society, destroying liberty in the process.

Stephen's belief in the opposition between liberty and equality underscores a fundamental division between the old Utilitarian and Manchester Liberals, and the new social liberalism that emerged in England during the latter part of the nineteenth century. The old or classical liberalism – that of Locke, Burke, Tocqueville and Fitzjames Stephen – assumed that liberty and equality are antithetical. The new liberalism – expounded by such men as T. H. Green and L. T. Hobhouse – contended that liberty is inseparable from equality, that liberty is meaningless without the equal economic and social means necessary for its pursuit. In contrast to the *laissez-faire* individualism of the classical liberal school, the new liberals, sometimes referred to as collectivists, advocated positive intervention by the State to provide the means for human improvement. The State, it was assumed, has a moral duty to provide the best life for its citizens. This assumption furnished a rationale for the socialist legislation in England during the latter part of the Victorian era. If Stephen's critique is on the mark, Mill's later works placed him in the camp of the new liberalism.[80] Stephen was also undoubtedly aware of Mill's flirtation with socialism in the later editions of his *Principles of Political Economy*, first published in 1848. Mill, Stephen believed, had strayed too far in his revision of Bentham, and was in fact an apostate. He had modified the liberal individualist ethic in the direction of the welfare State. Essentially, then, *Liberty, Equality, Fraternity* was an appeal from an old liberal to the new liberals to return to the fold.

Before launching his attack, Stephen lays the groundwork by expounding the Utilitarian theory of justice. According to this theory, justice is inseparable from utility. Like Bentham and Austin, Stephen believes that 'the justice and the expediency of a law are simply two names for one and the same thing'.[81] Only those who subscribe to the unverifiable theory of the intuitive rights of man can distinguish between a just and an expedient law. Mill recognised this, and he devoted a chapter of *Utilitarianism* to demonstrating that justice is grounded in utility.[82] Accordingly, Stephen holds that Mill ought to agree that equality is just only in so far as it is expedient.

The kind of equality which Stephen accepts is judicial equality, otherwise known as equal treatment before the law. He defines it as 'the impartial application of a law to the particular cases which fall under it'.[83] According to the distinguished constitutional lawyer A. V. Dicey, equality of this kind is a fundamental principle of the English Constitution.[84] Here Mill and Stephen were in agreement. But in the essay *Utilitarianism* Mill went beyond mere legal equality and advocated social equality, arguing that justice implied not merely that everyone should be treated equally, but that they should be afforded equal opportunities for improvement:

> Bentham's dictum 'everybody to count for one, nobody for more than one', might be written under the principle of utility as an explanatory commentary. The equal claim of everybody to happiness in the estimation of the moralist and the legislator involves an equal claim to all the means of happiness, except in so far as the inevitable conditions of human life, and the general interest in which that of every individual is included, sets limits to the maxim, and those limits ought to be strictly construed.... All persons are deemed to have a right to equality of treatment except where some recognized social expediency requires the reverse, and hence all social inequalities which have ceased to be considered expedient assume the character not of simple inexpediency but of injustice, and appear so tyrannical that people are apt to wonder how they ever could have been tolerated.[85]

Stephen and Mill, then, split on the question of social equality. Stephen argued that social equality is inexpedient, and that Mill therefore erred in supporting it. But his case against Mill suffers from a common misconception. He failed to perceive the distinction between substantive equality and equality of opportunity. Mill never maintained that all persons are equal in every respect. In fact he would have agreed with Stephen that, because people are not substantively equal, equal opportunity would lead to inequality of condition. What Mill did suppose was that, given equal opportunity, the inevitable inequalities among men might be placed upon more rational and equitable grounds. Accordingly, he advocated the removal of all unjust legal and social impediments to human improvement. He argued for equal opportunity in such areas as employment, public office, the suffrage and education. He wanted, in short, the abolition of special privilege.

But even this equality Stephen considered a danger. As a liberal of the old school, he believed that the establishment of equal opportunities would entail legislation which was a threat to individual freedom, inasmuch as it encouraged men to look to government to satisfy needs which ought to be met by private initiative. Stephen's Evangelical belief in individual responsibility prevented him from accepting the view that inequalities are the product of society. Many social conditions which the new liberalism found intolerable Stephen regarded as inevitable. He denied that men could be made more nearly equal by social reform: 'To try to make men equal by altering social arrangements is like trying to make cards of equal value by shuffling the pack. Men are fundamentally unequal, and the inequality will show itself, arrange society as you like.'[86] As Stephen saw it, inequality was the result not of society, but of natural limitations.

Stephen believed that Mill was mistaken in assuming that, despite substantial inequalities such as age, talent, education, knowledge and wealth, justice demands that all men should be treated as if they were equal. He also recognised that the danger in a democracy lies in the fact that men are prone to think that because they are equal in some respects they are equal in all. Since men are equally free, they claim to be absolutely equal. Such presumptive equality, Stephen feared, might serve as a justification for the masses to overturn the entire social order. Government and law must be adapted to the actual conditions of society at a given period. Social reform is beneficial only in so far as it reflects changes in society. For the law to presume substantive equality between men regardless whether it actually exists is inexpedient and dangerous. Laws cannot make men equal; but, as men do in fact become more equal, they can change the laws:

I think that if the rights and duties which laws create are to be generally advantageous, they ought to be adapted to the situation of the persons who enjoy or are subject to them. They ought to recognize both substantial equality and substantial inequality, and they should from time to time be so moulded and altered as always to represent fairly well the existing state of society. Government, in a word, ought to fit society as a man's clothes fit him. To establish by law rights and duties which assume that people are equal when they are not is like trying to make clumsy feet look handsome by the help of tight boots. . . . Rights and duties should be so moulded as to clothe, protect, and sustain society in the position which it naturally assumes.[87]

Stephen was prepared to accept a limited notion of social equality. A supporter of the English class system, he would allow for a proportionate equality based upon the substantive distinctions between men, in which there would be equality only within the several classes:

If the object were to secure the greatest amount of equality, the way to do it would be by establishing a system of distinctions, a social hierarchy corresponding as nearly as possible to the real distinctions between men, and by making the members of each class equal among themselves.[88]

Stephen added that, if it were possible to determine 'with unfailing accuracy' the intrinsic differences between men and group them accordingly, the solution to the problem of reconciling individual self-interest and the common good would be found.

A nation in which every one held the position for which he was best fitted, and in which every one was aware of the fact, would be a nation in which every man's life would be passed in doing that which would be at once most agreeable to himself and most beneficial to his neighbours, and such a nation would have solved at all events several of the great problems of life.[89]

But Stephen conceded that such an ideal can only be approximated Mill might have replied that the best way to fulfil the ideal would be to provide for equal opportunity, the sole method by which the valid distinctions between men may be ascertained.

Stephen devotes a number of pages to attacking the doctrine of equality between the sexes advanced in Mill's *Subjection of Women* –

'a work from which I dissent from the first sentence to the last'.[90] Stephen's views were clearly influenced by the legal and social conception of women that prevailed in his day. The Victorian woman could not vote, hold office, attend a university or enter a profession. Once married, she was civilly dead according to common law. Having no separate legal status, she could not inherit or own property, and until 1857 divorce required a special Act of Parliament.

Stephen attempts to establish that 'men and women are not equals, and that the laws which affect their relations ought to recognize this fact'.[91] Men owe their superiority not only to their strength but also to their 'greater vigour of character' and 'greater intellectual force'.[92] Stephen errs by again neglecting to distinguish between equality of substance and equality of opportunity. Mill correctly saw that the inferiority of women is not inherent, but the product of social influences, especially their inadequate education. But Stephen's scepticism regarding the educability of human beings led him to fail to perceive that the social position of women in his day was more the product of nurture than nature. Moreover, he was guilty of equating what is with what ought to be. For Stephen, it seems, the mere fact that for centuries women had been held in subjection furnished proof that their inequality was expedient.

Stephen went so far as to contend that Mill's doctrine of sexual equality is inconsistent with the institution of marriage. Applying the Hobbesian conception of sovereignty to the family, he concludes that the marriage contract necessarily involves the subordination of one party to the other.[93] As in the State, the government of the family must rest ultimately with one party. Since sovereignty by its nature cannot be shared, it must reside with the husband. Stephen would not think of giving it to the wife. He fails to recognise that, though in theory the government of the family belongs to the husband, there may be many instances where, because of a variety of circumstances, it belongs to the wife. Of course, Stephen adds, he does not mean to suggest that the husband has a right to enslave his wife or inflict cruel treatment upon her. While a wife should be subject to her husband, she must not be subjugated. Yet Stephen insists that on important family questions, such as place of residence or the scale of living, the wife should defer to her husband.

Though Stephen's position on women is conservative by today's standards, we must remember that his views were typical of his era. Indeed, Mill was virtually a voice crying in the wilderness. Moreover, a cogent argument has recently been made that, were it not for the influence of Harriet Taylor, Mill's close companion for many years who later became his wife, even he might not have seen fit to extend his social theories to the woman question.[94] At the same time, we should note that Stephen's opposition to Mill's ideas on sexual equality stemmed largely from his recognition of the revolutionary legal and social changes that would be entailed in putting them into effect.

One of Mill's most appealing arguments in support of sexual equality is that the subjection of women originated during the early stages of civilisation when physical force ruled the world. But history demonstrates, he claimed, that human progress has diminished the role of force in favour of reason and discussion. Indeed, the 'law of the strongest' had been 'entirely abandoned' in the most advanced nations of the world.[95] Sir Henry Maine, in his *Ancient Law* (1861) had said that 'the movement of the progressive societies has hitherto been a movement from status to contract'.[96] And Mill, obviously influenced by Maine, declared that in the modern world people are no longer born into a fixed status, but should be free to engage in whatever pursuits they please. Again, Stephen responds by pointing to the facts. Force is a constant: 'Disguise it how you will, it is force in one shape or another which determines the relations between human beings.'[97] The only thing that Maine's dictum about the passage from status to contract proves is that force changes its form. The natural inequalities between persons are displayed in different forms from one generation to another, but they cannot be obliterated.

And what is all this nonsense about progress? Stephen says that Mill is too sanguine in his view of human history. Though he does not entirely deny Mill's assumption that the progress of society involves changes for the better, Stephen can give only a qualified endorsement of the results. He saw clearly the distinction between moral progress and scientific and technical progress. His conception that good and evil are often inextricably mixed precluded his partaking in one of Victorian England's prevailing enthusiasms:

> I think that the progress has been mixed, partly good and partly bad. I suspect that in many ways it has been a progress from

strength to weakness; that people are more sensitive, less entertaining and ambitious, less earnestly desirous to get what they want, and more afraid of pain, both for themselves and others, than they used to be. If this should be so, it appears to me that all other gains, whether in wealth, knowledge, or humanity, afford no equivalent. Strength, in all its forms, is life and manhood. To be less strong is to be less of a man, whatever else you may be.... I do not myself see that our mechanical inventions have increased the general vigour of men's characters, though they have, no doubt, increased enormously our control over nature. The greater part of our humanity appears to me to be a mere increase of nervous sensibility in which I feel no satisfaction at all.[98]

VI

After attacking the idea of social equality, Stephen considers the notion of political equality – democracy, or the equal distribution of political power. In this case his arguments are not aimed directly at some work of Mill, who shared his apprehension over the emerging democracy, and who recognised the limitations of parliamentary government. Yet Stephen believes that the logic of Mill's doctrines of liberty, equality, and fraternity leads inexorably towards democracy.

In the years following his return from India, Stephen became a trenchant critic of the English system of parliamentary government. He also emerged as the most severe antagonist of democracy during the second half of the nineteenth century. His work in India, we have seen, confirmed his belief in efficient and benevolent rule. He was convinced that England's representative institutions were subject to certain inherent weaknesses which encumbered efficient government. Frederic Harrison, the English Positivist, thought that India had indeed too great an influence upon Stephen; he wrote to John Morley that Stephen 'writes like a man who has been touched with "Punjab Heat" '.[99] It is true that Stephen sometimes drew analogies between India and England which ignored the profound differences in the culture and history of the two countries. But he thought that in India he had found a combination of effective and benevolent government that was wanting in his own country. Many of Stephen's criticisms of democracy and parliamentary government anticipated those of

Sir Henry Maine's *Popular Government* (1885) and W. E. H. Lecky's *Democracy and Liberty* (1895). Stephen had the opportunity to read the proofs of the articles which later constituted Maine's *Popular Government*, and thought they were 'one of the very best things he ever wrote'.[100] Together with Stephen's *Liberty, Equality, Fraternity*, the works of Maine and Lecky constitute the most important anti-democratic thought in England during the late Victorian era.[101]

Stephen did not intend to propose a substitute for democracy; he readily acknowledged its eventual triumph. Nevertheless, he saw no reason to rejoice: 'The waters are out and no human force can turn them back, but I do not see why as we go into the stream we need sing Hallelujah to the river god.'[102] There were certain misconceptions and dangers related to universal suffrage which could not be ignored. The underlying premise of democracy was fallacious: government can never be in the hands of the majority. Stephen's political realism convinced him that, because the State is founded upon power, all government necessarily rests in the hands of a minority. This perception was to become the salient theme in the writings of elite theorists such as Gaetano Mosca, Vilfredo Pareto and Robert Michels at the turn of the century. To Stephen's mind, democracy – in the sense of equal distribution of political power – is a myth. It has nothing whatever to do with equality:

> Legislate how you will, establish universal suffrage, if you think proper, as a law which can never be broken. You are still as far as ever from equality. Political power has changed its shape but not its nature. The result of cutting it up into little bits is simply that the man who can sweep the greatest number of them into one heap will govern the rest. The strongest man in some form or other will always rule. If the government is a military one, the qualities which make a man a great soldier will make him a ruler. If the government is a monarchy, the qualities which kings value in counsellors, in generals, in administrators, will give power. In a pure democracy the ruling men will be the wirepullers and their friends; but they will no more be on an equality with the voters than soldiers or Ministers of State are on an equality with the subjects of a monarchy. Changes in the form of a government alter the conditions of superiority much more than its nature.

'Liberty, Equality, Fraternity' 155

What is important, then, are the qualities which determine leadership:

> In some ages a powerful character, in others cunning, in others powers of despatching business, in others eloquence, in others a good hold upon current commonplaces and facility in applying them to practical purposes will enable a man to climb on to his neighbours' shoulders and direct them this way or that; but in all ages and under all circumstances the rank and file are directed by leaders of one kind or another who get command of their collective force.[103]

Since all government is necessarily the rule of elites, Stephen contended that England should be ruled by an aristocracy of talent. He thought that the best government was one that provided rule by the wise, the moral and the capable. In essence, government is too important and too complicated to be left in the hands of the multitude. In Stephen's view, the greatest objection to universal suffrage is that it 'tends to invert what I should have regarded as the true and natural relation between wisdom and folly. I think that wise and good men ought to rule those who are foolish and bad.'[104] Mill too believed in government guided by the enlightened few. But, unlike Stephen, his conception of liberty induced him carefully to circumscribe the degree of influence which an elite may rightfully exercise over the majority. Stephen, on the other hand, thought that such limitation undermined good government.

> To say that the sole function of the wise and good is to preach to their neighbours, and that every one indiscriminately should be left to do what he likes, and should be provided with a rateable share of the sovereign power in the shape of a vote, and that the result of this will be the direction of power by wisdom, seems to me to be the wildest romance that ever got possession of any considerable number of minds.[105]

What Stephen feared most about democracy was that by dividing political power into little pieces it would give opportunities for demagogues and unscrupulous 'wirepullers and their friends' to cater to popular fears and commonplaces.[106] Such men would rise to leadership merely by sweeping a majority of votes together. Rule by the wise and the good in the interests of the many would be exchanged for rule by the corrupt in the interests of the few. England might then be prey to the very form of tyranny that Mill himself had envisaged.

Democracy being inevitable, the only recourse was to suggest ways in which popular institutions might be reconciled with efficient government. Only a few pages of *Liberty, Equality, Fraternity* are devoted to the subject of parliamentary government. Stephen undoubtedly believed that it would have been inappropriate to embark upon a lengthy discussion of specific institutional reforms within a work dealing with general principles. He deferred an extensive treatment of concrete proposals for two lectures delivered before the Edinburgh Philosophical Society in 1873, which we shall consider in our final chapter.

Stephen never anticipated that he would one day find himself in close agreement with the negative views of parliamentary government which he had denounced earlier in his friend Thomas Carlyle. Thoughout the 1860s and 1870s, the two men continued to exchange opinions on politics and society in the course of their Sunday afternoon walks through Chelsea. They were often accompanied by another well-known anti-democrat, James Anthony Froude. Leslie Stephen once confided to Oliver Wendell Holmes the fear that in his politics Fitzjames had been 'a good deal corrupted by old Carlyle',[107] but he later acknowledged that his brother's conclusions had been reached by a different route.[108]

VII

Fraternity — the third article of the popular democratic faith — supplied the foundation for the doctrines of liberty and equality. Stephen charges that, as with liberty and equality, fraternity or the sentiment of general love for mankind had become popularly regarded as an absolute, regardless of utility. The road to anarchy is paved with misplaced sentiment. Stephen regards fraternity as dangerous because it encourages a sentimental view of life and excessive discontent with social institutions. He suggests that we maintain a proper perspective:

> That upon some terms and to some extent it is desirable that men should wish well to and should help each other is common ground to every one. At the same time I cannot but think that many persons must share the feeling of disgust with which I for

one have often read and listened to expressions of general philanthropy. Such love is frequently an insulting intrusion. . . . I know hardly anything in literature so nauseous as Rousseau's expressions of love for mankind when read in the light of his confessions. 'Keep your love to yourself, and do not daub me or mine with it', is the criticism which his books always suggest to me. . . . It is not love that one wants from the great mass of mankind, but respect and justice.[109]

This time Stephen directs his fusillade against certain parts of Mill's *Utilitarianism*, in which Mill sought to establish a basis for the Positivist Religion of Humanity. The Positivist programme for a secular religion that worshipped mankind and rejected the supernatural conveniently corresponded with the Utilitarian greatest-happiness principle. After defining Utilitarianism as the system of morality which holds that actions are right to the extent that they produce happiness or pleasure, wrong to the extent that they produce unhappiness or pain, Mill proceeded to examine its ultimate sanction: what will induce men to do right? He located the foundation of Utilitarianism in 'the social feelings of mankind', the desire to be at unity with one's fellows, which forms 'a natural basis of sentiment for utilitarian morality'.[110] He rejected the system of politics and morals propounded by Comte, the patriarch of Positivism, as dangerous to human liberty and individuality, but he found great efficacy in his Religion of Humanity.[111]

Stephen opposed the Positivist attempt to raise social benevolence to the status of a religion.[112] He did not deny that human happiness stems largely from benevolent feelings, but he had serious misgivings about Mill's endeavour to elevate these feelings to form a new religion, 'a sort of secondary orthodoxy', which would supplant the traditional supernatural religion.[113] Stephen contended that fraternity was based upon an inaccurate conception of man. Mill and the Positivists assumed, of course, that all men are good and therefore worth loving. To Stephen, this view was sheer sentimentality, since it attributed to men qualities they simply did not possess. He explained the essential difference between himself and Mill:

He thinks otherwise than I of man and of human life in general. He appears to believe that if men are all freed from restraints and put, as far as possible, on an equal footing, they will naturally treat each other as brothers, and work harmoniously for their common good. I believe that many men are bad, a vast majority of men indifferent, and many good, and that the great mass of indifferent people sway this way or that according to circumstances, one of the most important of which circumstances is the predominance for the time being of the bad or good. I further believe that between all classes of men there are and always will be real occasions of enmity and strife, and that even good men may be and often are compelled to treat each other as enemies either by the existence of conflicting interests which bring them into collision or by their different ways of conceiving goodness.[114]

The Religion of Humanity is, moreover, founded upon an inaccurate psychology. Stephen maintains that, as a Utilitarian, Mill should recognise that men are moved primarily not by social sentiments but by self-love, 'the fountain from which the wider forms of human affection flow and on which philanthropy itself is ultimately based'.[115] Stephen believes that man is incapable of the self-sacrifice required by the doctrine of fraternity. Humanitarianism is enlightened self-interest in disguise: 'Humanity is only I writ large, and love for Humanity generally means zeal for my notions as to what men should be and how they should live.'[116] He offers what he considers a more practical approach to the attainment of happiness:

> The man who works from himself outwards, whose conduct is governed by ordinary motives, and who acts with a view to his own advantage and the advantage of those who are connected with himself in definite, assignable ways, produces in the ordinary course of things much more happiness to others (if that is the great object of life) than a moral Don Quixote who is always liable to sacrifice himself and his neighbours.[117]

Stephen spells out the practical effect of this egoistic psychology. John Plamenatz has written of the conflict in Utilitarian moral theory between its individualist psychology and its prescriptive happiness principle.[118] If men are moved primarily by self-interest, how is one to reconcile them to the common good? Some have refused to see any conflict. Thus Alexander Pope versified that 'true self-love and social are the same', Mandeville wrote a poem with 'Private Vices, Public Benefits' as its subtitle, and Adam Smith trusted in an 'invisible hand' to reconcile conflicting interests. But the Utilitarians could not ignore the conflict between the individual and society. Bentham believed that individual egos do not naturally harmonise, but must often be reconciled by the legislator. Stephen maintains that it is erroneous to suppose that either a moralist or a legislator desires to promote equally the happiness of everyone affected by his morals or law. The standards of happiness necessarily originate not in the people but in the legislator and moralist, who impose their views upon them either by power or the force of argument. 'The utilitarian standard is not the greatest amount of happiness altogether . . . but the widest possible extension of the ideal of life formed by the person who sets up the standard.'[119]

Not only is the Religion of Humanity ill founded, but it would also prove ineffective. At a time when the old certainties of religion were breaking down under the onslaught of science, the Positivists attempted to replace the dwindling supernatural sanction for morality with a natural one. Stephen argued that their attempt was destined to fail. We have seen that he believed all government and morals to be founded ultimately upon religion. And no religion, he thought, could be effective without a supernatural sanction. Since Positivism denied the existence of the Deity and a future state, it could not effectively maintain society. 'Considered as an organized religion,' Stephen exclaimed, 'it is superfluous to those who like it, and impotent as against those who like it not.'[120]

According to Stephen, religión – belief in God and a future state – exercises a profound effect upon morals. Without religion morality would no doubt continue to exist, but men would tend to be guided by immediate self-interest. He insists that religion provides the only adequate sanction for duty and virtue. We must not underestimate the results of the present decline of religion; it could eventually pave the way for despotism:

> We cannot judge of the effects of Atheism from the conduct of persons who have been educated as believers in God and in the midst of a nation which believes in God. If we should ever see a generation of men, especially a generation of Englishmen to whom the word God had no meaning at all, we should get a light upon the subject which might be lurid enough. Great force of character, restrained and directed by a deep sense of duty, is the

noblest of noble things. Take off the restraint which a sense of duty imposes, and the strong man is apt to become a tyrant and oppressor.[121]

Because Stephen believed that a false religion could not in the long run be useful, the question of the truth of Christianity loomed large in his mind. He held the question in abeyance within *Liberty, Equality, Fraternity* on the grounds that all the facts had not yet been examined. In the next chapter we shall discuss Stephen's religious thought at length. Here it is sufficient to note that he contends that Christianity does not lend support to the doctrine of fraternity. He maintains that there is a strong probability for the existence of God and a future state. But to say that God is a benevolent being, disposed to promote absolutely the happiness of man, is to contradict the experience of life. Awe, not love, is the correct feeling which man should have for God.[122] But is not humanitarianism, quintessentially expressed in the Sermon on the Mount, fundamental to Christianity? Stephen replies that the Christian religion has a 'terrible' as well as a philanthropic side. 'Christian love is only for a time and on condition. It stops short of the gates of hell, and hell is an essential part of the whole Christian scheme.'[123] Stephen detested that part of Christianity which sanctified weakness and suffering. He also perceived a radical inconsistency between the moral code propounded in the Sermon on the Mount and the code which regulates actual life. His views drew sharp criticism from some contemporaries as being too harsh. Richard Holt Hutton, editor of the *Spectator*, called him 'a Calvinist with the bottom knocked out'.[124] Echoing this sentiment, Frederic Harrison described his creed as 'Calvinism *minus* Christianity'.[125]

After many pages of vigorous dialectic, Stephen concludes his attack upon Mill by expressing the hope that he has succeeded in demonstrating two propositions with respect to the doctrines implied by the phrase 'Liberty, Equality, Fraternity':

> First, that in the present day even those who use those words most rationally – that is to say, as the names of elements of social life which, like others, have their advantages and disadvantages according to time, place, and circumstance – have a great disposition to exaggerate their advantages and to deny the existence, or at any rate to underrate the importance, of their

disadvantages. Next, that whatever signification be attached to them, these words are ill-adapted to be the creed of a religion, that the things which they denote are not ends in themselves, and that when used collectively the words do not typify, however vaguely, any state of society which a reasonable man ought to regard with enthusiasm or self-devotion.[126]

VIII

Liberty, Equality, Fraternity created a stir among English Liberals and Positivists. It is unfortunate that Mill, who died at Avignon in 1873, never had a chance to respond to Stephen's thorough attack. Before his death, however, he did manage to read the work in the form of Stephen's unsigned articles as they appeared in the *Pall Mall Gazette*. Alexander Bain, Mill's close friend, related that when Mill read the articles he remarked that their author 'does not know what he is arguing against, and is more likely to repel than to attract people'.[127] Stephen and Mill knew one another personally; but, as Leslie Stephen attested, their relationship was never cordial. And the withdrawal of Stephen from the celebrated Governor Eyre case in 1868 had increased their estrangement. Stephen thought Mill was 'cold as ice' and 'a walking book'.[128] Mill reciprocated his antipathy: his correspondence reveals that he considered Stephen brutal, vain and peremptory.[129]

Nevertheless, Stephen responded to Mill's death with a moving obituary in the *Pall Mall Gazette*. Though he declines to retract or modify any of his recent criticisms, Stephen expresses his sincere respect for Mill. He acknowledges that Mill was one of the greatest and most influential thinkers of his day, the foremost representative of English Utilitarianism, and the author of seminal works on logic and political economy. Yet even great men are not always correct in their judgements. The source of Mill's errors, Stephen suggests, was not a deficiency of intellect, but an excessive sensibility. Mill's sentimental view of man and society vitiated his later writings. Yet Stephen cannot condemn Mill as a man. He perorates with an uplifting note of tribute:

> When [Mill] died one of the tenderest and most passionate hearts that ever set to work an intellect of iron was laid to rest. May he rest in peace, and find, if it be possible, that his knowledge was less complete than he perhaps supposed, and that

there was more to be known than was acknowledged in his philosophy.[130]

The most important responses to *Liberty, Equality, Fraternity* appeared within the pages of the *Fortnightly Review* in 1873, and were written by John Morley and Frederic Harrison. Morley had been Mill's foremost disciple and, like his mentor, he sympathised with various aspects of Positivism. Harrison was a jurist, a leading English Positivist, and a prominent supporter of the working-class reform movement. The *Fortnightly*, under Morley's able editorship since 1867, had been a principal organ of Millite and Positivist thinking since its founding in 1865.[131] Never one to shy away from a good battle, Stephen ventured to respond to some of the criticisms of Morley and Harrison in the Preface and footnotes to the second edition of his work in 1874.

Morley was offended particularly by Stephen's assault upon Mill's doctrine of liberty. He agreed with Mill that the only safeguard against a tyranny of the majority in a democracy lay in regarding liberty as a positive value. After the passage of the Reform Act of 1867, which enfranchised many of the working class, the middle and upper classes feared a destruction of the social order. Morley conceived the role of the *Fortnightly* as that of intellectually preparing for the political and social changes necessary in an age of growing democracy. During this period, liberalism was in the throes of a doctrinal crisis as the division between the old individualist liberalism and the new egalitarian liberalism became more apparent.[132] With traditional liberalism under serious attack, and the working class gradually becoming aware of its new power, Morley believed that individual liberty was endangered. He disagreed with Stephen's contention that Mill's principle of liberty would promote the very evils that it was intended to prevent. 'In truth', he confessed, 'the stream is setting rather strongly the other way just now – which is all the better reason why one should maintain the true doctrine.'[133]

It is not surprising that Morley viewed Stephen's work with alarm. At a time when liberty was being threatened, Stephen attacked it as a mere negation and enthroned authority in its place. Accordingly, after reading *Liberty, Equality, Fraternity*, Morley sent a copy to Frederic Harrison, and requested that he compose a rebuttal:

I will send you Stephen's book to-morrow. I wish specially that you would make up your mind in two or three days whether you will deal with it, or not, and then let me know. He is becoming insufferable, and ought to be stamped upon. You are the man to do it, because you have as firm a grasp of the matter as he has, and you can make him ridiculous in a different way from that in which he makes himself ridiculous. So try to bring yourself under the yoke of composition once more.[134]

One can imagine Morley's disappointment with Harrison's reply. For Harrison found himself in agreement with a great deal in Stephen's book. He confessed that, though he greatly admired Mill's works *On Liberty* and *The Subjection of Women*, 'the principles which lie at the root of both of them are I think as truly metaphysical as the social contract, and as likely in inferior hands to prove disastrous to thought and society'.[135] In essence, he concurred with Stephen's attack upon Mill's sentimentalism: 'Every true positivist is a real conservative, and I am wishing for the time when as conservatives our time will come to defend the immortal institutions of men against sentimental sophists, noble or ignoble.'[136] Like Stephen, Harrison believed that in a time of increasing democracy, authority had to be stressed. As he saw it, the great political problem of the age was 'to found Authority without oppression upon a Public Opinion without Democracy'.[137]

As a confirmed Positivist, Harrison naturally found fault with Stephen's attack upon the Religion of Humanity as an inadequate sanction for morality and religion. He therefore informed Morley that he would answer Stephen's challenge, but that he would concentrate only upon those sections of *Liberty, Equality, Fraternity* in which Stephen attempted to establish the grounds for a supernatural religion.[138] Harrison pointed out in detail to Morley where he agreed and disagreed with Stephen's book:

> I think he is in the main right, and he has done a good work. I do not say that he has not done it with a bludgeoning Philistinism which is a little trying, and that he has not made some bold fallacies – but I don't wish to detract from a really good and useful argument, in which he is successful. I think – although I dislike his way of putting it and see how much he leaves out – as against Mill he is successful and even triumphant.

1. What he says of Liberty is right. Mill has talked about abstract and absolute right, and has idealised the individual in a way that is metaphysical nonsense and also extremely anarchical. Stephen fairly demolishes all this. Mill's plea for the sacredness of individual liberty is a dangerous sophism. . . . Stephen does not quite hit the true ground that society is a natural thing and you can only ask what is good for it and its members and not the whirligig of *rights* – but practically he hits the right line in asking. He is as near the truth as a politician or lawyer need be, though not as clear as a philosopher should be.

2. What he says about Equality is admirable. His argument as to the equality of the sexes is a little brutal but *so far as it goes* is unanswerable. It leaves out the finer positive argument for women's superiorities, but it does justice and no more than justice for men's. And there again he is as right as a mere legislator or lawyer need be – far more right than Mill's subversive paradoxes.

3. As to Fraternity, I am not quite sure, but I think Stephen is fairly right. I don't know what becomes of his Christianity, but that is his affair. Of course he utterly misunderstands Comte's Humanity which he imagines to be all men including W. E. G. [Gladstone]. This of course is ridiculous. And I am not sure that Comte would not agree with Stephen as to the hollowness of the democratic bluster about 'a man is a brother'.[139]

Since Harrison was unable to deliver the broad attack upon Stephen that he had requested, Morley felt constrained to undertake an independent defence of Mill. He therefore published an article entitled 'Mr. Mill's Doctrine of Liberty' in the *Fortnightly* in 1873.[140] There is no need to review either his criticism or Stephen's retorts in detail. The article, consisting in part of a reprise of Mill's arguments in favour of individual liberty, adds nothing new to Mill's position. Morley concurs with Mill that liberty, to be meaningful, must be regarded as a positive value, as the means to human excellence. He concedes the vagueness of the distinction between self-regarding and other-regarding acts. But he maintains that the only way to protect a minority from an oppressive majority is to distinguish between actions which affect other people directly, and those which affect them only indirectly.

IX

After a second edition in 1874, Fitzjames Stephen's *Liberty, Equality, Fraternity* remained virtually inaccessible for nearly a century until it was republished in 1967. The work was well received in its day. The *Saturday Review* hailed it as 'one of the most valuable contributions of political philosophy which have been published in recent times'. Both the *Athenaeum* and the *Quarterly Review* saw it as a necessary complement to Mill's doctrine of liberty.[141] Stephen, in emphasising authority, dealt with one side of a question which was already considered from the other side by Mill. Among Stephen's contemporaries, A. V. Dicey described his work as 'a strenuous assault' which 'certainly shows that Mill had diverged considerably from Bentham'.[142] Henry Sidgwick found it unsatisfactory in many respects, but conceded that Stephen was on the mark in attacking the absolute manner in which Mill expounded his views.[143] America's Charles Eliot Norton characterised Stephen's book as 'an excellent contribution to non-sentimental political discussion'.[144] In our own century, Sir Ernest Barker, referring to 'Stephen's splendid single star', believed that the book was 'the finest exposition of conservative thought in the latter half of the nineteenth-century'.[145] Harold Laski, not inclined to be sympathetic to Stephen's political views, read the work and confided to Oliver Wendell Holmes that 'Mill seems to have very thin blood beside those sledge-hammer blows'.[146] Most recently, it was acclaimed by a reviewer in *The Times Literary Supplement* as 'something of a Victorian classic'.[147]

Yet *Liberty, Equality, Fraternity* has never attained the popularity of *On Liberty*. Had Stephen been asked to speculate why Mill's essay received so many more favourable readers, he might have responded that Mill told them what they wanted to hear. Stephen failed to satisfy the needs of the leading schools of political thought in his day. He wrote at a time when classical liberalism, which prevailed in England during most of the nineteenth century, was evolving inexorably into the Welfare State philosophy. Proponents of this new thought naturally found Stephen's liberalism outmoded. At the same time, the traditional liberals, who drew their principal inspiration from Mill, were offended by Stephen's severe critique of their mentor. During a period when liberal society was threatened by growing socialism and an increasingly centralised State, they believed that Mill's views on liberty ought to be staunchly defended rather than attacked. Nor was Stephen at home in the conservative camp. Though late in life he found himself closer to them on certain issues, he never stopped agreeing with Mill that they were the 'stupid' party, unable to meet the challenges of the day.[148] Thus Stephen suffered the fate of most men out of step with their age: unable to attract any school of thought, his ideas failed to bear fruit in his lifetime.

Certainly, Mill's essay has been favoured by its tremendous moral appeal. To his disadvantage, Stephen was never tolerant of popular commonplaces, and his writing is pervaded by a sceptical view of human nature. Liberty, he declared, is a negative, dependent upon circumstances and founded upon compulsion. Equality is meaningless except in so far as substantive equalities in fact exist. And fraternity is an impractical and sentimental worship of an absurd abstraction. Mill was undoubtedly correct when he said that Stephen would repel many readers. But Stephen knew very well what he was attempting to refute, and he retained the courage of his convictions. As a political realist, he insisted that, because of the malady of human nature, we must endure what we cannot cure and make the best of things as they are.

8 An Honest Doubter

I

A sense of foreboding is evident throughout *Liberty, Equality, Fraternity*. Along with the rise of democracy, the decline of religion originated what we have termed a crisis of Victorian thought. Stephen, it will be recalled, believed that all government and morals are founded ultimately upon a religion, which must be supernatural rather than secular. Unlike the Positivists and rationalists of his time, he rejected the notion that morals could be divorced from religion. In his essay 'The Utility of Religion' Mill declared that, once the Religion of Humanity is accepted, one may dispense with Christianity, God and belief in an afterlife. Stephen was not as confident. In the interest of truth, he was willing to accept the fall of Christianity, but he feared the consequences. A. W. Benn therefore exaggerated when he called him 'the most thorough rationalist of the age'.[1] The firmly convinced leaders of rationalist thought in England during the 1870s were T. H. Huxley, W. K. Clifford and Leslie Stephen.

Because Fitzjames Stephen believed that the utility of religion depended upon its truth, he contended that the truth of Christianity was a question of paramount importance, to be decided only by a thorough study of the evidence. When he wrote *Liberty, Equality, Fraternity* this question still had not been resolved. 'The witnesses have been called,' he observed, 'the counsel have made their speeches, and the jury are considering their verdict.'[2] In his spiritual development, Stephen began as an Evangelical, grew to accept the views of the liberal Broad Church and, though retaining his belief in God and a future life, gradually lost faith in Christianity. Its fate preoccupied many other leading minds during the latter half of the Victorian age, and Stephen's contribution to the debate was significant.

Stephen's religious thought was profoundly influenced by his father's liberal Evangelicalism. A brief account of Stephen's early

167

upbringing is given in an autobiography begun late in life and never completed. His father, Sir James Stephen, was a pious Evangelical with 'a natural turn for asceticism'.[3] Though his 'sceptical intellect' led him to conclude that the historical evidence for Christianity was weak, he 'never allowed himself to think freely on religious subjects, though he thought about them incessantly, divining with singular ingenuity all sorts of reasons for not following the obvious roads which led to disbelief'.[4] When questioned about conflicting statements in the Bible, he conceded the difficulties but insisted that Christianity was founded on faith. A precocious child, Fitzjames did his best to follow his father's counsel, but he later recollected that 'nothing could make a deeper impression on me than these reluctant admissions, torn from him as they were by arguments of which he was too honest to deny the force though not bold or truth-loving enough to measure the full force'.[5]

But the elder Stephen was actually more sceptical than his son recognised. Writing late in life and after he himself had rejected Christianity, Fitzjames gave no credence to revealed religion and wished that his father had trusted more to his reason. But Sir James Stephen was more liberal than most Evangelicals of his day, and only a profound sense of his responsibility to teach his children about God prevented him from revealing to them how open-minded he really was. Throughout his life he associated freely with men of decidedly different religious views, even atheists. He once said that he 'never met with a single man who, like myself, had passed a long series of years in a free intercourse with every class of society who was not more or less what is called a Latitudinarian'.[6] That is, he rejected dogmatism and insisted that religion must not be divorced from the world. While he served as Colonial Under-Secretary, the elder Stephen wrote at leisure a number of essays on religious figures for the *Edinburgh Review* which were later published as *Essays in Ecclesiastical Biography* (1850). Characterised by broad understanding and brilliant style, they are portraits of both Catholics and Protestants: Hildebrand (Pope Gregory VII), Saint Francis of Assisi and Ignatius Loyola receive the same sympathetic treatment as Wilberforce, Wesley, Baxter and Luther.

In his Epilogue, Sir James expressed some views which led to a rift with the Evangelicals. Seeking to transcend the conflicting interpretations of Scripture that gave rise to sectarianism, he insisted that the first duty of man is to love God. The belief that 'God is light' and that 'God is love', shared by those who were the subjects of the essays, might serve as the basis of 'a catholic Church and of a true Christian Unity'.[7] He also disavowed the cardinal doctrine of Evangelicalism – Hell. Acknowledging that many abandon Christianity because they cannot reconcile God's goodness with the belief in eternal punishment, he suggested that the doctrine rests upon insufficient evidence and is not necessary to a Christian faith. These opinions drew criticism from contemporary Evangelicals, but Sir James believed that he was consistent with the tradition of his spiritual ancestors, William Wilberforce and the men of Clapham.

Sir James thought that the Claphamites represented the best of Evangelicalism, the rank and file being narrow and intolerant. Wilberforce and his followers had learned to accommodate themselves to the world in order to reform it. That they were able to work with Utilitarians and men of other creeds for social improvement showed that they refused to draw a sharp line between saint and sinner, the Church and the world. In his essay 'The Clapham Sect', a name that he made popular, Sir James praised their open-mindedness:

> Absolute as was the faith of Mr. Wilberforce and his associates, it was not that the system called 'Evangelical', should be asserted by them in the blunt and uncompromising tone of their immediate predecessors. A more elaborate education, greater familiarity with the world and with human affairs, a deeper insight into science and history, with a far nicer discernment of mere conventional proprieties, had opened to them a range of thought, and had brought them into relations with society, of which their fathers were comparatively destitute. Positiveness, dogmatism, and an ignorant contempt of difficulties, may accompany the firmest convictions, but not the convictions of the firmest minds.[8]

Sir James Stephen was ascetic by temperament. As Leslie later wrote, his father was 'a living categorical imperative'.[9] He was 'one of the few people to whom it was the same thing to eat a dinner and to perform an act of self-denial'.[10] He once smoked a cigar and found it so enjoyable that he never smoked another. He relished snuff until one day he found it superfluous. When Fitzjames was a young boy his mother asked, 'Did you ever know your father to do a thing because it was pleasant?' To which the precocious child responded, 'Yes, once – when he married you.'[11] Fitzjames's mother, the daughter of John Venn of Clapham, was a pious woman, but she was 'too placid and sensible to have any sort of religious fervour'.[12] Though in later years she retained her faith, she accepted the deviations of her children from orthodoxy with equanimity.[13] Like other Evangelicals, the Stephen children were taught to love God, read the Bible, and keep the Sabbath. Though the house was pervaded by 'a faint smell of asceticism', Fitzjames insisted that 'we were not the least bit ascetic'.[14] The children never attended plays or balls – which their father thought were 'not convenient' – but they were not taught that these recreations were sinful.[15] The Stephen household was not blighted by the ever-present sense of sin, or by the bleak and narrow atmosphere suffered by men such as Edmund Gosse, Samuel Butler and John Ruskin. The Stephen children never felt that their religion was forced upon them; rather, they regarded it as a normal part of life.[16]

Stephen's first mature religious thought occurred during the years he was a student at King's College, London. His father's influence, Leslie Stephen tells us, had 'removed a good deal of the true evangelical dogmatism'.[17] Hence we find Fitzjames sympathetic to the Broad Church movement – the spiritual descendant of Latitudinarianism – led at that time by Frederick Denison Maurice, chaplain at Lincoln's Inn, a professor at King's College, and later a well-known Christian socialist. Perhaps the greatest Anglican theologian of the century, Maurice was an impressive preacher who attracted a large audience. Stephen attended his sermons and read most of his works while he was at the college and later when he was studying for the bar. In his book *The Kingdom of Christ*, Maurice maintained that all religions contain a degree of truth, erring – he was fond of Coleridge's dictum – not in what they affirm but in what they deny. In his *Theological Essays*, Maurice boldly rejected the doctrines of atonement and eternal punishment, and was consequently dismissed from his professorship in 1853.

Though Stephen was devoted to his teacher, he could not accept Maurice's metaphysics. Soon after leaving Cambridge, Fitzjames became a disciple of Bentham and John Stuart Mill. Mill was then at the height of his influence. As Leslie wrote, 'The young men who graduated in 1850 and the following ten years found their teaching in Mill's *Logic*, and only a few daring heretics were beginning to pick holes in his system.'[18] In the face of Mill's denial of innate truths and his reverence for facts, Maurice's vaporous theology appeared chimerical. Indeed, Fitzjames said that Maurice's works convinced him that 'the only intelligible version of theology which could be given, was at once stupid and mischievous'.[19] On another occasion, he affirmed that, though he greatly respected Maurice's piety, 'I wholly and entirely disagreed with him as far as I understood him.'[20]

While studying for the bar, Stephen also read W. R. Greg's *Creed of Christendom* (1851), which attacked the historicity of the Bible. He read other works by Greg and, though the arguments were not new to him, he later said that 'they were pretty nearly the first books in that sense which I did not mentally rebel against, and reject, and they marked a sort of epoch in my ways of thinking though they did not convince me'.[21] In later life, Stephen came to know Greg and considered his works 'much too orthodox for me'.[22] Paradoxically, though Greg's work had contributed to subverting the scriptural basis for Christianity, the man considered himself a devout Christian. Stephen quipped that he was like a disciple of Christ 'who had heard the Sermon on the Mount, and who died before the Resurrection'.[23] Thus by the 1850s Stephen's philosophy was a combination of Utilitarianism and diluted Evangelicalism.

II

In March 1860 there appeared in England a volume entitled *Essays and Reviews* which at once raised a storm of protest. Written by seven Broad Churchmen – six members of the clergy and one layman – it was an attempt to reconcile Christianity with modern scholarship.[24] Orthodox religion was cracking under the attacks of natural science and historical criticism. Geology and the doctrine of evolution had undermined the biblical theory of a special creation. Charles Lyell's *Principles of Geology* (1830-3) had convincingly argued that the earth was much older than Genesis had led men such as Archbishop Usher to believe. The idea of the mutability of species, popularised by the immensely successful *Vestiges of Creation* (1844) by Robert Chambers, received a new impetus with the publication of Darwin's *Origin of Species* in 1859.[25] Moreover, the so-called 'higher criticism' of the Bible spread from Germany and found fertile ground in England. David

Friedrich Strauss's *Das Leben Jesu* (1835) had been translated by George Eliot in 1846, and increasing numbers of people were reading Scripture with a critical eye. Though Strauss did not deny the historical Jesus, he insisted that his divinity was a myth fashioned by his enthusiastic disciples to fulfil the Hebrew prophecies.

The authors of the *Essays and Reviews* were Frederick Temple (Headmaster of Rugby and future Archbishop of Canterbury), Rowland Williams (Vice-Principal and Professor at St David's College, Lampeter), Benjamin Jowett (the future Master of Balliol), Mark Pattison, Baden Powell and H. B. Wilson of Oxford, and C. W. Goodwin of Cambridge. Contending that the Bible should be read 'like any other book', Jowett summed up the theme of the group best: 'The time has come when it is no longer possible to ignore the results of criticism.'[26] The essayists were immediately denounced as the 'Septem contra Christum'. Their conclusions seem innocuous today, but what was disturbing then was that they were written not by infidels but mainly by clergymen. In fact, the essayists wrote with a constructive intent. Seeing that traditional religion was fighting a losing battle with science and history, they sought to preserve the core of Christianity by distinguishing between what was essential for belief and what could be regarded as accretions.

The Positivist Frederic Harrison argued that, though their view of the Bible was rational, the essayists had no business remaining in the Church. They had not gone far enough, but were attempting to support a 'crumbling edifice'.[27] Samuel Wilberforce, Bishop of Oxford since 1844, and known today for his debate with T. H. Huxley over Darwinism at the annual meeting of the British Association in 1860, led the attack from the orthodox side. He moved to have the Anglican bishops condemn the *Essays and Reviews* synodically in Convocation.

Fitzjames Stephen entered the controversy by serving as counsel for Rowland Williams, who was tried for heresy in the Arches Court of Canterbury for his contribution to the volume. Fitzjames had long been familiar with the writings of the school being attacked. Indeed, Leslie said that when his brother read Jowett's commentary on the Epistle to the Romans he found it far more orthodox than he himself could pretend to be.[28] Williams was charged with denying that the Bible was inspired. In his essay 'Bunsen's Biblical Researches' he disputed the canonicity of the books of Daniel, Jonah, Revelation, the Epistle to the Hebrews and the Second Epistle of St Peter. He also denied that Jonah and Daniel had written the books attributed to them. Throughout December 1861 and January 1862, Stephen diligently prepared his case. After the trial he published a volume containing his arguments.[29] The brief was a brilliant and extremely well-researched effort, which manifests the same scrupulous attention to both analysis and history as characterises all his legal works.

Stephen's defence rested on four principal contentions: (1) the issue before the court was purely legal; (2) the law upon this subject must be that of the Thirty-Nine Articles, the Rubrics and the Formularies, and not passages from Scripture; (3) the Articles purposely left it open to clergymen to hold that the Bible 'contains' but does not 'constitute' divine revelation; and (4) the Anglican clergy have long been free to apply criticism to decide what part of Scripture 'contains' the word of God.

Stephen insists that the question is not whether Dr Williams was correct in his opinions, but whether he was forbidden by law to express them as a clergyman. The court cannot be expected to decide the truth of his views. To do so would convert it into a court of theology, requiring it to pass judgement on every passage in the Bible.[30] Stephen argues that the sixth, seventh and twentieth Articles determine the canonicity of Scripture – what books constitute the Bible – but leave open the questions of inspiration and interpretation. Since no claim is made that the Bible is absolutely the word of God throughout, Williams was exercising a liberty sanctioned by the Thirty-Nine Articles.

The next point Stephen sought to establish is that the questions of inspiration and interpretation were 'designedly and intentionally'[31] left open by the Articles. He argues that the Westminster Confession of 1643, in which the sixth article was revised to declare that the Bible constituted entirely the word of God, was not upheld when the Articles were ratified during the Restoration in 1662. He concludes that the issue of inspiration was deliberately left undecided 'because the authors of the Articles knew well the danger of drawing any harsh line between that truth which God reveals to man through Scripture, and that which God reveals to man through reason'.[32]

What is more, English history shows that the eminent divines of the Anglican Church have exercised this liberty with impunity. Throughout the seventeenth and eighteenth centuries, English clergymen freely denied either the infallibility or the circumstantial accuracy of the Bible. They were likewise given latitude on the question of canonicity. Stephen cites a number of authorities to support these contentions, including Hooker, Chillingworth, Jeremy Taylor, Bishop Butler, Tillotson, Warburton, Paley and Whately. During the eighteenth century, the doctrine that the Bible was substantially but not totally true served as the defence of the Church against deists such as Bolingbroke, Voltaire and Hume. By the end of the century liberal Protestantism was victorious, enabling Edmund Burke confidently to exclaim, 'Who reads Bolingbroke now?'

Stephen thought that the English Reformation was a great victory for freedom of individual reason and conscience. Its leading principle was that true religion must be founded upon evidence. He argued the Williams case on the issue of this same religious liberty – that is, whether the law permits the English clergy 'to use their minds'.[33] The implication was clear: the Reformation was as much on trial as Williams. Aware that the public was prejudiced against his client's acquittal, Stephen concluded with a declaiming peroration, appealing to the court to consider the gravity of the issue before it:

> My lord, I feel no fear, for I am sure that your lordship will look beyond the cynical and ignorant clamour; you will look beyond the obscure advocate to whom you have listened with so much patient indulgence; you will look to the very right and truth of the cause itself; for be it attacked how it may, and be it defended how it will, it is a cause which might dignify the greatest genius that ever wore these robes; which might enlist the warmest sympathies of the human heart; for it is the cause of learning, of freedom, and of reason – the freedom of the freest, and the reason of the most rational church in the world.[34]

Despite the brilliance of Stephen's plea, Williams was convicted on two counts of heresy. But ultimate victory came in 1864, when he was acquitted on appeal to the Judicial Committee of the Privy Council. The Williams case was one of the most famous of Stephen's career and, though it did not increase his legal business, it enhanced his reputation. He had played an instrumental role in a significant triumph for religious liberalism in England. The case also tells us something of his religious ideas at that time. Leslie

Stephen said that, although his brother had been acting as an advocate, his contention that the Bible contains but does not constitute revelation was substantially his own.[35]

Prosecution having failed, the Church undertook its own measures. Bishop Wilberforce finally succeeded in having the *Essays and Reviews* condemned by the Convocation of Canterbury in 1864. At the same time Edward Pusey, a former leader of the Oxford Movement, drew up a declaration, signed by nearly 11,000 clergymen, that the Church of England maintains 'without reserve or qualification' the inspiration and divine authority of Scripture.[36] Pusey refused to accept the decision of the Privy Council acquitting Williams, and called for the institution of a new Court of Appeal, composed exclusively of ecclesiastics, to decide all religious disputes. Some years earlier, he had protested the famous Gorham judgement of 1850 in which the Council upheld the legal right of a clergyman, G. C. Gorham, to remain in his parish despite his unorthodox view of baptism. Stephen thought that this decision was highly important as proving that there are open questions on points of doctrine within the Church of England.[37]

III

During the 1860s Stephen contributed several more articles on religion to *Fraser's Magazine*. Since the editor of the *Saturday*, J. D. Cook, endeavoured to steer clear of theological controversy, Stephen had been unable to comment directly upon the religious issues that continued to preoccupy him. He relished his new opportunity, since 'it enables me to say all sorts of things that I had been cooking up in my mind for years'.[38] From 1861 on, *Fraser's* was under the efficient editorship of James Anthony Froude, who allowed his writers considerable freedom. When the *Cornhill* refused to continue publishing John Ruskin's articles on political economy, Froude welcomed them to his magazine. Stephen and Froude became intimate friends, and in later years they frequently vacationed together in Ireland and Devon.

Stephen contributed to still another controversy with a review of John Henry Newman's now classic *Apologia Pro Vita Sua* in 1864. This brilliant and moving spiritual autobiography was the ultimate product of a quarrel between Newman and the Christian socialist and novelist Charles Kingsley. In January 1864 an anonymous review of Froude's *History of England* (vols VII and VIII) had appeared in *Macmillan's Magazine*, containing the following passage:

> Truth, for its own sake, had never been a virtue with the Roman clergy. Father Newman informs us that it need not, and on the whole ought not to be; that cunning is the weapon which Heaven has given to the Saints wherewith to withstand the brute force of the wicked world which marries and is given in marriage. Whether his notion be doctrinally correct or not, it is at least historically so.

Thirty years earlier, Newman had been the central figure of the Oxford Movement, a reaction within the Church of England to political and religious liberalism. Stemming from Oxford, where Newman delivered sermons as Vicar of St Mary's, the movement reached its height in the late 1830s. Among its other prominent members were John Keble, Pusey, Hurrell Froude and W. G. Ward. The movement began in 1833 with Keble's famous 'National Apostasy' sermon, protesting the intrusion of the English government in Church affairs by its suppression of ten Irish bishoprics. To safeguard the English Church, Newman fashioned the so-called *Via Media* between Roman Catholicism and Evangelicalism. He contended that the Church of England was truly catholic and apostolic, deriving its authority from the Apostles, while avoiding the errors of both Rome and Protestantism.

For nearly a decade Newman walked a tightrope between Rome and Protestantism, until he wrote the fatal Tract XC in 1841, arguing that the Thirty-Nine Articles did not conflict with Catholic doctrine, but opposed only 'the dominant errors of Rome'. Most interpreted this as removing the distinction between the Anglican and Roman Churches. Convinced of the untenability of his views, Newman resigned from St Mary's in 1843, converted to Rome within two years, and was eventually made a cardinal in 1879. His conversion led many to infer that he had been dishonest, that only a lack of moral courage had prevented him from surrendering to Popery years earlier.

Newman was shocked when he read the insinuating passage in *Macmillan's*. He immediately wrote to the magazine, calling attention to 'a grave and gratuitous slander', and complaining that the accusation was not substantiated by reference to specific words he had written.³⁹ Kingsley wrote to Newman identifying himself as the author, saying that he had in mind many passages from Newman's works, particularly the sermon 'Wisdom and Innocence'. Kingsley proposed a public apology, unsatisfactory to Newman since it would have aggravated the original insult by implying that he had been confronted with extracts from his works and merely differed from Kingsley in his interpretation of them. A brief apology appeared in the February issue of *Macmillan's*, in which Kingsley, still alluding to Newman's writings, expressed regret for having mistaken his meaning. Newman responded by challenging him to prove his allegation. Kingsley then wrote a pamphlet, *What, Then, Does Dr. Newman Mean?*, in which he produced some of Newman's texts and reiterated the charge that he did not value truth. To settle the controversy definitively, Newman proceeded to set down the history of his religious opinions in the *Apologia*. He worked at a feverish pace, writing from morning to night, and produced within ten weeks a work of more than 500 pages, which he published in weekly instalments. His effort was a popular success and vindicated him in the eyes of many of his countrymen.

Stephen agreed with many other readers that the contest was unequal and that Kingsley had handled himself ineptly. Surveying the controversy for the *Saturday*, he argues that what Kingsley said about Newman and the Roman clergy is correct, but that he failed to prove it. Stephen concedes that 'Mr. Kingsley's habit of mind is a very unfortunate one for a serious investigation of truth . . . he is apt to be careless in investigating the grounds of what ought to be his judgments, but which are his prejudices.'⁴⁰ In his review of the *Apologia*, Stephen attempts to succeed where Kingsley failed. He admits that 'every word that the author says of himself and his opinions bears upon it the stamp of truth'.⁴¹ Though Newman did not intend to distort the truth, Stephen believes that his religious system is intellectually dishonest or sophistical, in that his arguments are those which can be acceptable only to those committed to 'a foregone conclusion', and not to those in search of the truth.⁴² Stephen submits that 'Dr. Newman got to Rome honestly enough as far as anything like fraud was concerned, yet the considerations which finally decided him were of a sentimental rather than a rational kind.'⁴³ Some years later, having read many of Newman's works, he repeated this judgement:

Newman is one of those people who pass their lives in a passionate effort to work out a result which at the bottom of their hearts they know is not true. His reason goes one way and his feelings the other, and he forces his reason to follow his feelings instead of regulating his feelings by his reason. I do not call this honest – though perhaps it is a question of words.[44]

At least one historian of the Oxford Movement has concurred with Stephen's contention.[45]

In tracing the development of his beliefs, Newman said that dogma was the fundamental principle of his religion, and that liberalism, or 'the anti-dogmatic principle and its developments', was his life-long enemy. He reserved further discussion of liberalism to a note appended to the second edition of the *Apologia* in 1865, where he defined it as 'false liberty of thought . . . the mistake of subjecting to human judgements those revealed doctrines which are in their nature beyond and independent of it'.[46] He concluded by setting forth eighteen propositions and their inferred consequences which he considered to be the cardinal tenets of modern liberalism. Among the things he condemned were Biblical criticism, State interference with the Church, Benthamism, and the doctrine of popular sovereignty.

Stephen took issue with Newman in an article for the *Saturday*, alleging that the modern liberal has no quarrel with revealed dogmas. But the liberal maintains that the question whether a dogma has been revealed is a matter of fact, to be decided according to the common rules of evidence.[47] Stephen also calls attention to the sceptical nature of Newman's arguments. Newman concedes that the palpable evil of the world appears to disprove the existence of a Deity. Were it not for the voice of his conscience, he confesses, 'I should be an atheist, or a pantheist, or a polytheist, when I looked into the world.'[48] Newman also makes the admission, fatal from Stephen's viewpoint, that human reason supports atheism. Though 'correctly exercised' it leads to belief in God, the soul and a future reward, 'as it acts in fact and concretely in fallen man, its tendency is towards simple unbelief in matters of religion'.[49] This argument, with the evidence one way and the conclusion another, suggests to Stephen the inference that 'if Dr. Newman was thoroughly honest he would be an atheist'.[50]

Newman based his faith upon the doctrine of probability, which he claimed to have derived from Butler's *Analogy of Religion* (1736), a long popular defence of Christianity against deism. He also thought that probability could serve as the grounds for certitude in religious belief. The *Apologia* contains a summary of his position:

> My argument is in outline as follows: that the absolute certitude which we were able to possess, whether as to the truths of natural theology, or as to the fact of a revelation, was the result of an assemblage of concurring and converging probabilities, and that, both according to the constitution of the human mind and the will of its Maker; that certitude was a habit of mind, that certainty was a quality of propositions; that probabilities which did not reach to logical certainty, might create a mental certitude; that the certitude thus created might equal in measure and strength the certitude which was created by the strictest scientific demonstration.[51]

Stephen submitted that this argument might be tenable if the probabilities relied upon by Newman were independent.[52] He offered as an example the question whether a person was at a given place at a certain time. If one person testifies that he saw him then and there, if another says he saw him heading in that direction shortly before that time, and if another person observed him leaving shortly afterwards, their independent testimonies combine to establish the probability of the person's whereabouts. But Newman errs, Stephen alleged, in founding his religion on dependent rather than independent probabilities. The probability of Christianity depends upon the probability of the existence of God, and the probability of Roman Catholicism depends upon both the existence of God and the truth of Christianity. If the probability of the existence of a Deity, the truth of the Christian religion and the truth of Romanism depend upon each other, then the probability of the last must be less than the first two. Even if the probabilities were independent, Newman would arrive at a result fatal to his theory, since theism and the fact of the divine mission of Christ may be established without resorting to Romanism.

Stephen returned to Newman in an article for *Fraser's*, 'On Certitude in Religious Assent', in response to W. G. Ward's praise of Newman's *Grammar of Assent* (1870) in the *Dublin Review*. This book was Newman's most important philosophical venture, and marked another episode in his battle with liberalism. He attempted to show that the certitude with which many sincere Christians hold their faith is reasonable even though it is based upon evidence insufficient for scientific proof. Many certitudes, he asserted, are founded upon informal proofs rather than strict logic. He made an important distinction between a 'notional' and a 'real' assent. The former is purely intellectual, and is given to abstract truths or ideas; the latter involves the 'whole man', and is more vivid and intense. Newman opposed the rationalist assumption that assent must be proportionate to the empirical evidence, that one must accept no more than what is demonstrable. He further distinguished between assent, which is absolute and certain, and inference, which leads to mere conditional acceptance. In all instances, assent is preceded by inference. To explain how certitude is arrived at in religious matters, he introduces the so-called 'illative sense', the faculty by which men, in response to an accumulation of converging probabilities, come to hold the dogmas of Christianity unconditionally.

Stephen naturally found this entirely sophistical. He protested that Newman's 'illative sense' is really a leap of faith, 'the function of which appears to be to draw positive conclusions from insufficient premisses'.[53] Though he agreed with Newman that the basic truths of natural religion – the existence of God and of a future state – are probable, he argued that, unless the conclusions are supported by evidence, we cannot pass from probability to certitude. The intensity and certainty with which we hold a doctrine have no necessary relation to its truth.

> Turn and twist as you will, you can never really get out of the proposition that the Christian history is just as probable as the evidence makes it, and no more; and that to give a greater degree of assent to it, or, if the expression is preferred, to give an unreserved assent to the proposition that it has a greater degree of probability than the evidence warrants, is to give up its character as an historical event altogether.[54]

It is clear from the foregoing that Stephen and Newman held differing conceptions of the role of faith in religion. Newman subscribed to the medieval formulation *credo ut intelligam:* one believes first, and then seeks to buttress this faith with understanding; whenever the conclusions of reason and faith conflict, reason must surrender. Stephen, on the other hand, belonged to the liberal religious tradition which insisted that faith may never conflict with reason. All dogma must rest upon substantial probability. Faith alone, without the restraint of reason, might be used to exercise a tyranny over the minds of men. Man has the choice of either confining his conclusions to matters which can be verified by experience, in which case he must forsake many important questions as insoluble, or he must be satisfied with probable solutions which are necessarily subject to error and revision. Stephen chose the latter course.[55]

Even though late in life Stephen came to doubt the adequacy of language to convey truth in philosophical matters, he found absolute scepticism untenable.[56] On the basis of probability, he thought he was justified in believing in the existence of God and a future state. The fault of Newman, he insisted, was that he was willing to attribute to the dogmas of his creed a greater degree of probability than the evidence warranted. Unlike Newman and many of his other contemporaries, Stephen did not retreat from the conclusions of science. He realised that only by an honest and courageous study of the facts can man attain salvation. To gain salvation, one must be willing to risk losing it.

Stephen recognised that in most branches of knowledge we must be satisfied with no more than probability.[57] His agnostic contemporary W. K. Clifford published a famous essay entitled 'The Ethics of Belief' contending that it is actually immoral to believe anything on insufficient evidence, for such credulity violates our duty to mankind of never surrendering our critical faculty.[58] Consequently, in religious matters, where we are seldom without doubt, we must suspend judgement. Stephen was unwilling to go as far as Clifford. The great American philosopher William James, in his widely celebrated essay 'The Will To Believe', introduced the notion of the 'forced option': on certain momentous questions, it is simply impossible not to make a choice. Though by remaining sceptical we may avoid errors if religion is false, we lose the truth if religion is true. In similar fashion, Stephen maintained that if, ignoring probability as a guide, we suspend our judgement on religious questions, this is only another way of answering them, fraught with its own consequences.[59] Whatever our decision, we must follow our conscience and have courage.

IV

Stephen reviewed some other books which had a bearing on this continuing controversy about religion. In 1865 appeared the *History of the Rise and Influence of the Spirit of Rationalism in Europe*, by the young disciple of Buckle, W. E. H. Lecky. Four years later he published an equally impressive *History of European Morals from Augustus to Charlemagne*. Together these works, though unjustly neglected today, established him as a pioneer in intellectual history. In the *Rationalism*, Lecky applied the historical method to trace the growth of secular thought in art, science, morality, and politics. Stephen confesses that it is difficult not to overpraise the book.[60] Yet, notwithstanding a lucid style and enormous erudition, it suffers from some grave misconceptions. Its great defect is that 'it is a lukewarm defence of great truths'.[61] Instead of setting up truth as 'the ultimate object and test of all thought whatever', Lecky merely determines whether a particular opinion is consistent with the sentiments of the day, and avoids the question of whether these sentiments are well founded.[62]

Lecky also made what Stephen considers to be a false distinction between rationalism and theology, implying that religion and reason are incompatible. Since all thought is reasoning, the true distinction is between correct and incorrect reasoning. The difference between a person who believes in witchcraft and one who does not is that one is right and the other wrong, not that one is a rationalist and the other a theologian.[63] Reason acting upon available information should be the sole cause of our opinions. The difference between one age and another consists in the different amounts of knowledge and experience they possess. By means of electricity and magnetism, Stephen contends, we explain many facts which in past ages either went unexplained or were attributed to supernatural agents. Lecky alleged that the disbelief in witchcraft was attributable to 'the spirit of the age. . . . It is the result not of any series of definite arguments or of new discoveries, but of a gradual, insensible, yet profound modification of the habits of thought prevailing in Europe.'[64] Protesting that Lecky's 'spirit of rationalism' was too vague and metaphysical, Stephen charges him with introducing 'into speculation by a new door one of those purely fictitious beings which it ought to be our object to exorcise and finally dispose of'.[65]

Next in Stephen's polemical path was an anonymous life of Christ published late in 1865 and entitled *Ecce Homo*.[66] Its bold presentation of Christ in purely human terms caused a stir among the orthodox. The work was summarily denounced by Lord Shaftesbury as 'the most pestilential book ever vomited, I think, from the jaws of hell'. J. R. Seeley, soon widely acknowledged as the author, later suggested that the book's enormous success was in large part owing to Shaftesbury's intemperate remark.[67] Seeley attempted to show that Christ instituted a universal Church or society and gave it a body of laws – the Sermon on the Mount. Stephen contends that the work is sheer fiction, 'a novel, and not even a good novel, under a critical disguise'.[68] He charges that Seeley fails to evaluate his biblical sources critically, since he merely assumes their truth and proceeds to establish that Christ founded a temporal theocracy and gave it a constitution. But nowhere in the Bible does Christ explicitly say that he intends to found a universal society on earth. Historical criticism has, moreover, shown that the Sermon on the Mount was not delivered at one place and time, but was the essence of several homilies given at a variety of places and over an extended period. Seeley's credulity leads Stephen to conclude that *Ecce Homo* was written by 'a sheep in wolf's clothing',[69] an orthodox believer posing as a rationalist.

On this occasion, Stephen also gives his view of the truth of the Gospel.[70] The prudent man, he says, will recognise that there are strong arguments on both sides of the question. Hence Stephen gives only 'a qualified assent' to the truth of Scripture. Though he has what he terms 'an honest doubt' concerning Christianity, he feels justified in worshipping in the Church to which he belongs until evidence settles the question.

By this time, it is clear, Stephen has relinquished his earlier conviction that the Bible, despite some errors, is substantially true. In a review of the writings of the American theologian Theodore Parker, he says that Christianity includes many falsehoods and that it will take years of difficult inquiry to separate the wheat from the chaff.[71] Elsewhere, in 'Women and Scepticism', he outlines the position which a reasonable woman, or any layman, may adopt regarding the great religious controversies of the day.[72] Despite her lack of special training, a woman has good reason to accept natural religion or theism – the belief in God and in a future state. Theism has never been disproved and its truth is suggested by its usefulness. It serves as the foundation upon which 'the whole framework of society is based' and furnishes the only satisfactory explanation of the physical and moral world.[73] A woman has as valid a reason to believe theism as she has to believe any of the moral and social doctrines of her age. In politics, law and the administration of justice, we act upon the information available, while reserving the right to revise our opinions upon further evidence. Theism should be handled in like fashion. A woman would also be prudent to adopt the revealed religion of the Gospels. The Church of England, derived from Scripture, is useful in that it gives an institutionalised form to natural religion and provides prayers and rituals enabling the faithful to worship God. But Stephen concedes a weakness in revealed religion. Modern scholarship has induced many competent and sincere people to doubt the truth of Christianity altogether. Until a consensus is reached among those qualified to judge, the layman and laywoman had best remain within established positions of revealed faith and doubt.

V

During this period, stretching from the *Origin of Species* to the Franco-Prussian War, the temporal power of Pius IX was threatened by Italian nationalism. At the same time, the Catholic Church was faced with the challenge of meeting the secular principles of the nineteenth century. The English Ultramontanes – notably Henry Manning, W. G. Ward and Cardinal Wiseman – were Catholics who supported the Papacy both in its claim to temporal sovereignty and in its opposition to modern science and scholarship. In 1864 Pius IX attempted to check liberalism, both in religion and politics, by issuing the encyclical *Quanta Cura* with the famous Syllabus of Errors' as an appendix. The 'Syllabus' was a compendium of propositions which had been condemned by the Church in previous years as representing 'the principal errors of our time'. One such proposition was that 'the Roman Pontiff can, and ought to, reconcile himself and come to terms with progress, liberalism and modern civilization'. The 'syllabus' became a source of controversy within the Church, and was opposed by leading Catholics such as Lord Acton in England and Döllinger in Germany. Even Newman questioned its binding power. But their views did not prevail. The liberal Catholic movement was finally defeated in 1870, when the Vatican Council promulgated the decree on papal infallibility, declaring the Pope infallible when speaking *ex cathedra* on matters of faith and morals.

Stephen expressed himself on 'English Ultramontanism' in an article for *Fraser's* in 1865 that takes issue with the contributions of Manning and Wiseman to a collection of *Essays on Religion and Literature*.[74] Theirs was a simple position: whenever science and theology conflict, science must be in error because theology is divinely revealed. They falsely assume, Stephen charges, that what they understand to be revealed truth is universally accepted. He again insists that the reasonable man does not deny revelation, but holds that historical and scientific criticism is the only means to determine what has actually been revealed, 'that science is the measure of theology, and that theology cannot possibly be the measure of science'.[75] Manning and Wiseman declare that they are not enemies of true science; but the difficulty, as Stephen is quick to point out, is that they define true science as that which agrees with their religious beliefs. To support their position the English Ultramontanes must adopt the absurd view that human knowledge is divided into separate departments, each with its own standard of truth. In one of his sermons Newman saw no difficulty in the fact that, while in science the earth moves round the sun, in theology the sun moves round the earth. Stephen argues that truth is one and that the rules of evidence are universal:

> If the word 'truth' means different things according as it is applied to theology or science, then a contradiction between the two is of no importance. Things theologically true may be scientifically false. The sun may go round the earth in a theological sense, and the earth round the sun in a scientific sense. The facts related in the Apostles' Creed may all be true theologically, whilst scientifically they are utterly false. Divorce, theologically considered, may be wicked; scientifically, it may be right. What is true whilst you are praying becomes false when you leave church. There is one creed for Sunday, another for Saturday. One code of morals as between priest and priest; another as between priests and men of the world.[76]

Stephen was one of the most vigorous opponents of Roman Catholicism in his day. Leslie cites one of his brother's letters, in which Fitzjames says that 'large parts of the [Catholic] theology are not only silly, but, I think, cruel and immoral to the last degree. I think the doctrine of eternal damnation so wicked and so cruel that I would as soon teach my children to lie and steal as to believe in it.'[77] Like his friend Froude, Fitzjames saw the Reformation as a victory of reason over Popery. Their dislike and suspicion of Catholicism were shared by many Englishmen, particularly after several followers of the Oxford Movement, including Manning, followed Newman to Rome. This antipathy increased after the so-called Papal Aggression of 1850, in which Pius IX, to cope with the growing number of English Catholics, restored the Catholic hierarchy in England. Stephen rejoiced that the Roman Church no longer wielded the power that brought about the Inquisition. All signs indicate, he said, that most Europeans view theology merely as a matter of opinion.

Henry Manning, Archbishop of Westminster from 1865, published a pamphlet in 1873 entitled *Caesarism and Ultramontanism*.[78] With an eye on the decree on papal infallibility, he attempted to establish the Roman Church as a divine institution, independent of civil powers and infallible in matters of faith and morals. Stephen again jumped into the fray with a review of the pamphlet for the *Contemporary Review*, and produced his most penetrating attack upon Catholicism.[79] He argues that the absolute sovereignty over the mind which the Catholic Church claims must be based on strong evidence. It must be established 'beyond all reasonable doubt' that God exists, that the historical statements of the Apostles' Creed are accurate, that Christ founded a Church with the constitution and powers which the Catholics claim for their Church, and that the Roman Catholic Church is the Church so established.[80] Examining each of these propositions, Stephen acknowledges that there is a strong probability of the existence of God; but he insists that this probability cannot support inferences about a Church. Biblical scholarship has made it impossible to say that the truth of the history of Christ as given in the Apostles' Creed is free from reasonable doubt. While it may be wise to assume that the Gospels are true and to continue with an established and useful form of worship, Stephen holds that the available evidence does not warrant a Church exercising absolute authority over the minds of men. He concludes that, even if the Apostles' Creed were historically accurate, the New Testament contains no unequivocal evidence either that Christ founded a Church or, if he did, that the Roman Catholic Church is the true Church. Stephen was convinced that, if Christianity were to survive, it would do so in the form of Protestantism.[81]

VI

Stephen's interest in religion did not slacken during his years in India. Indeed, he said that one of the main reasons he went there was to gain experience that might shed light on the great speculative questions. He sought aid in the writings of the ancients. After his return from India his appetite for reading was, as always, insatiable. He plunged into a rereading of the classics. Aeschylus, Demosthenes, Plato, Aristotle and Cicero were devoured at a rapid pace. In 1873 he wrote that one of his ambitions was to write a book, 'which I have had so many years in my mind', giving his 'final thoughts on religion, law, government and morals'.[82]

By the time Stephen returned to England, the 'qualified assent' to Christianity which he had maintained throughout the 1860s was no longer tenable in the face of the latest criticism. Like many of his contemporaries, he found that the struggle between religious orthodoxy and science had proved unequal. His brother Leslie had already abandoned belief in Christianity and soon emerged as one of the leading agnostics of England. Fitzjames himself stopped going to church, and now denied the divinity of Christ:

> I have been carrying on my speculations a great deal lately at various times, and I must own I have come to very definite negative results about it all. The more I think the matter over the more impossible does it appear to me to believe, and the more immoral to continue to pretend in any degree to believe, the supernatural side of Christianity.[83]

In a letter to W. W. Hunter, Stephen offered a succinct statement of his religious views:

> I do not believe the New Testament narrative to be true. To my mind, the whole history of Christ, in so far as it is supernatural, is legendary. As to the Christian morals, I cannot regard them

as either final or complete. As to natural religion, I think its two great doctrines – God and a future state – more probable than not; and they appear to me to make all the difference to morality. Take them away and Epicureanism seems to me the true and proper doctrine.[84]

Soon after his return in 1872, Stephen was invited to become a member of the Metaphysical Society.[85] Founded in 1869 by John Knowles and Tennyson, its sixty-two members included some of the greatest minds of Victorian England: Bagehot, W. K. Clifford, J. A. Froude, Gladstone, Frederic Harrison, R. H. Hutton, T. H. Huxley, Manning, Morley, Ruskin, Seeley, Henry Sidgwick, Leslie Stephen, John Tyndall and W. G. Ward. Mill declined an invitation to join, on the grounds that the questions with which the group proposed to deal were better considered by Socratic dialogue than by discussion in a large assembly.[86] He was probably correct. Nevertheless, the meetings generated much enthusiasm and illustrate the intellectual preoccupations of the day. The Society became a forum for the battle between the rationalists and the theists. It was at that time, for the purpose of their discussions, that Huxley coined the word 'agnostic'.[87] The members of the Society met nine times a year in London to hear and debate papers which they wrote on religious and philosophical questions. A total of ninety-five papers were submitted, many of which were published in either the *Contemporary Review* or the *Nineteenth Century*, both edited by Knowles. No new truths were discovered and no disputes were settled, but the discussions helped to clarify the various positions. In 1880, when it appeared that nothing more could be derived from the debates, the Society was dissolved.

Between 1874 and 1879, Stephen contributed seven papers, more than any other member except R. H. Hutton. Stephen's papers were aimed directly at the orthodox theists: 'Necessary Truth', 'Mysteries', 'Proof of Miracles', 'What Is a Lie?', 'The Effect of the Decline of Religious Belief on Morality', 'Authority in Matters of Opinion' and 'The Utility of Truth'. In each instance, he took the position of an empiricist in philosophy and a liberal in religion.

Two of Stephen's more interesting encounters were with W. G. Ward and Gladstone. Ward claimed that the mind was endowed with innate ideas or 'necessary truths' such as time, space and number. Stephen retorted that the mind possesses no knowledge independent of sense experience.[88] The dispute with Gladstone centred on a book by Sir George Cornwall Lewis, *On the Influence of Authority in Matters of Opinion*. Lewis held that a large proportion of the opinions of mankind are derived from the authority of experts, but that this authority has only limited application to questions of religion. Gladstone argued that authority does apply in religion, and he attempted to show that the consent of civilised mankind makes the acceptance of Christianity necessary. When doctrinal disputes arise, individuals are similarly bound to comply with the decisions of the more competent leaders of the Church of England. Stephen protested that there is no general agreement among the experts on religion and that the subject-matter is not one upon which we can exercise our senses. Gladstone errs, he said, in offering the consent of mankind as proof of the truth of Christianity. 'Great religious problems cannot be decided by voting on them.'[89]

Needless to say, Stephen's powerful logic intimidated some members of the Society. One historian has concluded that Stephen exercised a dominating influence during its most productive years.[90] Contemporary testimony lends credence to this view. R. H. Hutton referred in a reminiscence to Stephen's 'mighty bass that always exerted a sort of physical authority over us'.[91] On one occasion, after Stephen had delivered a critical paper on miracles, his salvo was greeted by a long silence. Gladstone took a piece of paper, scribbled some lines in Greek and passed it to Lord Arthur Russell. They were from the *Iliad*: 'Then did the whole assembly fall into deep silence, marvelling at the words of Diomede, tamer of horses.'[92] Frederic Harrison praised Stephen's 'sledge-hammer common sense', but thought that 'the Society lost something of its urbanity and more of its cohesion when Fitzjames Stephen introduced into metaphysics the style of the *Saturday Review* or a court of law'.[93] Nevertheless, Harrison also recalled the 'memories of energy, sterling sense, and downright *bonhomie* Fitzjames left to his friends'.[94]

Stephen thus emerged in the 1870s as a formidable antagonist of Christianity. All his adult life, he insisted that the Christian religion was only as strong as the evidence. Like a judge on the bench, he waited for the facts to pile up and modified his views accordingly, keeping to the probabilities and giving the accused (God) the benefit of the doubt. Stephen's greatest fear was that in the battle against Christianity, a victory for rationalism might be pyrrhic. Since a decline in religion would be accompanied by a decline in morals, the social order would be severely threatened. At a time when the triumph of democracy appeared inevitable, he believed that England could ill-afford the loss of the religious sanction. Stephen spent the last part of his life wrestling with the problem of finding a sanction for morals to replace that formerly exercised by religion.

9 The Last Sanction

I

Fitzjames Stephen, as we know, was one of many liberal intellectuals – including Matthew Arnold, Robert Lowe, Henry Maine, W. E. H. Lecky, and Walter Bagehot – who became critical of their creed during the 1860s and 1870s in response to the growth of democracy. The important fact is that it was not the old liberals but liberalism which underwent a fundamental change of belief. The downfall of the British Liberal Party is usually understood to have originated with the Home Rule crisis in 1886, when the Whigs under Lord Hartington and the Radicals under Joseph Chamberlain went over to the Conservative side in protest against Gladstone's Irish policy. But the roots of the division can be seen in the philosophical differences that became manifest among liberals much earlier, especially after the Reform Act of 1867.[1] The new liberals, more attuned to the popular mood of the day, won out, and Stephen spent the last part of his life lamenting what he called 'the Paradise Lost of Liberalism'.[2] As he wrote in the 1880s, 'The old maxims of government, the old Liberalism .... have been and are being utterly given up, and in their place is being erected a tyrannical democracy which will change the whole face of society and destroy all that I love or respect in our institutions.'[3] During these years the contrast between Indian and English politics became most apparent to Stephen. Whereas in India he had witnessed orderly, efficient and benevolent government, at home he saw an increasing tendency towards socialism and anarchy. As he wrote to his friend Lord Lytton, Viceroy from 1876 to 1880, India was 'the best corrective in existence to the fundamental fallacies of Liberalism'.[4]

In 1873 Stephen became a candidate for Parliament. Though not his first time, it was his last. He had made an unsuccessful bid for the Liberal seat for Harwich in 1865. His decision to stand again as a Liberal, this time for Dundee (in Scotland), was made in the hope that a seat might further his goal of codifying the criminal law and because his friend Lord Coleridge told him that if elected he would probably be appointed Solicitor General. Campaigning was distasteful to Stephen; it brought to the surface his distrust of popular enthusiasms: 'My dislike of the business is not the least due to weakness or over-delicacy, but to a deep-rooted disgust at the whole system of elections and government by constituencies like this.'[5] This antipathy he retained throughout his life. Not surprisingly, Stephen was defeated in his bid for a parliamentary seat, receiving the least number of votes among three candidates.

During Stephen's campaign, a local newspaper sought to discredit his liberalism by printing some extracts from *Liberty, Equality, Fraternity*. To this day, many believe that since this work is a forceful critique of Mill, Stephen was not a liberal. But we have shown that Stephen directed his assault not against liberalism in the old, classical sense, but against elements of the new liberalism which he perceived in some of Mill's writings. The split within the liberal ranks was underscored by a campaign paper, the *Torch*, published by Stephen's supporters, which contrasted his views with those of a new-liberal opponent, one Edward Jenkins:

> Mr. Stephen's liberalism is the liberalism of self-help, of individualism, of every form of conscious industry and energy. It is the only liberalism which has the smallest chance in Scotland. The liberalism of Mr. Jenkins is the liberalism of state aid, of self-abasement, and indolence.[6]

Like many contemporaries, Stephen feared the growing strength of Gladstonian liberalism. In 1876 Gladstone came out of retirement as leader of the Liberal Party to play a major role in the agitation against the Bulgarian atrocities. Stephen naturally opposed the atrocities, but he was disgusted by the way Gladstone could return to power merely by appealing to cheap popular sentiment. He later denounced the Liberal leader as 'the mouthpiece of blind and furious passions', the servant of 'King Mob'.[7] Gladstone's famous Midlothian campaign, in which he stumped the country in an appeal for votes, was met only by contempt from Stephen, who described him as 'positively revolutionary ... on the high road towards the destruction of nearly everything which I for one, and I suppose many thousand others chiefly like and value in English life and society'.[8] The victory of the Liberals in 1880 constituted a triumph of the masses over 'the respectable and wealthy part of English society'.[9]

To Stephen, the danger of modern liberalism was that it 'taught the public that there is no such thing anywhere as legitimate authority'.[10] Echoing the article he had written for the *Cornhill* almost twenty years before, Stephen defined a liberal as 'a man of an enlarged and educated mind', superior to 'the phrases which catch the ears of vulgar people', who recognises the value of 'great institutions and great enterprises'. Instead, he lamented, liberalism has come to mean 'the small dissenter way of looking at all national and international affairs'.[11] By the 1880s he believed that Britain was in a state of emergency. In a series of letters to *The Times*, he attacked Gladstone's Home Rule policy on the grounds that it threatened to disrupt the unity of the Empire and promote social revolution at home.[12] In a private letter he protested that 'the House of Commons appears to me to have gone mad. . . . It is full of a general notion . . . that the fact that an institution exists, is a presumption against its being allowed to continue to exist.'[13]

Disraeli believed that Stephen would have made an ideal Tory leader. 'It is a thousand pities', he wrote in 1881, 'that J. F. Stephen is a judge; he might have done anything and everything as leader of the future Conservative party.'[14] Had he known Stephen better, Disraeli would have concluded otherwise. 'The truth is,' Stephen had written in 1875, 'I am neither Tory nor Liberal. I simply hate English politics, and do not concern myself with them at all.'[15] On another occasion, he described himself as having 'fallen between the Liberal and Conservative stools'.[16] Like Bagehot, he found himself 'between sizes' in politics.

Stephen's distaste for popular politics made him an enemy of the party system as it had come to be. He had lost faith in one party and had no respect for the other:

> I am very sorry for it, but the men now at the top of the Conservative tree are all of them people whose political creed was chosen when the Conservative party was emphatically the stupid party, and when to be a Conservative meant to be opposed to pretty well all the main intellectual movements of the day.[17]

Along the same lines:

> I am deeply disgusted with the Liberal party. They seem to be ceasing to represent in any way the intellectual side of politics, and to be appealing to about the narrowest and most paltry of all popular prejudices in a manner which is as offensive to me as the matter which they preach. I am delighted to see them involved in failures of every description, but I must fairly say that I do not see much to admire in the Conservative party, when one gets away from India.[18]

The redeeming feature of the Conservative Party, in Stephen's view, was that under Disraeli it had been dedicated to maintaining the British Empire. In 1876, by means of the Royal Titles Act, Disraeli had Parliament confer upon Queen Victoria the title of Empress of India. It will be recalled that Stephen supported his policy of protecting British interests in India by resisting the expansion of Russian influence in Afghanistan. But Stephen found little to applaud in Disraeli's domestic programme of State-sponsored 'Tory Democracy'. In the wake of the 1867 Reform Act, Disraeli saw the political advantage of social reforms to improve the living conditions of the newly enfranchised working classes. Like the new liberals, progressive Tories conceived the State as a positive agent for human improvement. Stephen and his contemporaries were witnessing the death of Liberal England. Divorcing himself from politics, Stephen was convinced that he could be more influential outside Parliament.[19] During the 1870s, therefore, he was preoccupied with advocating reforms in the structure of English government and codification of the criminal law.

II

In our discussion of *Liberty, Equality, Fraternity* we noted that Stephen devoted only a few pages to the subject of parliamentary government. He reserved a much more extensive treatment for two lectures delivered before the Edinburgh Philosophical Society in 1873 and published in the *Contemporary Review*.[20] His thesis bears a marked resemblance to that set forth by Mill in his essay *Considerations on Representative Government* (1861). This is significant because it shows that Stephen's criticisms of the parliamentary system were no more severe than those of the nation's leading liberal. If Mill had departed from the original school of liberalism in his work *On Liberty*, *Representative Government* constitutes his return to the fold. Mill holds that while representative government is best, because it places sovereignty in the entire community, the common people are unfit to govern themselves. He carefully distinguishes between controlling the government and actually governing. The proper function of a representative assembly is to 'watch and control' the business of government, which should be entrusted to 'a specially trained and experienced Few'.[21] He goes on to advise that, in order to safeguard against the abuse of power by the majority, the franchise should also be weighted in favour of knowledge and intelligence, determined by occupation and education.[22]

In his lectures, Stephen argues that there are certain inherent defects in the parliamentary system which impair both legislation and executive government. The increasing complexity of society makes special knowledge and experience necessary for the effective administration of public affairs. Accordingly, opportunity must be provided for the most capable men to rule. They must also be afforded the means to devote themselves steadily and systematically to the general welfare. Some degree of continuity, discretionary authority and provision for the conception and execution of comprehensive legislative schemes is essential for good and efficient government. But parliamentary institutions, Stephen maintains, do not provide for these requisites. Instead, endless discussion, constant statement, reiteration and explanation hinder the process of governing.[23] Party organisation, the basis of the parliamentary system, also severely impairs governmental efficiency. Persons seeking office are compelled to assail the policies of incumbents with an eye more to the next election than to the best interests of the nation. And the incumbents, faced with uncertain tenure, must tailor their policies to popular taste, neglecting important matters which often take several years to establish. The danger is that politics is reduced to nothing but advocacy. In addition, the party system involves a deplorable waste of talent, as one-half of the nation's most capable men are obliged to devote their energy and talents to fighting the other half.[24] Under such a system, it is virtually impossible for Parliament to legislate satisfactorily upon the important subjects before it.

Cabinet government also leaves much to be desired.[25] Stephen glances back wistfully to centuries past when the executive power resided in a king ruling with the advice of the Privy Council – an administrative body whose members were more or less permanent. Over the years, Parliament has gradually gained supremacy and the monarchy has been reduced to a cypher. Under the present system of Cabinet government, the prime minister is given little power, and the Ministry is entirely dependent upon Parliament for its existence. Although England cannot restore a powerful monarchy, Stephen insists that king-like powers, 'subject of course to distinct and weighty responsibility', are essential for the executive to carry out the necessary functions of government.[26] He even intimates that a British Prime Minister would govern more effectively if entrusted with power similar to that of an American President. The parliamentary system has converted the British executive government into an aggregate of unconnected departments, each like a state unto itself, with no co-ordination or central control. Administrative continuity is, moreover, lacking. Stephen points out that since 1830 Britain had had sixteen Prime Ministers and fourteen distinct Ministries. Obviously, he does not believe that the so-called 'efficient' elements which Bagehot singled out for praise in the English Constitution – Parliament and the Ministry – are the most effective or beneficial means for governing a country. 'No one can justify, though he may explain, upon historical grounds, an arrangement by which the whole government of the country is vested in a popular assembly like the House of Commons ruling as king through a committee which may be dismissed at a moment's notice.'[27]

Stephen's sense of history prevented him from suggesting that the parliamentary system be abolished. His understanding of the role of power in politics led him to concede that sovereignty was firmly in the hands of Parliament. Nor did he disclaim or underestimate the benefits which popular institutions had bestowed over the centuries upon the English people.[28] For one thing, they had enabled England to avert the revolutionary solutions to political and social issues which had ravaged the Continent. Yet parliamentary government with a democratic suffrage is subject to the great danger – one which Stephen pointed out on several occasions – that the uneducated masses may fall prey to clever and unscrupulous wirepullers who will pander to their tastes and prejudices in order to gain power.[29] So far,

England had avoided this danger because it has been blessed with a class of wise and responsible men dedicated to the general welfare. 'If, however, the personal character of English politicians should ever be seriously lowered, it is difficult not to feel that the present state of the constitution would give bad and unscrupulous men a power for evil hardly equalled in any part of the world.'[30]

If government is too serious to be left to the demagogue, it is also too complex to be left to the incompetent. Stephen deplores that under the current system the ablest politicians must strive to devise measures which are interesting and comprehensible to the mass electorate. At the same time, many speculative men wish to limit the government to police matters, denying that it can profitably interfere in anything else. Stephen is undoubtedly referring here to the school of radical individualists, the most prominent being Herbert Spencer.[31] In both extremes – the prevailing theory of democracy and that of radical individualism – the argument is that the management of public affairs must be entrusted to the majority. The commonplace is that this function constitutes an ideal education, fostering independence and an interest in the general welfare. Stephen does not deny the value of either a wide interest in public affairs or government by consent: 'I had too much experience of the results of their absence in India to have any particular illusions about absolute government.'[32] Yet he fails to see the virtue in encouraging people to do things the wrong way. Since government requires uncommon knowledge and skill, he insists that 'it is a great mistake to treat public business to any considerable extent as an educational process, and to set to do it not those who are best qualified to transact it, but those for whom it is supposed to supply the best education'.[33]

Stephen suggested some specific reforms which would partially remedy the defects he pointed out. Essentially, he wanted to divorce politics from administration and guarantee to a trained elite the tenure necessary to devote themselves to the business of government. The Home Office, the Colonial Office, the War Office, the Admiralty and the India Office, he thought, had much to gain from tenure free from the vicissitudes of popular opinion. He also called for the creation of a Legislative Department, to prepare for parliamentary consideration numerous matters that require extended time, expert knowledge and special talent.[34] Stephen cited a passage from Mill, 'the most distinguished advocate of Parliamentary Government', to show that he also had such severe reservations about its effectiveness as to advocate giving Parliament the assistance of a separate legislative commission. In his *Autobiography*, Mill indicated that his *Considerations on Representative Government* raised questions which must be decided soon:

> The chief of these is the distinction between the function of making laws, for which a numerous popular assembly is radically unfit, and that of getting good laws made, which is its proper duty, and cannot be satisfactorily fulfilled by any other authority; and the consequent need of a legislative commission as a permanent part of the constitution of a free country, consisting of a small number of highly-trained political minds, on whom, when Parliament has determined that a law should be made, the task of making it should be devolved, Parliament retaining the power of passing or rejecting the Bill when drawn up, but not of altering it otherwise than by sending proposed amendments to be dealt with by the commission.[35]

To ensure that England would be supplied with a permanent source of knowledge and talent, Stephen suggested some reforms in the Civil Service.[36] He would introduce greater circulation within the offices of its upper ranks, so as to enable the officers to profit from the experience that comes from functioning under various forms of responsibility, and to make them more receptive to new ideas. The permanent heads of the important administrative departments should be recruited from the ablest men in the country, paid upon the same scale as judges, and be regarded as counsellors to the Cabinet Ministers rather than mere clerks. He was confident that such reforms would furnish England with an efficient and stable bureaucracy competent to carry on the extremely complicated matters of government. Clearly, Stephen's proposals were inspired by the British Government of India. It was a continual source of pride to him that a minority of devoted and well-trained civil servants could effectively and benevolently govern a vast sub-continent. He had every reason to believe that the bureaucracy would continue to be staffed by able men. In 1855 the Civil Service Commission had been instituted, and in 1870 an order in council during Gladstone's first Ministry opened all government offices, except the foreign service, to competitive examination.

Stephen was not unmindful of the evils that often attend bureaucratic government. He adverted to the prevalent English fear that it might destroy 'the vigour and originality' of the nation and subject it to 'the leaden rule of a small body of officials'.[37] To these abuses he could have added that bureaucracies are inclined to become resistant to change, and the endless accumulation of administrative procedure often precludes efficiency. Perhaps Stephen thought that Parliament might check these abuses. Besides, it must be conceded that mankind has yet to devise a form of government that does not involve some tendency to abuse. He was also aware of the perils of vesting unrestricted power in officials. The examples of the French and the German bureaucracies, he acknowledged, had instilled into his countrymen a fear of centralisation and bureaucracy. Yet, relying on the English liberal tradition, he believed that such apprehension was needless; he was sure that no system by which the government sought to supervise the individual in every important aspect of his life would be tolerated in England.[38] Besides, none of his proposals would require Parliament to give up its sovereignty to the bureaucracy. His desire was only that Parliament, in recognition of the need for special knowledge, should exercise its power through trained agents. This would ensure the rule of England with the guidance of the wise and the capable.

III

Stephen also sought to convince the English that they had much to gain by giving to themselves what they had bestowed upon India: an orderly and intelligible system of law. We have seen that during the 1860s he was willing to postpone codification because he recognised that such a comprehensive reform would not be accepted at that time. In its place, he favoured a revision of the Consolidation Acts of 1861 by a combination of parliamentary legislation and judicial decisions, co-ordinated by a new department of government to be called the Ministry of Justice. In 1863 Lord Westbury, then Lord Chancellor, was instrumental in the passage of the Statute Law Revision Act, which simplified the Statute Book by repealing obsolete laws and arranging and classifying those which remained in force.[39] At his direction, a Royal Commission was instituted in 1866 to investigate the expediency of a general digest of English law, both common and statute. The idea of codification was greeted with enthusiasm in Parliament and the press. Yet, even though the Commission reported favourably in 1867 and instructed some barristers to prepare digests, the project was abandoned when none of the specimens submitted met with approval. Thus the plan for a system of English law received another setback.[40]

Before the English law could be codified, certain obstacles had to be overcome. The task was obviously of such magnitude that it would take several years to complete. But, under the parliamentary system, measures originating with one Ministry were often discontinued by the next. Since a code was not an issue that aroused popular support, and, since governments were born and toppled over more immediate and pressing concerns, codification never became the cause of either political party. The work, moreover, demanded such special skill and prolonged attention that Parliament could not undertake it alone. But, being the supreme legislative body, Parliament was reluctant to delegate the legal reform to another agency. There was, besides, a deeply ingrained belief among the English that codification would impair the so-called elasticity of the common law. They prided themselves on their flexible, unwritten Constitution. Had it not enabled them to undertake gradual reform while Europe suffered revolutions? Finally, there were many judges who saw a code as a threat to the discretionary power permitted them under the prevailing legal system.

In spite of all, Stephen, fresh from his extraordinary success in codifying the Anglo-Indian law, sought to revive the cause of codification at home. In November 1872, he delivered before the Social Science Association a speech which was later published in the *Fortnightly Review* as 'Codification in India and England'.[41] After giving a general description of Anglo-Indian law, he attempted to point out the advantages of a code for England. Indian experience, he said, shows what in practice is meant by codification: it is the expression of the law in plain words and arranged in a perspicuous form.[42] Like Bentham, Stephen saw no utility in a system of law so massive and intricate as to be unintelligible even to the vast majority of lawyers. A code would enable every lawyer to have a precise and systematic knowledge of the principles and details of several branches of law. It would also reduce the law to a form readily understandable to the educated layman. As if his own Indian codes were not enough, Stephen offered the extraordinary codifying efforts of Edward Livingston and David Dudley Field in the United States as evidence that a criminal code was feasible for England.

Stephen then considered the best method for codifying. It is impossible, he argued, to discuss codification bills as ordinary bills before Parliament. 'A popular assembly might as well try to paint a picture as to discuss, section by section, a penal code or a law about contracts.'[43] At the same time, Stephen knew that Parliament would never delegate its legislative power. He suggested, therefore, the appointment of a commission to draft the codifying bills, each bill to be drawn by a single person, and then considered by the entire body. The bill should then be published in the press, with criticism invited from competent sources. After a bill had been drafted, criticised and settled, it should be submitted to the Lord Chancellor and the law officers who, if satisfied, should introduce it in Parliament. It should then be referred to a select committee of either House, which should include the commissioner who originally drafted the bill. The committee should then report to the House, and the bill take its normal course. The advantage of this system, Stephen contended, was that it provided a permanent body to work on codification while not infringing the sovereignty of Parliament. A systematic reform of the law is impossible when it depends entirely upon a Chancellor and law officers whose tenure is limited by the fortunes of a given Parliament. A permanent body would permit codification bills to carry over from session to session, thus avoiding the consequences of a change of Ministry – 'the rock on which so many schemes of law reform have split'.[44]

Stephen also addressed himself to the charge that codification would deprive the English law of its cherished elasticity. This was probably the most difficult objection to overcome, and he found it necessary to return to it later in a chapter of his *History of the Criminal Law of England*.[45] His opponents argued that the English law is in a state of continuous development and that judicial decisions, by which the law is adjusted to particular circumstances, make it increasingly definite and precise by settling previously undetermined questions. A code, they alleged, would destroy the flexibility and hinder the growth of the common law by shackling the discretionary powers of the judges. Stephen held that the object of codification is not to reduce the law upon a given subject to a form that would enable the judge or lawyer to settle every legal question. Even the best code would not relieve them of the task of applying general legal principles to facts. A code would assist the judge to exercise his authority by stating the law in a comprehensible and orderly fashion instead of leaving it to be discovered each time by research. Stephen insisted, moreover, that no code should or could be final, and that any code should be redrawn periodically to keep pace with new enactments.[46] Hence there is no reason why codification should hinder the growth of the law. Stephen also argued that the elasticity of the common law was exaggerated. When called upon to deal with a new set of circumstances, the judge is bound by precedents set by previous decisions and is by no means free to decide according to his own views of justice and expediency. Since a code merely records decided cases and parliamentary legislation, it cannot deprive the judge of any discretionary power he currently enjoys. It merely changes the form of statement of the rules by which he is bound.

Stephen's hopes were raised in the autumn of 1872 when Lord Coleridge, then Attorney General, instructed him to draw up an evidence code for England, modelled on his Indian Evidence Act. But the project was stillborn. Coleridge succeeded in introducing the bill only on the last day of the session of 1873, just before the first Gladstone Ministry fell and Parliament was dissolved. The bill was not reintroduced and was never made public.[47] Stephen was also engaged at this time in drawing up the Homicide Law Amendment Bill of 1874. The Capital Punishment Commission of 1864 had called attention to the inadequacy of the definition of murder, and recommended a reduction in the number of crimes subject to capital punishment. Shortly after his return from India, Stephen was requested by the Recorder of London, Russell Gurney, who had been approached by John Bright, to assist him by drawing up a bill defining the offence of murder.

Stephen immediately set to work and 'boiled down' – to use his favourite phrase – the existing homicide law from a length of 232 pages, as it appeared in 'Russell on Crimes', to seven, eliminating much confusion and intricacy in the process. In accord with his aim to distinguish between law and morals, he rejected the old definition of murder – 'killing with malice aforethought' – as vague and misleading, and defined the crime with reference to its intention rather than its motive.[48] Gurney introduced the bill into Parliament in 1874, and it was referred to a select committee composed of Chief Justice Cockburn, Baron Bramwell and Mr Justice Blackburn – with Stephen appearing as the principal witness. The committee criticised the bill strongly and, despite Stephen's vigorous defence, it was finally dropped.[49] The main objection was that the bill was only a partial measure. Since homicide involves principles relating to other branches of law, to codify only one branch would lead to confusion. The committee argued that it was unwise to begin 'to codify with the Law of Homicide and above all ... [to delegate] such a duty to a Select Committee of the House of Commons'. Yet, as Sir Leon Radzinowicz has pointed out, the prospect of codification was not dead. *The Times* thought that 'the Codification of our entire Criminal Law' was still valuable; *The Economist* regarded Stephen as the likely 'Codifying Commissioner'. And his friend Coleridge remained steadfast in his conviction that there was 'no reason why the law of England should not be expressed in a Code'.[50]

Undaunted by his failure, Stephen embarked upon the ambitious project of codifying the law by 'private enterprise', bringing his scheme before the public in an article for the *Nineteenth Century*. Since codification involves the condensation and rearrangement of the law, Stephen maintained that it is essentially a 'literary problem'.[51] Consequently, he argued, the task can be competently performed by private individuals without Parliament's assistance, though subject to its final approval.

To show the utility and feasibility of a general code, Stephen had begun to digest parts of the law. This work was also related to certain of his professional concerns at that time. In December 1875 he was appointed Professor of Common Law at the Inns of Court, a position he held until he was made a judge four years later. As the subject of his first course of lectures, he chose the law of evidence. By the last quarter of a century of legal reform, the state of legal education in England was still deficient. Available lawbooks brought together a mass of authorities and cases in such a way as to make a general or scientific view of principles virtually impossible for the beginner to attain. To assist the studies of those attending his lectures, Stephen adapted the draft bill on evidence which he had prepared in 1872, and produced his *Digest of the Law of Evidence* (1876). His aim was to provide a statement of the law that would afford 'a precise and systematic' knowledge in a moderate period of time.[52] Stephen then moved on to the criminal law. Sometime in 1873 or 1874, as he recollected, he had been asked to prepare a second edition of his still popular *General View of the Criminal Law*. While engaged in this task, he regretted that there existed no authoritative statement of the law to which he might refer his readers.[53] To remedy this deficiency, he prepared a *Digest of the Criminal Law* (1877). Then, in 1883, came his *Digest of the Law of Criminal Procedure in Indictable Offences*. Stephen's digests were enthusiastically received, and are among his greatest legal achievements. Indeed, at the beginning of this century Sir Courtenay Ilbert wrote that they 'are, and seem likely to remain, the best guides to these subjects which can be obtained either by the English or by the foreign student'.[54]

Stephen also attempted to convince his countrymen of the desirability of certain other projects, designed to put their law in order.[55] The Yearbooks, a series of several hundred volumes of reports written in French and extending from the reign of Edward I to the reign of Henry VII, should be translated and printed in a convenient form. The State Trials should be published, and a collection should be made of the laws of the different parts of the British Empire. To supervise these endeavours, he recommended the creation of a Council of Legal Literature to work in cooperation with the Councils of Law Reporting and Legal Education.

After completing the criminal-law digest, Stephen thought that it might be converted into a penal code. He communicated this intention to Lord Chancellor Cairns and the Attorney General, Sir John Holker, and was requested to draft bills for a criminal code and a code of criminal procedure.[56] Holker introduced the bill during the session of 1878. It was favourably received, and referred after a second reading to a Royal Commission consisting of Lord Blackburn, Mr Justice Barry, Lord Justice Lush and Stephen. According to Frederick Pollock, Stephen's hope that the bill would succeed was not unreasonable: 'As late as 1879, indeed, there seemed to be a fair prospect of passing an English criminal code which would have been better than any then existing.'[57] Radzinowicz has referred to Stephen's bill as a 'most comprehensive measure in criminal legislation, surpassing anything ever attempted in this country [England] by one man or by any one commission'.[58] The Commission sat for seven months, from November 1878 to May 1879, and presented its report, written by Stephen, in June. Holker reintroduced the bill, substantially Stephen's original draft, but it was shelved after a second reading.

Introduced again at the beginning of the session of 1880, it was stalled by the dissolution of Parliament. In 1883, Sir Henry James, then Attorney General, introduced that part of the bill relating to criminal procedure, but it suffered strong opposition and foundered in committee. Stephen would never have another chance.

Not that he did not deserve one. Radzinowicz thinks that, 'as codes go, this one [the Draft Penal Code] was good, and worth the trouble of re-amending and revising; but its chances had been wrecked by the deeply rooted hostility against codification *per se* and its threat to common law'.[59] Despite his failure, Stephen proved his merits. According to Radzinowicz, 'He remains the greatest draftsman and codifier of criminal law this country [England] has ever produced, a worthy peer of the most prominent amongst Continental lawyers who have left their mark in this field.'[60] Stephen's draft code became influential throughout the British Empire: it was adopted by Canada, New Zealand, Queensland, Western Australia and Tasmania; and it served as the basis for the penal codes of several colonies.

IV

In 1879, twenty-five years after he had been called to the bar, Fitzjames Stephen was appointed a Judge of the High Court of Justice, Queen's Bench Division. He was finally reaping the harvest of his industry and talent. Stephen rejoiced over the prospect of not having to do his daily stint of journalism: 'Now I am free to turn my mind to objects which have long occupied a great part of it, so far as my leisure will allow. It is a very strange sort of joy.'[61] Two years before, in recognition of his distinguished service in India, he had been made a Knight Commander of the Star of India (KCSI). During this latter part of his life, Stephen received several other tributes: he was made doctor of laws at the Universities of Oxford and Edinburgh, an honorary Fellow of Trinity College, Cambridge, a corresponding member of the Institut de France, and an honorary member of the American Academy of Arts and Sciences.[62]

Though Stephen brought to the bench a vast knowledge of the law, he was not a great judge if by that term one implies the making of landmark decisions. None of Stephen's deserves that rank. But neither was he mediocre. As Radzinowicz says: 'The very qualities which he so conspicuously displayed in his writings, namely, an uncanny faculty for sifting the grain from the chaff, for brushing aside a multitude of details, irrelevant, inconsistent and confusing, and for dissecting out the nucleus of a legal argument, is also manifest in his judgements.'[63] Yet Radzinowicz found it necessary to qualify this praise: 'From whatever angle one looks at his judicial achievement, he cannot be placed in the front rank of the Victorian Bench and his judgeship only contributed in a moderate degree towards the pre-eminence to which he is so emphatically entitled as an authority on criminal law.'[64]

Because Stephen regarded the judge as 'the organ of the moral indignation of mankind', he acquired a reputation for severity. He was convinced that the criminal court is a school of morality. What he disliked most – and to which he directed his severity – was brutality and oppression.[65] The law, he thought, must protect the weak from the strong and provide a safeguard against the abuse of power. The convicted criminal deserved to be hated by the community. Stephen was therefore stern with those who had committed heinous crimes and he made little effort to hide his indignation. Yet Leslie Stephen tells us that his brother never compromised his strong sense of fair play. Fitzjames was 'one of the most magnanimous of men . . . incapable of being overbearing in social intercourse'.[66] Though he persistently extolled the virtues of strength and courage, 'many stories', Leslie reports,

> have been told me of the extreme care with which he would try to elicit the meaning of some muddled remonstrance from a bewildered prisoner, and sometimes go very near to the verge of what is permitted to a judge by giving hints which virtually amounted to questions, and so helping prisoners to show that they were innocent or had circumstances to allege in mitigation.[67]

Stephen's most notorious case was that of Mrs Florence Maybrick, accused in 1889 of murdering her husband by arsenic poisoning.[68] Public opinion was at first decidedly against her, as it was discovered that she had had a brief affair with a Mr Brierley. After a seven-day trial at the Liverpool Summer Assizes – in which she was eloquently defended by Sir Charles Russell, later Lord Russell of Killowen – the jury pronounced her guilty. Accordingly, Stephen sentenced her to death. He later said, in reviewing the more than 1200 criminal cases that had come before him between

1885 and 1889, that this was 'the only case in which there could be any doubt about the facts'.[69] The verdict raised a furor throughout England, and Stephen was met by an angry crowd as he left St George's Hall. The Home Office was flooded with petitions from all over the country, and protest meetings were held in London and Liverpool. One petition in Mrs Maybrick's favour was signed by several members of Parliament. In response to the popular clamour, the Home Secretary, possibly at Stephen's suggestion,[70] commuted the sentence to twenty years penal servitude. After a number of efforts to secure her release, Mrs Maybrick was finally reprieved and set free in 1904.

Stephen was severely attacked for his role in the case. Many believed that the evidence presented at the trial was insufficient to support a conviction, and that the jury had been misdirected by Stephen in reaching its verdict. A rumour circulated that he was mentally unfit for the bench. While at the Derby assizes in 1885 he had suffered a slight stroke which left him partly paralysed and disabled him for three months. The many years of overwork had taken their toll. While the charge that he was incompetent is false, the consensus is that at the Maybrick trial he failed to show his customary power of concentration and grasp of details. In his summation, which lasted two days, he made a number of errors in dates and facts. He was also accused of giving undue prominence to the possible motive arising from Mrs Maybrick's adultery, which was not in issue, and of assuming that her husband had died of arsenic poisoning, which had not been proved, instead of other causes. Nevertheless, he showed extreme care in eliciting all possible evidence for the defence and stressed the doubts remaining after the prosecution had concluded its case.

While serving on the bench, Stephen continued to write. He had by this time renounced regular journalism and was able to devote himself exclusively to work that interested him, but had hitherto been postponed for practical reasons. His concern with Indian affairs never waned. In 1885 he published *The Story of Nuncomar and the Impeachment of Sir Elijah Impey*, a fragment of a projected larger work on the impeachment of Warren Hastings, which exonerated Impey from the charge of corruption levelled by Macaulay. During these years Stephen also wrote his greatest legal book. Having completed the Draft Penal Code in 1878, he returned to the task of revising his *General View*, and found it inadequate in many areas. Instead of merely bringing the work up to date, he decided that it should be rewritten and expanded.⁷¹ In the space of three and a half years, during what leisure he could afford while fulfilling his rigorous judicial duties, he produced the three-volume *History of the Criminal Law of England* (1883). A remarkable achievement, it enhanced Stephen's already considerable stature in the field of law. For our purposes, a glance at the contents must suffice. It presents an account of the influence of Roman law upon that of England; a history of the English substantive criminal law and procedure from before the Norman Conquest to the late nineteenth century; and a history of the criminal courts, their procedure and jurisdiction. Stephen continues to show the relation between law, morals and society, arguing that changes in the sentiments of the community are reflected in the history of legislation and punishments. He defends capital punishment for severe offences, suggests revisions in the definitions of crimes, and advocates codification. There are also sections dealing with insanity and the law, with Anglo-Indian law, and a comparison between French and English criminal procedure.

The *History* was hailed as a masterpiece by the legal and intellectual community. Maitland thought that on the subject of the Middle Ages Stephen surpassed his predecessors: 'I am struck every time I take up the book with the thoroughness of his work and the soundness of his judgments.' ⁷² Ilbert saluted it as 'the most solid and permanent contribution to the English legal literature of the century'.⁷³ Stephen

> has laid down broadly the lines on which the literary and scientific treatment of English law ought to proceed, and has sketched the ground plan of a building which it remains for successive generations of lawyers, and jurists to complete; and for this reason, if for no other, his name will always hold a foremost place in the annals of English law.⁷⁴

In our day Radzinowicz has written that the *History* 'silenced at last the reproach against England for not possessing a key to the understanding of its criminal law'.⁷⁵

V

Throughout the 1870s, while advocating reforms in the law and in the structure of government, Stephen continued to ponder the ultimate questions. As we know, he had concluded that historical

Christianity was false; yet he feared the social consequences of a general decline of religion. 'My view', he wrote to Lord Lytton, 'is that we are in the early stages of a religious revolution, which you and I may live to see in its political and social bearing.'[76] In essence, Stephen shared the feeling of many an honest doubter of his day. A note of apprehension recurs throughout his letters during this period. 'I feel alarmed', he confessed to Lord Lytton, 'at the spread of my own opinions. I do not doubt their truth, but I greatly doubt the capacity of people in general to bear them.'[77] Stephen's fear is understandable. As we know, he believed that government is dependent upon morality and morality profoundly influenced by religion. The decline of religion, therefore. must inevitably lead to changes both in public morals and the principles of government.

In 1877 a paper which Stephen presented to the Metaphysical Society, 'The Influence on Morality of a Decline in Religious Belief' served as the subject of a symposium published in the *Nineteenth Century*.[78] Sceptics such as W. K. Clifford and T. H. Huxley were confident that morality had a basis independent of religion and would be virtually unaffected by the erosion of Christianity. Frederic Harrison, in true Positivist fashion, held that the Religion of Humanity could easily supplant supernatural religion. On the other hand, theists such as James Martineau and W. G. Ward were convinced that, because morality was dependent upon religion, the fall of Christianity would be accompanied by a precipitous decline in the standards of conduct. Both sides, Stephen thought, were partly right. He agreed with the sceptics that morality would survive, society being impossible without morals. At the same time, Christianity had had so much influence on European morals that with religion destroyed morality must necessarily be transformed. Christian morals cannot be preserved while denying the truth of Christian theology. The waning of Christianity would inevitably bring about a 'moral revolution' in which the standards of conduct would rest on secular grounds.

The prospect of a moral revolution greatly alarmed Stephen. He had criticised the Positivists severely because their secular religion failed to supply an adequate sanction for morality. If men ceased to believe in God and an afterlife, what would induce them to do good and avoid evil? Ever since his reluctant conclusion that Christianity was false, this question had haunted Stephen. He was ready to believe that love, friendship and benevolence would survive without religion. But he was not convinced that society could protect itself from the wicked. The ultimate sanction for morals, if it was no longer religion, must reside in the law.

Near the close of his *History of the English Criminal Law*, Stephen once again exhorts his countrymen to codify their criminal law, not the least reason being its 'immense moral importance'. Indeed, 'the criminal law may be described with truth as an expression of the second table of the Ten Commandments. The statement in the Catechism of the positive duties of man to man corresponds step by step with the prohibitions of a Criminal Code.'[79] Thus Stephen returns to a theme which informs much of his legal writing. Now that the influence of religion is rapidly declining, the criminal law must replace the Decalogue as the sanction for morals. Stephen insists upon the importance of this message:

> I think that there never was more urgent necessity than there is now for the preaching of such a sermon in the most emphatic tones. At many times and in many places crime has been far more active and mischievous than it is at present, but there has never been an age in the world in which so much and such genuine doubt was felt as to the other sanctions on which morality rests. The religious sanction in particular has been immensely weakened, and unlimited license to every one to think as he pleases on all subjects, and especially on moral and religious subjects, is leading, and will continue to lead, many people to the conclusion that if they do not happen to like morality there is no reason why they should be moral. In such circumstances it seems to be specially necessary for those who do care for morality to make its one unquestionable, indisputable sanction as clear, and strong, and emphatic, as words and acts can make it. A man may disbelieve in God, heaven, and hell, he may care little for mankind, or society, or for the nation to which he belongs, – let him at least be plainly told what are the acts which will stamp him with infamy, hold him up to public execration, and bring him to the gallows, the gaol, or the lash.[80]

VI

The final years of Stephen's life were darkened by sorrows and disappointments. His views on politics and religion grew progressively pessimistic; and he was frustrated in his attempt to get his countrymen to codify their law and reform the structure of their government. He saw England's national greatness waning and the Empire which he upheld seriously threatened. His disillusionment with current politics led him to recall that back in 1848 he had joined many of his age and class in wishing for a whiff of grapeshot to suppress the French revolution which toppled the government of Louis Philippe.[81]

At the same time, Stephen suffered personal tragedy. He was deeply affected by the deaths of his friends Henry Maine and George Venables in 1888, and that of Lord Lytton in 1891. The most grievous loss was that of his son James Kenneth, who was stricken by mental illness and died in an asylum in 1892. He had been a brilliant and promising graduate of Cambridge and the author of the charming volume of light verse *Lapsus Calami*. Despite these hardships Fitzjames never lamented his fate. He realised that life is a struggle, and accepted its trials. He never lost hope; it was against his nature. 'Despair', he once wrote in answer to a gloomy poem by Tennyson, 'is the vilest of words.'[82] Like many other Victorians, he found happiness in work. Indeed, as Leslie Stephen said, work was his religion.[83]

Stephen's health continued to deteriorate after the Maybrick case. He was stricken by another stroke during the assizes at Exeter in March 1890, and ordered to take a rest for three months. Some qualified observers thought that he had difficulty concentrating on cases. The man whose formidable intellect had earned him the respect of both friends and opponents was undergoing the loss of his powers. Doubts about his competence were raised in Parliament, and critical remarks appeared in the press. At the suggestion of Lord Coleridge, he consulted a physician, who urged him to resign. He did so in April 1891, and was awarded a baronetcy in recognition of a lifetime of achievement. In the ensuing few years he continued to work. He prepared a new edition of his *General View of the Criminal Law* in 1890, and he brought out a collection of some of his favourite *Saturday Review* articles, the *Horae Sabbaticae*, in 1892. His physical condition worsened, and early in 1893 he was unable to climb stairs. He was moved to Red House Park, in Ipswich, and died peacefully on 11 March 1894, shortly after his sixty-fifth birthday. He is buried at Kensal Green, beside his parents.

We have stressed Stephen's life-long preoccupation with the ultimate questions. He insisted that no thinking man can avoid such issues as the meaning of life, the existence of God and an afterlife. Refusing to face them is simply another way of answering them. Yet he believed that such questions are destined to remain 'riddles of the Sphinx'.[84] Probability, not certitude, is the most we can expect in any branch of knowledge. If a person chooses to believe in religion, he cannot prove beyond all reasonable doubt that he is right. Nor can we be certain that another who chooses not to believe is mistaken. Each must follow his reason and conscience and accept the consequences:

> We stand on a mountain pass in the midst of whirling snow and blinding mist, through which we get glimpses now and then of paths which may be deceptive. If we stand still, we shall be frozen to death. If we take the wrong road, we shall be dashed to pieces. We do not certainly know whether there is any right one. What must we do?[85]

In answer to this question, Stephen offers his creed, quoting part of the verse from the Book of Joshua which was inscribed on his father's tombstone: 'Be strong and of a good courage.' He continues:

> Act for the best, hope for the best, and take what comes. Above all let us dream no dreams, and tell no lies, but go our way, wherever it may lead, with our eyes open and our heads erect. If death ends all, we cannot meet it better. If not, let us enter whatever may be the next scene like honest men, with no sophistry in our mouths and no masks on our faces.[86]

This eloquent passage, from the peroration to *Liberty, Equality, Fraternity*, is Stephen's fitting epitaph. He spent the greatest part of his life combating commonplaces and sentimental dreamers. In the process, he engaged in controversy with Victorian England's brightest lights – Mill, Arnold, Carlyle, Dickens, Newman, Gladstone. Much that he wrote was unpopular. As one who found himself swimming against the tide of the late nineteenth century, he was not surprised by the opposition he met. 'Nothing of mine is ever popular', he wrote in 1890. 'Indeed I do not know how it should be, for my object has always been to show the weak side of all opinions which embody popular sentimentality of any sort.'[87] Courage was perhaps Fitzjames Stephen's most engaging quality. We may not always agree with him, we may even be offended by his vigour and his tone, but all his writings manifest a man who is unafraid to suffer the consequences of his own view of the facts. His works set forth many unpalatable truths. The mistake is to think he relished revealing them.

10 Epilogue

Unless we understand the thought of Sir James Fitzjames Stephen we will not have a full picture of the Victorian Age. A great dissenter, he spent most of his professional life criticising the utopian schemes and intellectual cant of his contemporaries. No one who studies Stephen's life and thought can fail to be impressed by the power and penetration of his mind, the range of his writings and accomplishments, and his moral courage. Though in his attempt to reconcile democracy and culture he found himself in a rearguard action, swimming against many currents of the nineteenth century, he relentlessly challenged the assumptions of liberals and conservatives alike. Perhaps more than any other man of his time, Stephen saw the perils of a blind devotion to such abstractions as liberty, equality and fraternity. Not that he enshrined order and authority in their place; he insisted that they too must be judged according to the criteria of time, place and circumstances. A liberal who was critical of his creed, Stephen's writings contain a refreshing dose of independence and imagination, unfortunately absent from much of the liberalism of his day.

Stephen belongs to the tradition of thought, which includes Hobbes and the early Utilitarians, that held that the science of politics must be founded upon the principle of utility rather than upon absolute and universal ideas. The hallmark of this tradition is a great respect for the rule of law and a profound distaste for sentimental thinking. Political realists, these thinkers saw that liberty is impossible without the rule of law. They knew that law without power is ineffectual, and power without law is tyrannical. They also believed that to attribute to all men outstanding qualities which only a few possess, or to assume that political and social schemes are beneficial merely because men conceive them is both sentimental and dangerous. Any institution or plan can be supported by ideas alone. The true test is to see to what extent ideas conform to experience and institutions promote general happiness.

Throughout this work we have insisted upon calling Stephen a liberal. To a great extent, liberal and conservative are relative terms which can be understood only in the context of the age in which they exist. A liberal of the first half of the nineteenth century was considered a conservative by the second. Stephen was a liberal in the classical sense. But in his own day a new type of liberalism undermined the classical position, causing Stephen and many of his generation to be regarded as conservatives. The important fact is that the views of the classical liberals remained the same; it was liberalism that changed.

Stephen's writings emphasise the important distinction between the old classical liberalism and the new social and democratic liberalism. The former, whose exponents included Locke, Montesquieu, the American Founding Fathers, Tocqueville and many of Stephen's contemporaries in Britain and Europe, advocated liberty and representative government, but distrusted the common man and feared democratic rule. Democratic liberalism, rooted in French Jacobinism and the inspiration for the revolutionary movements which swept Europe during the nineteenth century, called for universal suffrage and the fullest extension of equality, even at the expense of liberty. While the old liberal believed that the best government is that which governs least, the new liberal held that the best government is that which governs most.

Classical liberals of the Victorian Age, including Fitzjames Stephen, equated democracy with mediocrity and tyranny. Of the democratic governments which existed during the mid-nineteenth century, the United States was still young and showed little sign of disproving Tocqueville's unflattering report of its progress. In France, universal suffrage was instrumental in establishing the dictatorship of Napoleon III's Second Empire. Resistance to democracy was greater in England, but eventually the classical liberals were compelled to accept Reform Acts which substantially increased the suffrage. By the end of the century, democratic institutions were virtually triumphant throughout most of the Western world. The power of government over the lives of citizens increased enormously as the new liberals, supported by a widening electorate, passed a great body of social legislation. But recent times have witnessed a loss of confidence within the ranks of the new liberals. Just as the old liberals underwent a crisis in the late nineteenth century when they found that their philosophy no longer suited the demands of the age, liberals today have begun to break ranks. Many have come to realise that it is utopian to seek the solution to man's problems in big government. Modern liberalism is in grave trouble, and its social philosophy appears to be bankrupt.

One of the original attractions of the new liberalism in England was its claim to have an answer to the problem of poverty: government. In contrast, the classical liberals were accused of being insensitive to the plight of the poor. But the deficiencies of the classical liberals must be placed in historical perspective. During the first part of the nineteenth century, when their philosophy of small government was regnant, the old liberals believed that the solution to poverty was to instil into the lower classes the virtues of thrift and hard work, so that they might improve themselves by their own efforts. Like many of his liberal contemporaries, Stephen was also influenced by Evangelicalism, which concluded that poverty is the product more of sin than of society. It took a virtual revolution in political and social thinking to bring about the victory of the new liberal idea that the State must directly promote the welfare of its members. Stephen and his fellow classical liberals thought that such State paternalism was both dangerous and unnecessary: dangerous because it posed a serious threat to individual liberty; and unnecessary because, on the basis of the old philosophy, Britain had become the richest and most powerful nation in the world. Although poverty continued to exist, there was strong evidence that the condition of the poor had improved greatly since the early part of the century. To many, this was proof that Britain was on the verge of solving its social problems.

As a prophet Stephen had mixed success. England has survived the crisis in Victorian thought which resulted from the wane of religion and the success of democracy. But the issues raised by the crisis continue to preoccupy us today. In retrospect, Stephen was mistaken in his estimate of the effects of the decline of orthodox Christianity. Society has managed to survive the weakening of the supernatural sanction. Like Joseph de Maistre, with whom he was not inclined to agree on most points, Stephen felt compelled in the end to resort to the hangman as the last sanction for morals. He did so with the firm conviction that with the fall of religion the quality of human life would decline immeasurably. Stephen could not escape the problems of his time. When many contemporaries, including himself, were discarding their faith, he feared that a secular society would be unable to maintain itself. As a confirmed Benthamite, he had no recourse but to take refuge in the law.

Stephen perceived the important role played by law in the formation of political culture. Not only did the law provide a stable framework for the growth of civilisation, but it also provided a regular and acceptable channel for the expression of man's natural vindictive sentiments. While Stephen clearly underrated the opposition of his countrymen to codification, he shared the belief of other great jurists that a code was the only means of establishing a firm basis for a rational science of jurisprudence. He also perceived the reciprocal relationship between law and morals and was a leader in supporting decreased criminal liability for the insane. In addition, he has left a rich legacy of legal writings which alone would ensure him the esteem of posterity. Though his views on India may be judged negatively today, Stephen believed that those who had forged this segment of the British Empire had performed a noble and imperishable deed: that of bringing law and a measure of culture to a subcontinent that had known much carnage and despair.

Perhaps the most striking characteristic of Stephen's thought is its unity. Law, morality, politics and religion are intricately related in his writings. But, as the crisis of Victorian thought progressed, Stephen found to his dismay that the many strands which composed his own thought began to separate. While his desire to preserve its unity at a time of tremendous intellectual ferment has led some to consider him a conservative, the practical goals that he sought and the critical means that became his hallmark show him to have been essentially a classical liberal throughout his life. At the same time, he discerned the nature of the breakdown of the liberal consensus in England. His whole career was spent pursuing culture in the face of romantic idealism and social panaceas. He dedicated his life to the conviction that men can truly progress only when they are firmly grounded in reality.

Notes

Abbreviations (all works by Sir James Fitzjames Stephen, unless otherwise stated):

EB   *Essays by a Barrister* (1862).
History *History of the Criminal Law of England* (1883).
GV   *A General View of the Criminal Law of England* (1863). (2nd edn 1890; references are to the 1st edn, unless otherwise stated.)
HS   *Horae Sabbaticae* (1892).
Life   Leslie Stephen, *The Life of Sir James Fitzjames Stephen* (1895).
LEF   *Liberty, Equality, Fraternity*, ed. R. J. White (1967).

CHAPTER 1: CULTURE AND DEMOCRACY

1. G. K. Chesterton, *The Victorian Age in Literature*, Home University Library edn (London, 1966) p. 3.
2. Noel Annan, 'The Intellectual Aristocracy', in J. H. Plumb (ed.), *Studies in Social History: A Tribute to G. M. Trevelyan* (London, 1955) pp. 243–87.
3. James Fitzjames Stephen, 'Autobiographical Fragment', University Library, Cambridge, Add. MSS 7349 (1884) p. 37.
4. See the excellent study by Merle M. Bevington, *The 'Saturday Review', 1855–1868: Representative Educated Opinion in Victorian England* (New York, 1941). For a complete list of Stephen's contributions to the *Saturday*, see ibid., pp. 373–81.
5. Ibid., pp. 58–9.
6. Ibid., p. 59.
7. Ibid., p. 71.
8. Bevington, *The 'Saturday Review'*, p. 26.
9. Ibid., p. 25.

10. Anthony Trollope, *Autobiography*, ed. Frederick Page (London, 1950) p. 199.
11. Bevington, *The 'Saturday Review'*, p. 31. Emphasis as in original.
12. Leslie Stephen, *The Life of Sir James Fitzjames Stephen* (London, 1895) p. 177. (Hereafter cited as *Life*.)
13. Bevington, *The 'Saturday Review'*, p. 31.
14. Norton to James Russell Lowell, 1 Jan 1869; in Charles Eliot Norton, *Letters*, vol. I (Boston, Mass., 1913) pp. 313–14.
15. Bevington, *The 'Saturday Review'*, p. 35.
16. *Life*, p. 178.
17. John Morley, *Recollections*, vol. I (New York, 1917) p. 168.
18. Quoted in J. W. Robertson Scott, *The Story of the 'Pall Mall Gazette'* (Oxford, 1950) p. 148.
19. *Life*, p. 214. Leslie also lists the number of articles that his brother wrote for the *Pall Mall* from 1865 to 1878 (*Life*, pp. 213-14), see also Robertson Scott, *The 'Pall Mall Gazette'* p. 148.
20. Any attempt to assign the *Pall Mall* articles would call for detailed internal analysis (a task beyond the scope of this study), and would in no way alter our conclusions.
21. *Life*, p. 307.
22. *Life*, p. 96.
23. 'Liberalism', *Cornhill Magazine*, V (1862) 71.
24. Ibid.
25. Ibid., p. 72.
26. Ibid., p. 73.
27. Ibid., p. 80.
28. J. S. Mill, 'On Liberty', in *Utilitarianism, Liberty, and Representative Government*, Everyman's Library edn (New York, 1951) p. 166.
29. J. S. Mill, 'Tocqueville on Democracy in America', *Dissertations and Discussions*, vol. II (London, 1859) pp. 1–83.
30. 'Mr. Mill on Political Liberty', *Saturday Review*, VII (1859) 186, 213.
31. Ibid., p. 186.
32. Ibid.
33. Ibid., p. 187.
34. Ibid., p. 213.
35. 'Mr. Mill's Essays', *Saturday Review*, VIII (1859) 47.

36. 'Mr. Mill on Political Liberty', *Saturday Review*, VII (1859) 213.
37. Review in *Fraser's Magazine*, LIX (1859) 526–33.
38. G. O. Trevelyan, *Life and Letters of Lord Macaulay*, vol. II (London, 1876) pp. 456–7.
39. J. C. Rees, *Mill and His Early Critics* (Leicester, 1956) p. 9.
40. 'Mr. Mill on Political Liberty', *Saturday Review*, VII (1859) 214.
41. Ibid.
42. *Life*, p. 166.
43. 'Mr. Mill on Political Liberty', *Saturday Review*, VII (1859) 214.
44. Rees, *Mill and His Early Critics*, p. 17.
45. *Life*, p. 201
46. 'Mr. Carlyle', *Essays by a Barrister* [*EB*] (London, 1862) p. 242.
47. Ibid., p. 243.
48. Ibid.
49. Ibid., p. 249.
50. John Holloway, *The Victorian Sage: Studies in Argument* (London, 1953) chs 2 and 3.
51. *EB*, pp. 248–9.
52. Ibid., p. 251.
53. Ibid., p. 253.
54. *EB*, p. 247.
55. 'Mr. Carlyle', *Fraser's Magazine*, LXXII (1865) 790.
56. Ibid. Stephen also paid tribute to Benthamite Utilitarianism in a review of '[Nassau] Senior's Historical and Philosophical Essays', *Saturday Review*, XIX (1865) 479.
57. 'Mr. Carlyle', *Fraser's Magazine*, LXXII (1865) 793.
58. Ibid., p. 792.
59. 'Lord Macaulay', *EB*, p. 101.
60. Ibid., p. 99.
61. Ibid., p. 100.
62. 'Lord Macaulay's Works', *Saturday Review*, XXII (1866) 207.
63. 'The Function of Criticism at the Present Time', in Matthew Arnold, *Lectures and Essays in Criticism*, ed. R. H. Super (Ann Arbor, Mich., 1962) p. 266.
64. Ibid., p. 270.
65. Ibid., p. 264.
66. Ibid., pp. 264–5.
67. Ibid., p. 275.
68. *Letters, 1848–1888*, ed. George W. E. Russell (London, 1895), vol. I, p. 282.

69. 'Mr. Matthew Arnold and His Countrymen', *Saturday Review*, XVIII (1864) 683.
70. Ibid.
71. Stephen argued along the same lines in his article 'French and English Logic', *Saturday Review*, VII (1859) 460.
72. 'Mr. Matthew Arnold and His Countrymen', *Saturday Review*, XVIII (1864) 684.
73. 'Mr. Matthew Arnold amongst the Philistines', *Saturday Review*, XIX (1865) 235.
74. 'Mr. Arnold on the Middle Classes', *Saturday Review*, XXI (1866) 163.
75. Matthew Arnold, *Culture and Anarchy*, ed. with introduction by J. Dover Wilson (Cambridge, 1969) pp. 46–8.
76. Ibid., p. 11.
77. Ibid., pp. 53–4.
78. Ibid., ch. 3.
79. See Lionel Trilling, *Matthew Arnold* (New York, 1977) pp. 259–65.
80. 'Mr. Matthew Arnold on Culture', *Saturday Review*, XXIV (1867) 79.
81. Ibid.
82. Ibid.
83. Ibid.
84. For an excellent survey of the events leading up to the 1867 Reform Act, see the introduction by J. Dover Wilson to his edition of Arnold's *Culture and Anarchy*.
85. Ibid., p. xxvi.
86. *Life*, p. 224.
87. Asa Briggs, *The Age of Improvement, 1789–1867* (New York, 1960) p. 515.
88. Walter Bagehot, *The English Constitution*, World's Classics edn (London, 1968) p. 271.
89. 'Lord Palmerston', *Pall Mall Gazette*, 19 Oct 1865.

CHAPTER 2: THE STATE

1. Stephen to Lord Lytton, 21 Sep 1890, in *Horae Sabbaticae* [*HS*], 3 vols (London, 1892).
2. *Life*, p. 226.
3. *Life*, p. 123.

4. See Stephen's remarks on Mill's famous essays on Bentham and Coleridge, in 'Mr. Mill's Essays', *Saturday Review*, VIII (1859) 46.
5. *English Works of Thomas Hobbes*, 11 vols (London, 1839).
6. 'Hobbes's *Leviathan*', *HS*, vol. II, p. 20.
7. 'Hobbes on Government', *HS*, vol. II, pp. 1, 4.
8. Sir Frederick Pollock, *An Introduction to the History of the Science of Politics*, Beacon Press edn (Boston, Mass., 1960) p. 107.
9. *Leviathan*, ch. 11.
10. 'Hobbes's *Leviathan*', *HS*, vol. II, p. 29.
11. *Leviathan*, ch. 13.
12. Ibid., ch. 17.
13. 'Hobbes on Government', *HS*, vol. II, p. 5.
14. Ibid.
15. Ibid., pp. 6–7.
16. 'Sovereignty', *HS*, vol. II, pp. 55–6.
17. 'Hobbes on Government', *HS*, vol. II, p. 12.
18. Ibid.
19. Ibid., p. 11.
20. Michael Oakeshott's Introduction to *Leviathan*, Blackwell's Political Texts (Oxford, 1946) p. lvii.
21. 'Cobbett's Political Works', *HS*, vol. III, pp. 224–5.
22. 'Hobbes on Government', *HS*, vol. II, p. 11.
23. Ibid.
24. 'Sovereignty', *HS*, vol. II, p. 55.
25. Ibid., p. 63.
26. Ibid., p. 56.
27. Ibid.
28. Ibid., p. 69.
29. Ibid.
30. Writing for *Fraser's Magazine* in 1863, Stephen advocated British neutrality on the American Civil War. See 'England and America', *Fraser's Magazine*, LXVIII (1863) 419.
31. 'Sovereignty', *HS*, vol. II, pp. 63–4.
32. Ibid., p. 64.
33. Ibid., p. 66.
34. See the excellent study by Bernard Semmel, *The Governor Eyre Controversy* (London 1962); for Stephen's role see ch. 7, 'The Prosecution'. Leslie Stephen discusses his brother's contribution to the case in *Life*, pp. 227–31.

35. Stephen to his mother, 26 Mar 1867 (University Library, Cambridge, Add. MSS 7349).
36. 'Locke on Government', *HS*, vol. II, p. 150.
37. Ibid., p. 153.
38. 'Tom Paine', *HS*, vol. III, p. 187.
39. Ibid., p. 199.
40. J. S. Mill, *Autobiography*, World's Classics edn (London, 1940) p. 191.
41. 'Bossuet and the Protestants', *HS*, vol. II, p. 100.
42. See especially 'De Maistre – *Soirées de St. Petersbourg*' and 'De Maistre's *Principe Generateur*', *HS*, vol. III, pp. 250, 287.
43. 'Tom Paine', *HS*, vol. II, pp. 200–1.
44. John Morley, *Burke* (New York, 1879) p. 167.
45. 'Edmund Burke', *Saturday Review*, V (1858) 372.
46. 'Burke on the English Constitution', *HS*, vol. III, p. 116.
47. See A. M. Osborn, *Rousseau and Burke: A Study of the Idea of Liberty in Eighteenth Century Political Thought* (London, 1940), which argues convincingly that their principles are not opposed but similar, though they come to very different conclusions.
48. 'Burke on the French Revolution', *HS*, vol. III, p. 140.
49. Ibid., p. 142.
50. See, for example, the Preface to *Burke's Politics*, ed. Ross J. S. Hoffman and Paul Levack (New York, 1949); and Peter J. Stanlis, *Edmund Burke and Natural Law* (Ann Arbor, Mich., 1958).
51. 'Burke on the English Constitution', *HS*, vol. III, pp. 119–20.
52. Ibid., p. 122.
53. Ibid., p. 127.
54. 'Burke on Popular Representation', *Saturday Review*, XX (1865) 394.
55. 'Burke on the English Constitution', *HS*, vol. III, p. 129.
56. 'Burke on Popular Representation', *Saturday Review*, XX (1865) 395.
57. 'Burke on the French Revolution', *HS*, vol. III, pp. 147–8.
58. Ibid., p. 149.
59. 'Burke on Popular Representation', *Saturday Review*, XX (1865) 395.
60. Ibid.
61. Ibid.

62. Ibid.
63. 'Burke on the French Revolution', *HS*, vol. III, pp. 146–7.
64. Ibid., p. 147.
65. 'Burke and de Tocqueville on the French Revolution', *HS*, vol. III, p. 155.
66. Ibid., p. 164.
67. Ibid., p. 167.
68. 'Voltaire as a Theologian, Moralist, and Metaphysician', *HS*, vol. II, pp. 237–8.
69. 'Burke on the French Revolution', *HS*, vol. III, p. 150.
70. Ibid.
71. 'Burke and de Tocqueville on the French Revolution', *HS*, vol. III, p. 171.
72. 'Burke on the French Revolution', *HS*, vol. III, p. 152.

CHAPTER 3: THE POLITICS OF LITERATURE

1. 'The License of Modern Novelists', *Edinburgh Review*, CVI (1857) 125.
2. 'The Relation of Novels to Life', *Cambridge Essays*, 1855, p. 185.
3. In the same article Stephen criticised the sentimental novelist Charles Reade's *It Is Never too Late to Mend*, a severe attack on the English prison system. Stephen concluded that Reade was 'wrong in his facts, wrong in his law, and wrong in his logic' – *Edinburgh Review*, CVI (1857) 150.
4. Sir Leon Radzinowicz, *Sir James Fitzjames Stephen (1829–1894) and His Contribution to the Development of Criminal Law*, Selden Society Lecture (London, 1957) p. 12.
5. For an excellent discussion of Evangelical and Utilitarian attitudes toward literature, see Richard D. Altick, *The English Common Reader: A Social History of the Mass Reading Public 1800–1900* (Chicago, 1957) pp. 99–140.
6. Mill, *Autobiography*, p. 93.
7. *Cambridge Essays*, 1855, p. 148.
8. Ibid., pp. 187–92.
9. See George Orwell, 'Charles Dickens', *Inside the Whale* (London, 1940); in *Charles Dickens: A Critical Anthology*, ed. Stephen Wall (Baltimore, 1970) pp. 297–313.
10. 'Mr. Dickens as a Politician', *Saturday Review*, III (1857) 8.
11. Ibid.

12. 'The License of Modern Novelists', *Edinburgh Review*, CVI (1857) 131–2.
13. 'Mr. Dickens as a Politician', *Saturday Review*, III (1857) 8.
14. 'The License of Modern Novelists', *Edinburgh Review*, CVI (1857) 152.
15. Ibid., p. 156.
16. 'Mr. Dickens as a Politician', *Saturday Review*, III (1857) 9.
17. Ibid., p. 8.
18. Ibid.
19. 'The License of Modern Novelists', *Edinburgh Review*, CVI (1857) 134.
20. Ibid., pp. 132–3.
21. Wall, *Dickens: A Critical Anthology*, p. 290.
22. Leslie Stephen said that his brother was deeply offended because he believed that the character of Tite Barnacle was a caricature of their father and all those who had distinguished themselves in the Civil Service. See *Life*, p. 159.
23. 'The License of Modern Novelists', *Edinburgh Review*, CVI (1857) 128.
24. Ibid., p. 128.
25. 'Mr. Dickens as a Politician', *Saturday Review*, III (1857) 9.
26. Sir William Robertson Nicoll, *Dickens's Own Story* (London, 1923) p. 212. It was Nicoll who attributed the review to Stephen. See also George H. Ford, *Dickens and His Readers* (New York, 1965) p. 103.
27. Ibid.
28. 'A Tale of Two Cities', *Saturday Review*, VIII (1859) 741.
29. Ibid., p. 742.
30. Ibid.
31. Ford, *Dickens and His Readers*, p. 105.
32. Wall, *Dickens: A Critical Anthology*, p. 221.
33. Ibid.
34. Walter Bagehot, 'Charles Dickens', *Literary Studies*, Everyman's Library edn, vol. II (London, 1950) p. 189.
35. Ibid., p. 192.
36. Wall, *Dickens: A Critical Anthology*, p. 201.
37. Ford, *Dickens and His Readers*, p. 107. 'Mr Popular Sentiment' appears in *The Warden* (1855) ch. 15.
38. 'The Relation of Novels to Life', *Cambridge Essays*, 1855, p. 175.
39. Ford, *Dickens and His Readers*, pp. 55–6.

40. Ibid.
41. 'Light Literature and the *Saturday Review*', *Saturday Review*, IV (1857) 35.
42. 'Mr. Thackeray', *Fraser's Magazine*, LXIX (1864) 403.
43. 'Balzac', *Saturday Review*, IV (1857) 560.
44. Ibid., p. 559.
45. 'Manon Lescaut', *Saturday Review*, VI (1858) 65.
46. 'Light Literature in France', *Saturday Review*, IV (1857) 220.
47. 'Balzac', *Saturday Review*, IV (1857) 560.
48. Ibid.
49. Ibid.
50. 'Madame Bovary', *Saturday Review*, IV (1857) 40.
51. Ibid., p. 41.
52. Ibid.

CHAPTER 4: TOWARDS A SCIENCE OF SOCIETY

1. *Life*, p. 123.
2. Mark Pattison, *Memoirs* (London, 1885) p. 166.
3. 'English Jurisprudence', *Edinburgh Review*, CXIV (1861) 481.
4. Ibid., pp. 463–4.
5. Ibid., p. 471.
6. Ibid., p. 470.
7. Oliver Wendell Holmes, *The Common Law* (Cambridge, Mass., 1963) p. 5.
8. G. P. Gooch, *History and Historians in the Nineteenth Century* (London, 1935) p. 292.
9. 'Mr. Hallam', *EB*, p. 26.
10. Ibid., pp. 21–2.
11. Ibid., p. 22.
12. Ibid., p. 23.
13. Ibid., p. 27.
14. 'English Jurisprudence', *Edinburgh Review*, CXIV (1861) 478–9.
15. Sir Henry Maine, *Ancient Law*, Everyman's Library edn (London, 1965) p. 100.
16. 'English Jurisprudence', *Edinburgh Review*, CXIV (1861) 484.
17. Ibid., pp. 485–6.
18. *A General View of the Criminal Law of England* (London, 1863) p. 337. (Hereafter cited as *GV*.)
19. Ibid., pp. 329–30.
20. Ibid., p. 331.

21. Goldwin Smith, *The Study of History* (London, 1861); Charles Kingsley, *The Limits of Exact Science as Applied to History* (London, 1860).
22. See 'The Science of History' and 'Scientific Method Applied to History', two lectures published by Froude in *Short Studies on Great Subjects*, 2 vols (London, 1909).
23. 'Mr. Kingsley on the Study of History', *Westminster Review*, LXXV (1861) 161; 'Mr. Goldwin Smith on the Study of History', *Westminster Review*, LXXVI (1861) 157.
24. J. S. Mill, *A System of Logic,* 10th edn (London, 1879) vol. II ch. 11, p. 544.
25. 'Buckle's *History of Civilization in England*', *Edinburgh Review*, CVII (1858) 471.
26. 'The Study of History', *Cornhill Magazine*, III (1861) 668.
27. 'English Jurisprudence', *Edinburgh Review*, CXIV (1861) 465.
28. 'The Study of History', *Cornhill Magazine*, IV (1861) 32.
29. 'Buckle's *History*', *Edinburgh Review*, CVII (1858) 478.
30. Mill, *A System of Logic*, Bk VI ('On the Logic of the Moral Sciences') ch. 5.
31. David Hume, *A Treatise of Human Nature*, Everyman's Library edn (London, 1911) vol. I, Introduction, p. 5.
32. Mill, *A System of Logic*, Bk VI, ch. 7.
33. Ibid., ch. 8.
34. Ibid., ch. 10.
35. 'Buckle's *History*', *Edinburgh Review*, CVII (1858) 481.
36. Mill, *A System of Logic*, 5th edn (London, 1862) Bk VI, ch. 11.
37. 'The Study of History', *Cornhill Magazine*, IV (1861) 37–8.

CHAPTER 5: THE CRIMINAL LAW

1. *Life*, p. 203.
2. *Cambridge Essays*, 1857, pp. 1–63.
3. Sir William Holdsworth, *A History of English Law*, vol. XV (London, 1903–66) p. 290.
4. Sir Frederick Pollock, 'Sir James Fitzjames Stephen', *Encyclopedia Britannica*, XXV (1895) 884.
5. Radzinowicz, *Stephen and the Development of Criminal Law*, p. 22.
6. Preface to *GV*, pp. v–vi.
7. Ibid., pp. 1–3.
8. Ibid., pp. 4–7.
9. Ibid., pp. 7–8.

10. Ibid., p. 66.
11. Ibid., pp. 75–8.
12. Ibid., p. 81.
13. Ibid., p. 82.
14. Ibid., p. 90.
15. Ibid., pp. 81–2.
16. *History of the Criminal Law of England*, vol. II (London, 1883) p. 95 (hereafter cited as *History*); see also his judgement in the case of *Queen v. Tolson* (1889), 23 QBD 168.
17. *GV*, pp. 99–100.
18. Ibid., p. 100.
19. Ibid., p. 102.
20. Ibid., pp. 115–17.
21. Ibid., p. 99.
22. *History*, vol. II, pp. 81–2.
23. Ibid., p. 82.
24. Radzinowicz, pp. 34–5.
25. Report of the Capital Punishment Commission, cmd 3590, 1866, in *Parliamentary Papers*, Reports, 1866, vol. XXI, p. 1; Stephen's evidence, at pp. 254–61, 227–98. See also Stephen's articles 'Capital Punishment', *Fraser's Magazine*, LXIX (1864) 753; and 'Report of the Capital Punishment Commission', *Fraser's Magazine*, LXXIII (1866) 232.
26. 'The Punishment of Convicts', *Cornhill Magazine*, VII (1863) 189.
27. Radzinowicz, p. 35.
28. *GV*, p. 99.
29. Ibid., pp. 99–100.
30. (1843) 10 *Clark and Finnelly*, 200; 4 *State Trials*, NS, 847.
31. 10 *Clark and Finnelly*, 210.
32. *GV*, p. 96.
33. 'On the Policy of Maintaining the Limits at Present Imposed by Law on the Criminal Responsibility of Madmen', *Papers Read before the Juridical Society: 1855–1858* (London, 1858), vol. I, p. 67; 'Responsibility and Mental Competence', *Law Magazine and Review*, XVIII (1865) 26.
34. *GV*, p. 95.
35. *History*, vol. II, pp. 153 ff. Henry Weihofen, in his *Insanity as a Defense in Criminal Law* (New York, 1933) pp. 29–30, n. 40, thought that 'Sir James Stephen probably had a wider knowledge of forensic psychiatry than any other legal

commentator of his time. His discussion of the Opinion in M'Naghten's Case is one of the most searching criticisms on the subject.'
36. *History*, vol. II, p. 168.
37. *GV*, p. 10.
38. Ibid., pp. 153–4.
39. Ibid., p. 165.
40. Ibid., p. 203.
41. Ibid., p. 207.
42. Ibid., p. 208.
43. 'The Criminal Law and the Detection of Crime', *Cornhill Magazine*, II (1860) 696.
44. *GV*, p. 229.
45. Ibid., pp. 232–3.
46. Ibid., p. 232.
47. Ibid., p. 76.
48. Introduction to *A Digest of the Law of Evidence*, 4th edn (London, 1893) x–xi.
49. *GV*, pp. 235–6.
50. Ibid., p. 245.
51. Ibid., pp. 239 ff.
52. James Bradley Thayer, *A Preliminary Treatise on Evidence at the Common Law* (Boston, Mass., 1898) pp. 266–8, n. 1; John Henry Wigmore, *A Treatise on the Anglo-American System of Evidence in Trials at Common Law* (Boston, Mass., 1940) p. 297.
53. Maine's review of the Indian Evidence Act is reprinted in his *Village-Communities in the East and West*, 7th edn (London, 1895) pp. 295–330, at p. 305.
54. Introduction to *The Indian Evidence Act* (Calcutta, 1872) p. 55.
55. *GV*, pp. 284–94.
56. Ibid., p. 289.
57. Ibid., pp. 328–9.
58. 'Mr. Best on Codification', *Saturday Review*, II (1856) 545; second notice, ibid., p. 614. 'Law Reform', *Saturday Review*, I (1856) 252; second notice, ibid., p. 345.
59. Sir Courtenay Ilbert, *Legislative Methods and Forms* (Oxford, 1901) p. 111.
60. Ibid., p. 128.
61. *GV*, p. 150.
62. Ibid., p. 336.
63. Ibid., p. 152.

64. Ibid., p. 328.
65. Benjamin Cardozo, *The Nature of the Judicial Process* (New Haven, Conn., 1921).
66. *GV*, p. 328.
67. Ibid., p. 332.
68. Ibid., p. 333.
69. Jeremy Bentham, *Works*, vol. IX, pp. 597–612; cited in Benjamin Cardozo, 'A Ministry of Justice', *Harvard Law Review*, XXXV (1921–2) 113.
70. Ibid.; Roscoe Pound, 'Juristic Problems of National Progress', *American Journal of Sociology*, XXII (1917) 721, 729, 731.
71. *GV*, p. 336.
72. *Life*, p. 211.
73. *Law Magazine and Review*, XVIII (1864–5) 139–69, at p. 169.
74. *Fraser's Magazine*, LXIX (1864) 37–48, at pp. 47–8.
75. *Law Journal*, XXX (1895) 393–5.

CHAPTER 6: INDIA

1. *Life*, p. 233.
2. Ibid., p. 234 (Stephen to Emily Cunningham, 17 Mar 1869).
3. 'Autobiographical Fragment', p. 48.
4. Stephen to his mother, 10 Mar 1869.
5. Stephen to his mother, 14 Mar 1869.
6. Quoted in *Life*, p. 241.
7. In this analysis I am indebted to Eric Stokes, *The English Utilitarians and India* (Oxford, 1959) pp. 287–98; and R. Iyer, 'Utilitarianism and All That: the Political Theory of British Imperialism in India', in *St Antony's Papers*, no. 8: 'South Asian Affairs' (London, 1960).
8. Quoted in Stokes, *The English Utilitarians and India*, pp. 321–2.
9. For a survey and assessment of Stephen's work in India, see John Roach, 'James Fitzjames Stephen', *Journal of the Royal Asiatic Society*, Apr 1956, p. 1; and Stokes, *The English Utilitarians and India*, pp. 273–311.
10. For an excellent summary of codification in India, see Ilbert, *Legislative Methods and Forms*, pp. 129–55.
11. *History*, vol. III, p. 299.
12. Ibid., p. 300.
13. Ibid.

14. For a survey of Anglo-Indian Legislation during this period, see Sir Courtenay Ilbert, *The Government of India* (Oxford, 1915) pp. 94–107.
15. See Stephen's chapter 'Legislation under Lord Mayo', in Sir William Hunter, *Life of the Earl of Mayo*, vol. II (London, 1875) p. 182.
16. Ibid., p. 180.
17. Ibid., p. 181.
18. Ibid.
19. Ibid., p. 177.
20. *History*, vol. III, pp. 344–5.
21. Sir M. E. Grant Duff, *Sir Henry Maine: A Brief Memoir of His Life* (London, 1892) pp. 60–1.
22. Holdsworth, *A History of English Law*, vol. XI, p. 225.
23. James Bryce, *Studies in History and Jurisprudence*, Vol. I (Oxford, 1901) pp. 127-31.
24. Radzinowicz, p. 14.
25. Sir Frederick Pollock, Preface to *The Indian Contract Act* (London, 1905) p. v.
26. Pollock, 'Sir James Fitzjames Stephen', *National Review*, XXV (1895) 820–1.
27. Sir Courtenay Ilbert, 'Sir James Stephen as a Legislator', *Law Quarterly Review*, X (1894) 223–4.
28. 'Legislation under Lord Mayo', in Hunter, *Life of the Earl of Mayo*, vol. II, pp. 148–9.
29. Ibid., p. 161.
30. Ibid., p. 162.
31. Ibid., p. 164.
32. Ibid.
33. Ibid., p. 167.
34. Repr, in Maine, *Village-Communities in the East and West*, pp. 203–39.
35. Ibid., p. 231.
36. In Hunter, *Life of the Earl of Mayo*, vol. II, pp. 165–6.
37. Maine, *Village-Communities*, p. 230.
38. Stephen to Lord Lytton, 27 July 1876.
39. *Life*, p. 289.
40. Pollock, 'Sir James Fitzjames Stephen', *National Review*, XXV (1895) 821.
41. *Minutes on the Administration of Justice in British India*, Selections

from the Records of the Government of India, Home Department, no. 89 (Calcutta, 1872) p. 32.
42. Ibid., p. 106.
43. Ibid., p. 94.
44. Ibid., p. 30.
45. Ibid.
46. Ibid., p. 8.
47. Ibid., pp. 766–7.
48. In Hunter, *Life of the Earl of Mayo*, vol. II, p. 170.
49. Ibid., p. 171.
50. Ibid., p. 172.
51. Ibid., p. 173.
52. Ibid.
53. Ibid., p. 174.
54. 'Manchester on India', *The Times*, 4 Jan 1878, p. 3.
55. *The Times*, 1 and 2 Mar 1883; 2 and 9 Nov 1883.
56. *The Times*, 1 Mar 1883, p. 8.
57. Sir John Strachey, *India* (London, 1888).
58. *Nineteenth Century*, XIV (1883) 541–68.
59. Ibid., p. 542.
60. Ibid., p. 547.
61. Ibid., p. 551.
62. In Hunter, *Life of the Earl of Mayo*, vol. II, p. 174.
63. Ibid., p. 176.
64. Ibid., p. 174.
65. Ibid., pp. 168–9.
66. Ibid., p. 175.
67. Stephen to his mother, 10 Feb 1870.
68. Stephen to Lord Lytton, 6 Sep 1876.
69. *Life*, p. 243.
70. Stephen to Venables, 4 July 1870.
71. Stephen to Emily Cunningham, 12 June 1872; *Life*, p. 300.
72. Stephen to Emily Cunningham, 7 May 1872.
73. Stephen to Emily Cunningham, 15 July 1872.
74. Stephen to Emily Cunningham, 3 July 1874.

CHAPTER 7: LIBERTY, EQUALITY, FRATERNITY

1. Stephen to Emily Cunningham, 27 Apr 1872.
2. *Liberty, Equality, Fraternity*, ed. R. J. White (Cambridge,

1967). (Hereafter cited as *LEF*.)
3. *Life*, p. 307.
4. Stephen to Lord Lytton, 2 May 1876.
5. *LEF*, p. 24.
6. See above pp. 10–13.
7. Stephen to J. S. Mill, 3 Aug 1871.
8. Stephen to Emily Cunningham, 14 Mar 1873.
9. *LEF*, p. 53.
10. See Rees, *Mill and His Early Critics*.
11. John Morley, *Recollections*, vol. I (New York, 1917) p.55.
12. *LEF*, p. 53.
13. Stephen to Emily Cunningham, 12 Sep 1872.
14. Stephen to Emily Cunningham, 1 May 1872.
15. *LEF*, pp. 35–6.
16. *Life*, pp. 71, 87, 98.
17. *LEF*, p. 55.
18. Ibid., pp. 55–6.
19. Ibid., p. 166.
20. Ibid., pp. 176–7.
21. Ibid., p. 57.
22. Ibid.
23. Ibid., p. 58.
24. Ibid., p. 61.
25. Ibid., p. 65.
26. Ibid., p. 59.
27. Ibid., pp. 59–60.
28. Ibid., p. 66.
29. Ibid., p. 67.
30. Ibid., p. 72.
31. Ibid., p. 70.
32. Ibid.
33. Ibid., p. 71.
34. Ibid., p. 75.
35. Ibid., p. 74.
36. Ibid., p. 76.
37. Ibid., p. 78.
38. Ibid., pp. 78–9.
39. Ibid., p. 79.
40. Ibid., pp. 106–7.
41. See above, p. 9.

42. 'Mr. Mill's Doctrine of Liberty', *Fortnightly Review*, XX (1873) 234; repr. in John Morley, *Nineteenth Century Essays*, ed. Peter Stansky (Chicago, 1970) p. 125.
43. *LEF*, pp. 81–2.
44. See Arnold, *Culture and Anarchy*, ch. 4 ('Hebraism and Hellenism').
45. See above, p. 12.
46. *LEF*, p. 81.
47. Ibid., p. 81.
48. Ibid., p. 84.
49. Ibid., p. 82.
50. Arnold, *Culture and Anarchy*, p. 41.
51. *LEF*, p. 174.
52. Ibid., p. 170.
53. Ibid., pp. 172–3.
54. Ibid., p. 85.
55. Ibid., pp. 86–7.
56. Ibid., p. 87.
57. Ibid., p. 90.
58. Ibid., p. 95.
59. Ibid., p. 92.
60. Ibid., p. 90.
61. *Life*, pp. 326–7.
62. *LEF*, p. 98.
63. Ibid., p. 103.
64. Ibid., p. 164 and *passim*.
65. Ibid., p. 108.
66. Ibid., p. 115.
67. The works referred to are Milton's *Areopagitica* (1644) and Locke's *Letters Concerning Toleration* (1690, 1692).
68. Patrick Devlin, *The Enforcement of Morals* (Oxford, 1965); H. L. A. Hart, *Law, Liberty and Morality* (New York, 1963).
69. See Devlin, Preface to *The Enforcement of Morals*, p. vii.
70. *LEF*, p. 138.
71. Ibid., pp. 139–40.
72. Ibid., p. 140.
73. Ibid., p. 141.
74. Ibid., p. 151.
75. Ibid., p. 162.
76. Ibid., p. 188.
77. Ibid., p. 175.

78. Ibid., p. 174.
79. Ibid., p. 175.
80. In the recently published *On Liberty and Liberalism: The Case of John Stuart Mill* (New York, 1974), Gertrude Himmelfarb has persuasively argued that *On Liberty* is inconsistent with the bulk of Mill's other, more conservative works.
81. *LEF*, p. 184.
82. Ch. 5.
83. *LEF*, p. 181.
84. A. V. Dicey, *Introduction to the Study of the Law of the Constitution*, 9th edn (London, 1941) ch. 4.
85. *LEF*, p. 187.
86. Ibid., p. 208.
87. Ibid., pp. 191–2.
88. Ibid., p. 208.
89. Ibid.
90. Ibid., p. 188.
91. Ibid., p. 198.
92. Ibid., p. 194.
93. Ibid., pp. 195–6.
94. This contention is made by Gertrude Himmelfarb in her book *On Liberty and Liberalism*.
95. *LEF*, p. 198.
96. Ibid., p. 202.
97. Ibid.
98. Ibid., p. 199.
99. Harrison to Morley, 9 Apr 1873; quoted in George Feaver, *From Status to Contract: A Biography of Sir Henry Maine, 1822–1888* (London, 1969) p. 190.
100. Stephen to Lord Lytton, 7 Sep 1884.
101. See B. E. Lippincott, *Victorian Critics of Democracy* (Minneapolis, 1938).
102. *LEF*, p. 212.
103. Ibid., p. 211.
104. Ibid., p. 212.
105. Ibid.
106. Ibid., p. 211.
107. Leslie Stephen to Holmes, 24 Jan 1873; in F. W. Maitland, *The Life and Letters of Leslie Stephen* (London, 1906) pp. 230–1.
108. *Life,* pp. 201–2. Fitzjames also began a work on Carlyle for the English Men of Letters series, but abandoned it because,

as Leslie relates, 'he should have to adopt too frequently the attitude of a hostile critic' – *Life*, p. 203.
109. *LEF*, p. 221.
110. Ibid., p. 223.
111. For Mill's objections to Comte's authoritarianism, see his *Auguste Comte and Positivism* (London, 1865).
112. Stephen was especially critical of the absurd rituals concocted by Comte and his followers. See 'Positive Religion', *Saturday Review*, VII (1859) 567; and 'Congreve's Sermon on Positivism', *Saturday Review*, VII (1859) 304.
113. *LEF*, p. 226.
114. Ibid.
115. Ibid., p. 232.
116. Ibid., p. 238.
117. Ibid., p. 239.
118. John Plamenatz, *The English Utilitarians*, 2nd rev. edn (1958) p. 9.
119. *LEF*, p. 228.
120. Ibid., p. 134.
121. Ibid., p. 254.
122. Ibid., pp. 256–7.
123. Ibid., p. 259.
124. *Spectator*, 7 June 1873, p. 728.
125. See Frederic Harrison, 'The Religion of Inhumanity', *Fortnightly Review*, XIX (June 1873) 677–99, at p. 677.
126. *LEF*, p. 261.
127. Alexander Bain, *John Stuart Mill: A Criticism with Personal Recollections* (New York, 1882) p. 111.
128. *Life*, p. 316; see also Stephen to Emily Cunningham, 29 Dec 1873.
129. Himmelfarb, *On Liberty and Liberalism*, p. 286.
130. *Pall Mall Gazette*, 10 May 1873, pp. 1–2. The attribution is based on internal evidence, and on a letter from Frederic Harrison to John Morley, 12 May 1873 (Harrison Collection, Box no. 2, London School of Economics and Political Science).
131. See E. M. Everett, *The Party of Humanity: The 'Fortnightly Review' and its Contributors, 1865-1875* (Chapel Hill, NC, 1939).

132. On this subject see the excellent article by John Roach, 'Liberalism and the Victorian Intelligentsia', *Cambridge Historical Journal*, XIII (1957) 58.
133. Quoted in D. A. Hamer, *John Morley: Liberal Intellectual in Politics* (Oxford, 1968) p. 86.
134. F. W. Hirst, *Early Life and Letters of John Morley*, vol. I (London, 1927) p. 239.
135. Harrison to Morley, 8 Apr 1873.
136. Ibid.; also quoted in Feaver, *From Status to Contract*, pp. 188–9.
137. Frederic Harrison, 'The Revival of Authority', *Fortnightly Review*, XIX (1873) 2.
138. The resulting article was 'The Religion of Inhumanity', *Fortnightly Review*, XIX (1873).
139. Harrison to Morley, 8 Apr 1873; also quoted in Feaver, *From Status to Contract*, p. 188. Harrison later amplified his objections to Mill, using arguments remarkably similar to those of Stephen, in *Tennyson, Ruskin, Mill, and Other Literary Estimates* (New York, 1900) pp. 268–302.
140. *Fortnightly Review*, XX, 234.
141. *Saturday Review*, XXXV (1873) 517–18; *Athenaeum*, no. 2377 (17 May 1873) 627–8; *Quarterly Review*, June 1873, 178–89.
142. A. V. Dicey, *Lectures on the Relation between Law and Public Opinion in England during the Nineteenth Century* (London, 1905) p. 427n.
143. *The Academy*, IV (1873) 292.
144. Charles Eliot Norton, *Letters* (Boston, Mass., 1913) vol. I, pp. 468–9.
145. Sir Ernest Barker, *Political Thought in England: 1848–1914*, 2nd edn (London, 1928) p. 150.
146. Laski to Holmes, 12 Feb 1924; in *Holmes–Laski Letters, 1916–35*, ed. Mark D. Howe (Cambridge, Mass., 1953) vol. I, p. 592.
147. *TLS*, 3 Oct 1968, p. 1093.
148. Stephen to Lytton, 2 Apr 1880. Reference to the Conservatives as the 'stupid party' also appears in Mill's *Autobiography*, p. 245.

CHAPTER 8: AN HONEST DOUBTER

1. A. W. Benn, *The History of English Rationalism in the Nineteenth Century* (New York, 1962) vol. II, p. 237.
2. *LEF*, p. 259.
3. 'Autobiographical Fragment', p. 6.
4. Ibid., pp. 6–7.
5. Ibid.
6. *Life*, p. 56.
7. Sir James Stephen, *Essays in Ecclesiastical Biography* (London, 1850) vol. II, p. 503.
8. Ibid., p. 309.
9. *Life*, p. 63.
10. Ibid., p. 61.
11. Ibid., p. 63.
12. 'Autobiographical Fragment', p. 10.
13. *Life*, p. 41.
14. Ibid., p. 14.
15. Ibid.
16. Ibid., p. 62.
17. Ibid., p. 124.
18. Ibid., p. 123.
19. 'Autobiographical Fragment', p. 36.
20. See 'The Unknowable and the Unknown', *Nineteenth Century*, XV (1884) 918n.
21. Stephen to Lady Grant Duff, 17 Nov 1881.
22. Ibid.
23. Ibid., p. 213, n.1.
24. For excellent accounts of the controversy, see Owen Chadwick, *The Victorian Church* (1966–70) vol. II, pp. 75–97; and Basil Willey, *More Nineteenth Century Studies: A Group of Honest Doubters* (London, 1966) pp. 137–85.
25. Strangely enough, Stephen was indifferent to Darwinism. He insisted that, even if true, the theory of evolution is not necessarily inconsistent with Christianity. See 'General Jacob on the Progress of Being', *Saturday Review*, V (1858) 528.
26. Quoted in Willey, *More Nineteenth Century Studies*, p. 156.
27. Harrison published a review of the controversy, entitled 'Neo-Christianity', in the *Westminster Review* for October 1860.
28. *Life*, p. 185.
29. *The Defence of Dr Rowland Williams* (London, 1862).

30. Ibid., p. 9.
31. Ibid., p. 66.
32. Ibid., p. 107.
33. Ibid., p. 2.
34. Ibid., p. 331.
35. *Life*, p. 188. In his article on Fitzjames in the *Dictionary of National Biography*, Leslie Stephen said that his brother was chosen as Williams's counsel because of 'his sympathy with the general position of the Broad Church Party'. See *DNB*, vol. LIV (New York, 1898) p. 165.
36. Chadwick, *The Victorian Church*, vol. II, p. 84.
37. 'Dr. Pusey and the Court of Appeal', *Fraser's Magazine*, LXX (1864) 649.
38. Stephen to his mother, 2 Jan 1864.
39. For the Newman-Kingsley correspondence on this issue, see John Henry Cardinal Newman, *Apologia Pro Vita Sua*, ed. A. Dwight Culler (Boston, Mass., 1956 Appendix, pp. 369–84.
40. 'Dr. Newman and Mr. Kingsley', *Saturday Review*, XVII (1864) 254.
41. 'Dr. Newman's *Apologia*', *Fraser's Magazine*, LXX (1864) 266.
42. Ibid.
43. Ibid., p. 269.
44. Stephen to Emily Cunningham, 23 Sep 1874.
45. See Geoffrey Faber, *Oxford Apostles: A Character Study of the Oxford Movement* (London, 1936), for a suggestive Freudian analysis.
46. *Apologia*, p. 271.
47. 'Dr. Newman and Liberalism', *Saturday Review*, XIX (1865) 768–70.
48. 'Dr. Newman's *Apologia*', *Fraser's Magazine*, LXX (1864) 275.
49. Ibid.
50. Ibid., p. 280.
51. Ibid., p. 272; the summary appears in Chapter 1 of the *Apologia*.
52. Ibid., pp. 272–4.
53. 'On Certitude in Religious Assent', *Fraser's Magazine*, n.s., V (1872) 36.
54. *LEF*, p. 265.
55. Ibid., p. 263.
56. See his article 'Max Müller's Science of Thought', *Nineteenth Century*, XXIII (1888) 569, 743. For Stephen's criticism of

scepticism, see, for example, the following articles in his *Horae Sabbaticae*: 'The Scepticism of Bayle', 'Montaigne's Essays' and 'Hume's Essays'.
57. *LEF*, p. 266.
58. W. K. Clifford, *Lectures and Essays* (London, 1901) vol. II, pp. 163–205.
59. *LEF*, pp. 270–1.
60. 'Mr. Lecky on Rationalism', *Fraser's Magazine*, LXXII (1865) 537.
61. Ibid., p. 544.
62. Ibid., p. 539.
63. Ibid.
64. Ibid., p. 544.
65. Ibid., p. 542.
66. '*Ecce Homo*', pt 1, *Fraser's Magazine*, LXXIII (1866) 746; pt 2, LXXIV (1866) 29.
67. Seeley subsequently became Professor of Modern History at Cambridge University and the author of *The Expansion of England* (London, 1883).
68. '*Ecce Homo*', *Fraser's Magazine*, LXXIII (1866) 747.
69. Ibid.
70. Ibid., LXXIV (1866) 48–52.
71. 'Life and Writings of Theodore Parker', *Fraser's Magazine*, LXIX (1864) 243.
72. *Fraser's Magazine*, LXVIII (1863) 679.
73. Ibid., p. 682.
74. 'English Ultramontanism', pt 1, *Fraser's Magazine*, LXXI (1865) 671; pt 2, LXXII (1865) 1.
75. Ibid., LXXI (1865) 680.
76. Ibid.
77. Stephen to Emily Cunningham, 23 Sep 1874.
78. Repr. in Henry Manning, *Miscellanies* (London, 1877) vol. II, pp. 129–62.
79. 'Caesarism and Ultramontanism', *Contemporary Review*, XXIII (1873–4) 494, 989.
80. Ibid., pp. 503–4.
81. 'The Present State of Religious Controversy', *Fraser's Magazine*, LXXX (1869) 572.
82. Stephen to Emily Cunningham, 19 Mar 1873.
83. Stephen to his mother, 23 Jan 1872.

84. See F. H. Skrine, *Life of Sir William Wilson Hunter* (London, 1901) p. 214. The letter is dated 30 Apr 1873.
85. For an excellent account of the Society, see Alan W. Brown, *The Metaphysical Society: Victorian Minds in Conflict, 1869–1880* (New York, 1947).
86. Ibid., p. 23.
87. Leonard Huxley, *Life and Letters of Thomas H. Huxley* (New York, 1900) vol. I, pp. 343–4.
88. Stephen's paper was published as 'Necessary Truth', *Contemporary Review*, XXV (1874–5) 44.
89. 'Mr. Gladstone and Sir George Lewis on Authority in Matters of Opinion', *Nineteenth Century*, I (1877) 292.
90. Brown, *The Metaphysical Society*, p. 107.
91. Ibid., p. 61; see also R. H. Hutton, 'The Metaphysical Society: A Reminiscence', *Nineteenth Century*, XVIII (1885) 189.
92. Brown, *The Metaphysical Society*, p. 107.
93. Frederic Harrison, *Autobiographic Memoirs* (London, 1911) vol. II, p. 87.
94. Ibid., p. 112.

CHAPTER 9: THE LAST SANCTION

1. This thesis has been persuasively argued by John Roach in 'Liberalism and the Victorian Intelligentsia', *Cambridge Historical Journal*, XIII (1957) 58.
2. Stephen to Lady Grant Duff, 18 May 1883.
3. Stephen to Lady Grant Duff, 30 Apr 1886.
4. Stephen to Lord Lytton, 15 Mar 1878.
5. Stephen to his mother, 27 July 1873; *Life*, p. 345.
6. *Life*, p. 346.
7. Stephen to Lord Lytton, 1 Oct 1879.
8. Stephen to Lord Lytton, 25 Dec 1879.
9. Stephen to Lord Lytton, 14 Apr 1880.
10. Stephen to Lord Lytton, 8 July 1879.
11. Stephen to Lord Lytton, 23 Oct 1879.
12. *The Times*, 4, 5 and 21 Jan, 29 Apr, 1 Mar 1886.
13. Stephen to Lady Grant Duff, 20 Mar 1886.
14. Quoted in *Life*, p. 349.
15. Stephen to Emily Cunningham, 23 Mar 1875.
16. Stephen to Lord Lytton, 24 May 1877.

17. Stephen to Lord Lytton, 2 Apr 1880.
18. Stephen to Lord Lytton, 3 Feb 1880.
19. Stephen to his mother, 16 Aug 1873; Stephen to Lord Lytton, 21 June 1878.
20. 'Parliamentary Government', *Contemporary Review*, XXIII (1873–4) 1, 165.
21. See J. S. Mill, *Considerations on Representative Government*, ch. 5.
22. Ibid., ch. 8.
23. These arguments are summarised in *LEF*, pp. 215–16.
24. 'Parliamentary Government', *Contemporary Review*, XXIII (1873) 6–8.
25. Ibid., pp. 11–17.
26. Ibid., p. 14.
27. *LEF*, p. 215.
28. 'Parliamentary Government', *Contemporary Review*, XXIII (1874) 3.
29. Ibid., p. 169.
30. Ibid., p. 3.
31. Ibid., pp. 167–8. See also Herbert Spencer. *The Proper Sphere of Government* (London, 1842). Spencer sought to recall English liberals to the doctrine of *laissez-faire* in *The Man Versus the State* (London, 1884).
32. 'Parliamentary Government', *Contemporary Review*, XXIII (1874) 170.
33. Ibid.
34. Ibid., p. 180.
35. Ibid., p. 11; see also Mill, *Autobiography*, pp. 224–5.
36. 'Parliamentary Government', *Contemporary Review*, XXIII (1874) 180–1.
37. Ibid., p. 177.
38. Ibid., p. 178.
39. Ilbert, *Legislative Methods and Forms*, pp. 60–2.
40. Ibid., p. 127.
41. *Fortnightly Review*, XVIII (1872) 644; Stephen's address was summarised in the *Irish Law Times*, VI (1872) 572.
42. 'Codification in India and England', *Fortnightly Review*, XVIII (1872) 660.
43. Ibid., p. 665.
44. Ibid., p. 667.
45. See *History*, vol. III, pp. 347–67.

46. 'Codification in India and England', *Fortnightly Review*, XVIII (1872) 668.
47. See the Introduction to Stephen's *Digest of the Law of Evidence*, 2nd edn (London, 1876) p. iii; Ilbert, *Legislative Methods and Forms*, p. 127.
48. 'Codification in India and England', *Fortnightly Review*, XVIII (1872) 664–5.
49. *Life*, p. 353.
50. Radzinowicz, *Stephen and the Development of Criminal Law*, p. 19.
51. 'Improvement of the Law by Private Enterprise', *Nineteenth Century*, II (1877) 198, 205.
52. Introduction to *Digest of the Law of Evidence*, 2nd edn (London, 1876) p. v.
53. See Preface to the *History*.
54. Ilbert, *Legislative Methods and Forms*, p. 128.
55. 'Improvement of the Law by Private Enterprise', *Nineteenth Century*, II (1877) 205–15.
56. Ilbert, *Legislative Methods and Forms*, pp. 69–70, 127–8; see also the Preface to Stephen's *History*.
57. See his review of Leslie Stephen's *Life of J. F. Stephen*, 'Sir James Fitzjames Stephen', *National Review*, XXV (1895) 820.
58. Radzinowicz, *Stephen and the Development of Criminal Law*, p. 20.
59. Ibid., p. 21.
60. Ibid., p. 22.
61. Stephen to Emily Cunningham, 4 Jan 1879.
62. Radzinowicz, *Stephen and the Development of Criminal Law*, p. 40.
63. Ibid., p. 37.
64. Ibid., p. 39.
65. Ibid., p. 437.
66. Ibid., p. 438.
67. Ibid., p. 442.
68. See H. B. Irving (ed.), *Trial of Mrs. Maybrick*, Notable English Trials series (Philadelphia, 1912).
69. *GV*, 2nd edn (London, 1890) p. 173.
70. *Life*, p. 447.
71. See Preface to the *History*.
72. *Life*, p. 435.

73. Sir Courtenay Ilbert, 'Sir James Stephen as a Legislator', *Law Quarterly Review*, X (1894) 222.
74. Sir Courtenay Ilbert, 'The Life of Sir James Stephen', *Law Quarterly Review*, XI (1895) 386.
75. Radzinowicz, *Stephen and the Development of Criminal Law*, p. 24.
76. Stephen to Lord Lytton, 3 Feb 1880.
77. Stephen to Lord Lytton, 1 Oct 1879.
78. *Nineteenth Century*, I (1877) 331, 531. Stephen's arguments appear on pp. 331–3 and 545–6.
79. *History*, vol. III, p. 366.
80. Ibid., p. 367.
81. *Life*, pp. 107–8; 'Autobiographical Fragment', pp. 45–6.
82. *Life*, pp. 457–8.
83. Ibid., pp. 453–4.
84. *LEF*, p. 270.
85. Ibid., p. 271.
86. Ibid.
87. Stephen to Lord Lytton, 21 Sep 1890.

Bibliography

For a complete bibliography of Sir James Fitzjames Stephen the reader is referred to Sir Leon Radzinowicz, *Sir James Fitzjames Stephen (1829–1894) and His Contribution to the Development of Criminal Law*, Selden Society Lecture (London, 1957) pp.49–62. For a list of Stephen's contributions to the *Saturday Review*, see Merle M. Bevington, *The 'Saturday Review', 1855–1868: Representative Educated Opinion in Victorian England* (New York, 1941) pp. 373–81.

NB. Here and in the Notes, articles are located by the number of the page on which they commence.

I. MANUSCRIPT SOURCES

Writings of Stephen, University Library, Cambridge, Add. MSS. 7349 (on microfilm at Columbia University Library):
(1) 'Autobiographical Fragment' (1884);
(2) 'Choice of One of the Three Learned Professions, Law, Physics and Divinity' (1850);
(3) Letters of J. F. Stephen;
(4) 'The Nature of Belief' (1862);
(5) 'Unfinished Letter to His Children Stating His Religious Beliefs' (c. 1876).

Additional manuscript collection consulted:

The Frederic Harrison Papers, London School of Economics and Political Science. (The Frederic Harrison–John Morley correspondence.)

II. PUBLISHED WORKS OF FITZJAMES STEPHEN

Essays by a Barrister (London, 1862). A reprint of 33 articles contributed to the *Saturday Review*.

Defence of the Reverend Rowland Williams (London, 1862).
A General View of the Criminal Law of England (London, 1863; 2nd edn 1890).
Minute on the Administration of Justice in British India, selections from the Records of the Government of India, Home Department, no. 89 (Calcutta, 1872).
The Indian Evidence Act: With an Introduction on the Principles of Judicial Evidence (Calcutta, 1872).
Liberty, Equality, Fraternity (London, 1873; 2nd edn, with a new preface and notes, 1874; repr. with an introduction by R. J. White, Cambridge, 1967).
'[Indian] Legislation under Lord Mayo', in Sir William Wilson Hunter, *Life of the Earl of Mayo* (London, 1875) vol. II, 143–226.
A Digest of the Law of Evidence (London, 1876; 2nd edn 1881; 3rd edn 1887; 4th edn 1893).
A Digest of the Criminal Law (Crimes and Punishments) (London, 1877; 2nd edn 1879; 3rd edn 1883; 4th edn 1887; 5th edn 1894).
A Digest of the Law of Criminal Procedure in Indictable Offences (London, 1883).
A History of the Criminal Law of England, 3 vols (London, 1883).
The Story of Nuncomar and the Impeachment of Sir Elijah Impey, 2 vols (London, 1885).
Horae Sabbaticae, 3 vols (London, 1892). A reprint of 55 articles contributed to the *Saturday Review.*

III. ARTICLES BY STEPHEN CITED IN THIS BOOK

(Other than those included in *Essays by a Barrister* and *Horae Sabbaticae.*)

Cambridge Essays
'The Relation of Novels to Life', 1855, p. 148.
'The Characteristics of English Criminal Law', 1857, p. 1.

Contemporary Review
'Caesarism and Ultramontanism', XXIII (Dec 1873–May 1874) 497, 989
'Parliamentary Government', XXIII (Dec 1873–May 1874) 1, 165.
'Necessary Truth', XXV (Dec 1874 – May 1875) 44.

Bibliography

Cornhill Magazine
'The Criminal Law and the Detection of Crime', II (1860) 696.
'The Study of History', III (1861) 666; IV (1861) 25.
'Liberalism', V (1862) 70.
'The Punishment of Convicts', VII (1863) 189.

Edinburgh Review
'The License of Modern Novelists', CVI (1857) 124.
'Buckle's *History of Civilization in England*', CVII (1858) 465; CXIV (1861) 183.
'English Jurisprudence', CXIV (1861) 456.

Fortnightly Review
'Codification in India and England', XVIII (1872) 644.

Fraser's Magazine
'England and America', LXVIII (1863) 419.
'Women and Scepticism', LXVIII (1863) 679.
'Life and Writings of Theodore Parker', LXIX (1864) 243.
'Mr. Thackeray', LXIX (1864) 401.
'Capital Punishment', LXIX (1864) 753.
'Dr. Newman's *Apologia*', LXX (1864) 265.
'Dr. Pusey and the Court of Appeal', LXX (1864) 644.
'What Is the Law of the Church of England?', LXXI (1865) 225.
'English Ultramontanism', pt 1, LXXI (1865) 671; pt 2, LXXII (1865) 1.
'Mr. Lecky on Rationalism', LXXII (1865) 537.
'Mr. Carlyle', LXXII (1865) 778.
'Report of the Capital Punishment Commission', LXXIII (1866) 232.
'*Ecce Homo*', LXXIII (1866) 746; LXXIV (1866) 29.
'On Certitude in Religious Assent', n.s., V (1872) 23.

Nineteenth Century
'Mr Gladstone and Sir George Lewis on Authority in Matters of Opinion', I (1877) 270.
'A Modern "Symposium": the Influence on Morality of a Decline in Religious Belief', I (1877) 331, 531.
'Improvement of the Law by Private Enterprise', II (1877) 198.
'The Foundations of the Government of India', XIV (1883) 541.
'The Unknowable and the Unknown', XV (1884) 905.
'Max Müller's Science of Thought', XXIII (1888) 569, 743.

Saturday Review
'Law Reform', I (1856) 252.
'Mr. Best on Codification', II (1856) 545, 614.
'Mr. Dickens as a Politician' (review), III (1857) 8.
'*Little Dorrit*' (review), IV (1857) 15.
'Light Literature and the *Saturday Review*', IV (1857) 34.
'*Madame Bovary*' (review), IV (1857) 40.
'Light Literature in France', IV (1857) 219.
'Balzac' (review), IV (1857) 559.
'Edmund Burke' (review), V (1858) 372.
'Mr. Dickens' (review), V (1858) 474.
'General Jacob on the Progress of Being', V (1858) 528.
'*Manon Lescaut*' (review), VI (1858) 64.
'Mr. Mill on Political Liberty' (review), VII (1859) 186, 213.
'Congreve's Sermon on Positivism', VII (1859) 304.
'French and English Logic', VII (1859) 460.
'Positive Religion', VII (1859) 567.
'Mr. Mill's Essays' (review), VII (1859) 46, 76.
'*A Tale of Two Cities*' (review), VIII (1859) 741.
'Dr. Newman and Mr. Kingsley', XVII (1864) 253.
'Mr. Matthew Arnold and His Countrymen', XVIII (1864) 683.
'Mr. Matthew Arnold amongst the Philistines', XIX (1865) 235.
'Senior's Historical and Philosophical Essays' (review), XIX (1865) 479.
'Dr. Newman and Liberalism' (review), XIX (1865) 768.
'Burke on Popular Representation' (review), XX (1865) 394.
'Mr. Arnold on the Middle Classes', XXI (1866) 161.
'Lord Macaulay's Works' (review), XXII (1866) 207.
'Mr. Matthew Arnold on Culture', XXIV (1867) 78.

IV. WORKS BY STEPHEN'S CONTEMPORARIES

Arnold, Matthew, *Culture and Anarchy*, ed. with introduction by J. Dover Wilson (Cambridge, 1969).
——, *Lectures and Essays in Criticism*, ed. R. H. Super (Ann Arbor, Mich., 1962).
——, *Letters of Matthew Arnold, 1848–1888*, ed. George W. E. Russell, 2 vols (London, 1895).
Austin, John, *The Province of Jurisprudence Determined*, ed. H. L. A. Hart (London, 1954).

Bibliography

Bagehot, Walter, *The English Constitution*, World's Classics edn (London, 1968).
——, *Literary Studies*, Everyman's Library edn, 2 vols (London, 1950).
Bain, Alexander, *John Stuart Mill: A Criticism with Personal Recollections* (New York, 1882).
Buckle, Henry Thomas, *A History of Civilization in England*, 2 vols (London, 1857–61).
Carlyle, Thomas, *Chartism* (London, 1840).
——, *Latter-Day Pamphlets* (London, 1850).
——, *On Heroes and Hero Worship* (London, 1841).
——, *Past and Present* (London, 1843).
Clifford, W. K., *Lectures and Essays*, 2 vols (London, 1901).
Grant Duff, Sir M. E., *Sir Henry Maine: A Brief Memoir of His Life* (London, 1892).
Harrison, Frederic, *Autobiographic Memoirs*, 2 vols (London, 1911).
——, 'The Religion of Inhumanity', *Fortnightly Review*, XIX (1873) 677.
——, 'The Revival of Authority', *Fortnightly Review*, XIX (1873) 1.
——, *Tennyson, Ruskin, Mill, and Other Literary Estimates* (New York, 1900).
Hunter, Sir William Wilson, *Life of the Earl of Mayo*, 2 vols (London, 1875).
Hutton, R. H., 'The Metaphysical Society: a Reminiscence', *Nineteenth Century*, XVIII (1885) 177.
Lecky, W. E. H., *Democracy and Liberty*, 2 vols (London, 1896).
——, *History of the Rise and Influence of the Spirit of Rationalism in Europe* (London, 1865).
Maine, Sir Henry, *Ancient Law*, Everyman's Library edn (London, 1965).
——, *Lectures on the Early History of Institutions* (London, 1875).
——, *Popular Government* (London, 1886).
——, *Village-Communities in the East and West* (London, 1871).
Manning, Henry Edward (Cardinal), *Miscellanies*, 2 vols (London, 1877).
Mill, John Stuart, *Autobiography*, World's Classics edn (London, 1940).
——, *Dissertations and Discussions*, vols I–II (London, 1859), III (London, 1867), IV (London, 1875).
——, *On Bentham and Coleridge*, with introduction by F. R. Leavis (London, 1950).

——, *Principles of Political Economy*, ed. V. W. Bladen and J. M. Robson, vols II–III of *Collected Works* (Toronto, 1965).
——, 'The Subjection of Women', in *Essays on Sex Equality*, ed. Alice S. Rossi (Chicago, 1970).
——, *A System of Logic*, 10th edn (London, 1879).
——, *Utilitarianism, Liberty, and Representative Government*, Everyman's Library edn (London, 1940).
Morley, John, *Burke*, English Men of Letters series (New York, 1879).
——, 'Mr. Mill's Doctrine of Liberty', *Fortnightly Review*, XX (1873) 234; repr. in John Morley, *Nineteenth Century Essays*, ed. Peter Stansky (Chicago, 1970) pp. 111–38.
——, *Recollections*, 2 vols (London, 1917).
Newman, John Henry (Cardinal), *An Essay in Aid of a Grammar of Assent*, with introduction by Etienne Gilson (New York, 1955).
——, *Apologia Pro Vita Sua*, ed. with introduction and notes by A. Dwight Culler (Boston, Mass., 1956).
Norton, Charles Eliot, *Letters* (Boston, Mass., 1913) vol. I.
Pattison, Mark, *Memoirs* (London, 1885).
Seeley, J. R., *Ecce Homo* (London, 1865).
Spencer, Herbert, *The Man versus the State* (London, 1884).
——, *The Proper Sphere of Government* (London, 1842).
Stephen, Sir James, *Essays in Ecclesiastical Biography*, 2 vols (London, 1850).
Stephen, Leslie, *The English Utilitarians*, 3 vols (London, 1900).
——, *The Life of Sir James Fitzjames Stephen* (London, 1895; repr. New Jersey, 1972).
——, 'Stephen, James Fitzjames', *Dictionary of National Biography*, vol. LIV (New York, 1898) p. 165.
Tocqueville, Alexis de, *Democracy in America*, trs. Henry Reeve, 2 vols (London, 1862).
Trevelyan, G. O., *Life and Letters of Lord Macaulay* (London, 1876).
Trollope, Anthony, *Autobiography*, ed. Frederick Page (London, 1950).

V. SECONDARY WORKS

Albee, Ernest, *A History of English Utilitarianism* (New York, 1902).
Alexander, Edward, *Matthew Arnold and John Stuart Mill* (London, 1965).

Altholz, Josef, *The Liberal Catholic Movement in England* (London, 1962).
Altick, Richard D., *The English Common Reader: A Social History of the Mass Reading Public 1800–1900* (Chicago, 1957).
Annan, Noel, *Leslie Stephen* (London, 1951).
——, 'The Intellectual Aristocracy', in J. H. Plumb (ed.), *Studies in Social History: A Tribute to G. M. Trevelyan* (London, 1955) pp. 243–87.
Barker, Sir Ernest, *Political Thought in England, 1848–1914* (Oxford, 1959).
Benn, Alfred W., *The History of English Rationalism in the Nineteenth Century*, 2 vols (New York, 1962).
Bentham, Jeremy, *An Introduction to the Principles of Morals and Legislation*, Dolphin edn (New York, 1961).
Berlin, Isaiah, *Four Essays on Liberty* (Oxford, 1969).
Bevington, Merle M., *The 'Saturday Review', 1855–1868: Representative Educated Opinion in Victorian England* (New York, 1941).
Birkenhead, Earl of, *Fourteen English Judges* (London, 1926).
Blehl, Vincent F., and Connolly, Francis X. (eds), *Newman's Apologia: A Classic Reconsidered* (New York, 1964).
Bowle, John, *Politics and Opinion in the Nineteenth Century: An Historical Introduction* (New York, 1954).
Briggs, Asa, *The Age of Improvement, 1783–1867* (New York, 1960).
——, *Victorian People: Some Reassessments of People, Institutions, Ideas, and Events, 1851–1867* (London, 1954).
Brinton, Crane, *English Political Thought in the Nineteenth Century* (London, 1933).
Britton, Karl, *John Stuart Mill* (New York, 1969).
Brown, Alan W., *The Metaphysical Society: Victorian Minds in Conflict 1869–1880* (New York, 1947).
Bryce, James, *Studies in History and Jurisprudence*, 2 vols (Oxford, 1901).
Burrow, J. W., *Evolution and Society: A Study in Victorian Social Theory* (Cambridge, 1966).
Cardozo, Benjamin N., 'A Ministry of Justice', *Harvard Law Review*, xxxv (1921–2) 113.
——, *The Nature of the Judicial Process* (New Haven, Conn., 1921).
Chadwick, Owen, *The Victorian Church*, 2 vols (New York, 1966–70).
Chesterton, G. K., *The Victorian Age in Literature*, Home University Library edn (London, 1966).

Clark, George Kitson, *The Making of Victorian England* (Cambridge, Mass., 1962).
Clive, John, *Macaulay: The Shaping of the Historian* (New York, 1973).
Cox, R. G., 'The Reviews and Magazines', *The Pelican Guide to English Literature*, vol. VI: 'From Dickens to Hardy' (Baltimore, 1968) pp. 188–204.
Davidson, William, *Political Thought in England: The Utilitarians from Bentham to J. S. Mill* (New York, 1916).
Devlin, Patrick, *The Enforcement of Morals* (Oxford, 1965).
Dicey, A. V., *Introduction to the Study of the Law of the Constitution* 9th edn (London, 1939).
——, *Lectures on the Relation between Law and Public Opinion in England in the Nineteenth Century* (London, 1905).
Dunn, W. H., *James Anthony Froude*, 2 vols (Oxford, 1961).
Eastwood, R. A., and Keeton, G. W., *The Austinian Theories of Law and Sovereignty* (London, 1929).
Edwardes, Michael, *British India, 1772–1947* (London, 1967).
Everett, Edwin M., *The Party of Humanity: The 'Fortnightly Review' and Its Contributors, 1865–1874* (Chapel Hill, NC, 1939).
Faber, Geoffrey, *Oxford Apostles: A Character Study of the Oxford Movement* (London, 1936).
Feaver, George, *From Status to Contract: A Biography of Sir Henry Maine, 1822–1888* (London, 1969).
Fifoot, C. H. S., *English Law and Its Background* (London, 1932).
——, *Judge and Jurist in the Reign of Victoria* (London, 1959).
Ford, George H., *Dickens and His Readers* (New York, 1965).
Friedmann, W., *Legal Theory*, 5th edn (New York, 1967).
Friedrich, Carl J., *The Philosophy of Law in Historical Perspective* (Chicago, 1958).
Fuller, Lon, *The Law in Quest of Itself* (Boston, Mass., 1966).
Gooch, G. P., *History and Historians in the Nineteenth Century* (London, 1935).
'Graham, Evelyn', *Fifty Years of Famous Judges* (London, 1930).
Gross, John, *The Rise and Fall of the Man of Letters* (New York, 1969).
Halévy, Elie, *The Growth of Philosophic Radicalism*, trs. Mary Morris, Beacon Press edn (Boston, Mass., 1955).
Hall, Jerome, *General Principles of Criminal Law*, 2nd edn (Indianapolis, 1960).

Hamer, D. A., *John Morley: Liberal Intellectual in Politics* (Oxford, 1968).
Harding, Alan, *A Social History of English Law*, Penguin edn (Baltimore, 1966).
Hart, H. L. A., *Law, Liberty, and Morality* (New York, 1963).
Hearnshaw, Fossey J. C. (ed.), *The Social and Political Ideas of Some Representative Thinkers of the Victorian Age* (London, 1967).
Himmelfarb, Gertrude, *On Liberty and Liberalism: The Case of John Stuart Mill* (New York, 1974).
——, *Victorian Minds* (New York, 1968).
Hirst, F. W., *Early Life and Letters of John Morley*, 2 vols (London, 1927).
Hobbes, Thomas, *Leviathan*, ed. with introduction by Michael Oakeshott, Blackwell's Political Texts (Oxford, 1946).
Hobhouse, L. T., *Liberalism* (Oxford, 1904).
Hoffman, Ross J. S. and Levack, Paul (eds), *Burke's Politics: Selected Writings and Speeches of Edmund Burke on Reform, Revolution, and War* (New York, 1970).
Holdsworth, Sir William, *A History of English Law*, 16 vols (London, 1903–66).
——, *Charles Dickens as a Legal Historian* (New Haven, Conn., 1928).
——, *The Historians of Anglo-American Law* (New York, 1928).
——, *Some Lessons from Our Legal History* (New York, 1928).
——, *Some Makers of English Law* (Cambridge, 1938).
Holloway, John, *The Victorian Sage: Studies in Argument* (London, 1953).
Holmes, Oliver Wendell, *The Common Law* (Cambridge, Mass., 1963).
Holmes–Laski Letters, The, 2 vols, ed Mark de Wolfe Howe (Cambridge, Mass., 1953).
Holmes–Pollock Letters, The, 2 vols. ed Mark de Wolfe Howe (Cambridge, Mass., 1941).
Houghton, Walter E., *The Victorian Frame of Mind, 1830–1870* (New Haven, Conn., 1957).
Huxley, Leonard, *Life and Letters of Thomas H. Huxley*, 2 vols (New York, 1900).
Ideas and Beliefs of the Victorians: An Historic Revaluation of the Victorian Age, BBC talks (London, 1949).
Ilbert, Sir Courtenay, *The Government of India* (Oxford, 1915).

——, *Legislative Methods and Forms* (Oxford, 1901).
——, 'The Life of Sir James Stephen', *Law Quarterly Review*, XI (1895) 386.
——, 'Sir James Stephen as a Legislator', *Law Quarterly Review*, X (1894) 222.
Irving, H. B. (ed.), *Trial of Mrs. Maybrick*, Notable British Trials series (Philadelphia, 1912).
Iyer, R., 'Utilitarianism and All That: the Political Theory of British Imperialism in India', *St Antony's Papers*, no. 8: 'South Asian Affairs' (London, 1960) pp. 9–71.
Jenks, Edward, *A Short History of English Law* (London, 1912).
Keeton, G. W., and Schwarzenberger, G., *Jeremy Bentham and the Law: A Symposium* (London, 1948).
Kirk, Russell, *The Conservative Mind* (Chicago, 1967).
Knickerbocker, Frances W., *Free Minds: John Morley and His Friends* (Cambridge, Mass., 1943).
Laski, Harold J., *The Decline of Liberalism* (London, 1940).
Lippincott, Benjamin E., *Victorian Critics of Democracy* (Minneapolis, 1938).
Locke, John, *Two Treatises on Government*, ed. Peter Laslett (Cambridge, 1967).
Maitland, Frederic W., *Life and Letters of Leslie Stephen* (London, 1906).
Metcalf, T. R., *The Aftermath of Revolt: India 1857–1870* (Princeton, NJ, 1964).
Moore, R. J., *Liberalism and Indian Politics, 1872–1922* (London, 1966).
Neff, Emery, *Carlyle and Mill* (New York, 1926).
Nicoll, Sir William Robertson, *Dickens's Own Story* (London, 1923).
Nisbet, Robert, *The Quest for Community* (Oxford, 1973).
Osborn, A. M., *Rousseau and Burke: A Study of the Idea of Liberty in Eighteenth Century Political Thought* (London, 1940).
Packe, Michael St John, *The Life of John Stuart Mill* (London, 1954).
Peters, Richard, *Hobbes*, Penguin edn (Baltimore, 1967).
Pincoffs, Edmund, *The Rationale of Legal Punishment* (New York, 1966).
Plamenatz, John P., *The English Utilitarians*, 2nd rev. edn (Oxford, 1958).
——, *Man and Society*, 2 vols (London, 1963).

Pollock, Sir Frederick, *An Introduction to the History of the Science of Politics*, Beacon Press edn (Boston, Mass., 1960).
——, 'Sir James Fitzjames Stephen', *National Review*, XXV (1895) 817.
——, 'Sir James Fitzjames Stephen', *Encyclopedia Britannica*, 11th edn, vol. XXV, p. 884.
——, and Maitland, Frederic William, *The History of English Law*, 2 vols (Cambridge, 1895).
——, assisted by D. F. Mulla, *The Indian Contract Act* (London, 1905).
Pound, Roscoe, *Jurisprudence*, 5 vols (St Paul, Minn., 1959).
——, 'Juristic Problems of National Progress', *American Journal of Sociology*, XXII (1917) 721.
Radzinowicz, Sir Leon, *A History of English Criminal Law and Its Administration from 1750* (New York, 1948–68).
——, *Sir James Fitzjames Stephen (1829–1894) and His Contribution to the Development of Criminal Law*, Selden Society Lecture (London, 1957).
Rankin, Sir G., *Background to Indian Law* (Cambridge, 1946).
Rees, J. C., *Mill and His Early Critics* (Leicester, 1956).
Roach, John, 'James Fitzjames Stephen: a Study of His Thought and Life' (unpublished Ph.D. dissertation, University Library, Cambridge, 1953).
——, 'James Fitzjames Stephen', *Journal of the Royal Asiatic Society*, Apr 1956, p. 1.
——, 'Liberalism and the Victorian Intelligentsia', *Cambridge Historical Journal*, XIII (1957) 58.
Robertson, John M., *Buckle and His Critics: A Study in Sociology* (London, 1895).
Robertson Scott, J. W., *The Story of the 'Pall Mall Gazette'* (Oxford, 1950).
Sabine, George, *A History of Political Theory* (New York, 1961).
Semmel, Bernard, *The Governor Eyre Controversy* (London, 1962).
Skrine, F. H., *Life of Sir William Wilson Hunter* (London, 1901).
Somervill, D. C., *English Thought in the Nineteenth Century* (New York, 1936).
Southgate, Donald, *The Passing of the Whigs, 1832–1886* (London, 1962).
Spear, Percival, *The Oxford History of Modern India, 1740–1947* (Oxford, 1965).

St Aubyn, Giles, *A Victorian Eminence: The Life and Works of Henry Thomas Buckle* (London, 1958).
Stanlis, Peter J., *Edmund Burke and the Natural Law* (Ann Arbor, Mich., 1958).
Stokes, Eric, *The English Utilitarians and India* (Oxford, 1959).
Strachey, Sir John, *India* (London, 1888).
Strauss, Leo, *The Political Philosophy of Hobbes* (Chicago, 1952).
Thayer, James Bradley, *A Preliminary Treatise on Evidence at the Common Law* (Boston, Mass., 1898).
Thomson, David, *England in the Nineteenth Century*, Penguin edn (Baltimore, 1967).
Trilling, Lionel, *Matthew Arnold* (New York, 1977).
Vidler, Alec R., *The Church in an Age of Revolution*, Penguin edn (Baltimore, 1968).
Vinogradoff, Paul, 'The Teaching of Sir Henry Maine', *Law Quarterly Review*, XV (1904) 119–33.
Wall, Stephen (ed.), *Charles Dickens: A Critical Anthology*, Penguin edn (Baltimore, 1970).
Webb, R. K., *Modern England: From the 18th Century to the Present* (New York, 1968).
Weihofen, Henry, *Insanity as a Defense in Criminal Law* (New York, 1933).
Willey, Basil, *More Nineteenth Century Studies: A Group of Honest Doubters* (London, 1956).
——, *Nineteenth Century Studies* (London, 1949).
Woodward, E. L., *The Age of Reform, 1815–1870* (Oxford, 1938).
Young, G. M., *Victorian England: Portrait of an Age* (London, 1936).

Index

Acton, Lord, 184
'Adullamites', 23
Aeschylus, 187
Afghanistan, 13, 194
Altick, Richard D., 224 n.5
American Academy of Arts and Sciences, 205
American Revolution, 40, 42
Analogy of Religion (Butler), 178
Ancient Law (Maine), 31, 62, 65–7, 108, 152
Annan, Noel, 2
Apologia Pro Vita Sua (Newman), 175–81
Apostles' Creed, 185–6
Areopagitica (Milton), 10
Aristotle, 29, 187
Arnold, Matthew, ix, 2, 6, 7, 12, 18–24, 60, 125, 128, 136, 138, 191, 212
Arnold, Thomas, 18
Athenaeum, 165
Austin, John, 28, 62–4, 569, 75–6, 93–4
'Authority in Matters of Opinion' (J. F. Stephen), 188
Autobiography (J. S. Mill), 39, 198
Avignon, 161

Bacon, Sir Francis, 101
Bagehot, Walter, 4, 25, 56, 82, 128, 188, 191, 196
Bain, Alexander, 161
Balzac, Honoré de, 58
Bank Charter Act, 20
'Barbarians' (Arnold), 21
Barker, Sir Ernest, 165
Barry Mr Justice, 204

Bastille, 23
Battle of the Books (Swift), 21
'Baxter, Richard, 168
Beales, Edmond, 23
Bengal, 100, 115
Benn, A. W., 167
Bentham, Jeremy, ix, 20, 27–30, 41, 47, 71, 75, 77, 80–1, 90, 92–4, 99, 159, 165, 170, 200
Benthamism, *see* Utilitarianism
Bentinck, Lord William, 118
Bevington, Merle, 4
Bill of Rights (English), 40
Blackburn, Mr Justice, 203, 204
Blackstone, William, 64, 74, 76, 77, 79, 94
Bleak House, 52, 57
Bolingbroke, Lord, 174
Bombay, 98, 100, 115
Bonald, Viscount de, 40
Bossuet, Bishop, 40
Bracton, Henry de, 77
Bradlaugh, Charles, 23
Bramwell, Baron, 203
Brazil, 37
Briggs, Asa, 24–5
Bright, John, 3, 23, 24, 37, 113, 202
British Association, 172
British (English) Constitution, 18, 25, 27, 35, 36, 39, 41, 43–5, 54, 64–5, 82, 196
British Museum, 130
Broad Church, 167, 170–1
Brown, Alan W., 241 n. 85
Bryce, James (Lord), 4, 104
Buckle, Thomas Henry, 11, 41, 68–70, 72, 123

257

258   Index

Bulgarian atrocities, 192
'Bunsen's Biblical Researches'
  (Rowland Williams), 172
Burke, Edmund, 17, 26–7, 41–6, 140,
  147, 174
Burma, 101
Butler, Bishop, 174, 178
Butler, Samuel, 170

Caesar, Julius, 73
Caesarism and Ultramontanism
  (Manning), 186
Cairns, Lord Chancellor, 204
Calcutta, 98
Calvinism, 12–13, 136–7, 160
Cambridge Apostles, 2, 120, 125
Cambridge Essays, 51, 74
Cambridge Union, 22
Cambridge University, 2, 27, 61, 62,
  68, 170, 205, 211
Canada, 205
Capital Punishment Commission
  (1864), 82, 202
Cardozo, Benjamin, 94
Carlyle, Thomas, ix, 2, 5, 14–16, 24,
  37, 55, 72, 156, 212
Chadwick, Owen, 238 n. 24
Chamberlain, Joseph, 191
Chambers, Robert, 171
'Characteristics of the English
  Criminal Law' (J. F. Stephen),
  74, 86
Charlemagne, 133
Charles I, King of England, 130
Charter Act of 1833, 100, 106
Chartism (Carlyle), 15
Chartist movement, 23
Chesterton, G. K., 1
Chillingworth, William, 174
Christ, Jesus, 142–3, 171, 179, 183, 187
Christian Observer, 4
Cicero, 187
'Circumlocution Office', 54
Civil Service Commission, 198
Civil War (English), 27
Civil War (U.S.), 35
Clapham Sect, 2, 169
Clifford, W. K., 167, 181, 188, 209
Clive, Lord, 97

Cockburn, Chief Justice, 203
Code of Civil Procedure (Indian), 101
Code of Criminal Procedure (Indian),
  101, 103, 115
'Codification in India and England'
  (J. F. Stephen), 200
Coke, Sir Edward, 33, 64, 77, 101
Colenso, Bishop, 19
Coleridge, Lord, 192, 202–3, 211
Coleridge, Samuel Taylor, 39, 170
Colonial Office, 197
Comédie humaine, La (Balzac), 58
Commentaries (Blackstone), 64, 78
Comte, Auguste, 61, 123, 157, 164
Conservative Party, 23–4, 166, 193–4
*Considerations on Representative
  Government* (J. S. Mill), 194–5,
  198
Consolidation Acts (1861), 77, 93–4,
  199
Constitutional History of England
  (Hallam), 64
Contemporary Review, 186, 188, 194
Cook, John Douglas, 3–5, 175
Cornhill Magazine, 3, 7, 21, 69, 87, 175,
  193
Court of Chancery, 52, 53, 57
Cousin Bette, La (Balzac), 59
Cousin Pons, Le (Balzac), 59
Creed of Christendom (W. R. Greg), 171
Crimean War, 54
Criminal Appeal Act of 1907, 88
criminal law, 74–96 *passim*
Cuba, 37
Culture and Anarchy (Arnold), 7, 21, 22,
  24
culture and democracy, 1–25 *passim*
'Culture and its Enemies' (Arnold),
  21, 22
Cunningham, Emily (Stephen's
  sister-in-law), 98
Cunningham Henry (Stephen's
  brother-in-law, 98
Cunningham, Mary, *see* Mary Stephen

Dalhousie, Lord, 101
Danton, Georges Jacques, 15
Darwin, Charles, 37, 171, 184
Das Kapital (Marx), 54

Defoe, Daniel, 51
Delhi, 119
democracy, ix, 1–3, 7–10, 15, 18, 25, 32, 36, 48–9, 61, 75, 96, 126, 128–9, 131, 139, 146–7, 153–6, 162–3, 167, 190–1, 214–16
Democracy and Liberty (Lecky), 154
Democracy in America (Toqueville), 9–10
Demosthenes, 187
Derby, Lord, 24
Desmoulins, Camille, 15
Devlin, Patrick, 143
Devon, 175
Dicey, Alfred, Venn, 148, 165
Dickens, Charles, ix, 37, 50–7, 212
Dickens's Own Story (Nicoll), 225 n. 26
Dictionary of National Biography, 56
Digest of the Criminal Law (J. F. Stephen), 204
Digest of the Law of Criminal Procedure in Indictable Offences (J. F. Stephen), 204
Digest of the Law of Evidence (J. F. Stephen), 203
Disraeli, Benjamin, 23, 24, 50, 193–4
Dissertations and Discussions (J. S. Mill), 11
Döllinger, Johann Inganz, von, 184
Draft Criminal (Penal) Code (1878), 85, 204–5, 207
Dublin Review, 179
Dundee, 191

East India Company, 99, 101
Ecce Homo (Seeley). 183
Economist, The, 203
Edict of Nantes, 409
Edinburgh Philosophical Society, 156, 194
Edinburgh Review, 69, 168
Edinburgh University, 205
Education Act of 1870, 13
Education Commission (1858), also Newcastle Commission, 12, 74
Edward I, King of England, 204
'Effect of the Decline of Religious Belief on Morality, The' (J. F. Stephen), 188

'Effects of Observation of India on Modern European Thought' (Maine), 108
Eliot, George, 7, 123, 172
Elizabeth I, Queen of England, 134
English Common Reader, The (Altick), 224 n. 5
English Constitution, The (Bagehot), 25
'English Jurisprudence' (J. F. Stephen), 62
'English Ultramontanism' (J. F. Stephen), 185
English Utilitarians and India, The (Stokes), 230 n.7
equality, 32–3, 122–3, 146–56
Escott, T. H. S., 4
Essays (Macaulay), 17, 97, 207
Essays and Reviews, 171–2, 175
Essays by a Barrister (J. F. Stephen), 5, 64
Essays in Criticism (Arnold), 22
Essays in Ecclesiastical Biography (Sir James Stephen), 168
Essay on Religion and Literature, 185
Estates General (1789), 46
'Ethics of Belief' (Clifford), 181
'ethology', 71
Eton, 2
Evangelicalism, 2, 12, 38, 50, 98, 107, 136–7, 151, 167–71, 216
Eyre Defence Committee, 37
Eyre, Edward John, 37–8, 161

Faber, Geoffrey, 239 n. 45
Field, David Dudley, 201
Fielding, Henry, 51
Flaubert, Gustave, 59
Fortnightly Review, 91, 162, 164, 200
'Foundations of the Government of India' (J. F. Stephen), 116
Founding Fathers (American), 215
Fragment on Government, A (Bentham), 30
Francis, Saint, 168
Franco-Prussian War, 184
Fraser's Magazine, 48, 57, 82, 96, 175, 179, 185
fraternity, 122–3, 156–61, *passim*, 166

Frederick the Great (Carlyle), 16
Freeman, E. A., 4
French Revolution, 1, 8, 18, 39, 40–1, 43, 45–7, 55, 72, 122, 130
French Revolution, The (Carlyle), 14–15, 55
Freud, Sigmund, 81
Froude, Hurrell, 176
Froude, James Anthony, 14, 68, 156, 175, 176, 186, 188
'Function of Criticism at the Present Time' (Arnold), 18

Gardiner, S. R., 64
Gaskell, Elizabeth, 50
General View of the Criminal Law, 62, 67, 74–96 *passim*, 204, 207, 211
George III, King of England, 42, 67
Gladstone, William, ix, 6, 23, 99, 115, 120, 164, 188–9, 191–3, 198, 212
Glorious Revolution (1688), 28, 80
Goodwin, C. W., 172
Gordon, George, 37
Gorham, G. C., 175
Gosse, Edmund, 170
Government of India, The (Ilbert), 231 n. 14
Governor Eyre Controversy, The (Semmel), 222 n. 34
Grammar of Assent (Newman), 179–80
Grant Duff, Sir M. E., 4, 97, 103
Great Exhibition of 1851, 1
Green, J. R., 4
Green, T. H., 147
Greenwood, Frederick, 5–6
Greg, W. R., 171
Gregory VII, Pope, 168
Gurney, Russell, 202

Habeas Corpus Act, 40
Hale, Matthew, 64, 77
Hallam, Henry, 64–5
Harcourt, William, 3, 4
Hard Times, 52
Hardy, Thomas, 7
Harrison, Frederic, 37, 123, 153, 160, 162–4, 172, 188, 189, 209, 237 n. 139
Hart, H. L. A., 143

Hartington, Lord, 191
Hartley, David, 71
Harwich, 191
Hastings, Warren, 97, 207
'Hebraism' (Arnold), 136
Hegel, G. H. F., 81
Henry VII, King of England, 204
Henry VIII, King of England, 134
Himmelfarb, Gertrude, 235 n. 80
Hindus, 113, 118, 119
History of British India (James Mill), 109
History of England (J. A. Froude), 176
History of England (Macaulay), 17, 120
History of English Thought in the Eighteenth Century (Leslie Stephen), 26
History of European Morals from Augustus to Charlemagne (Lecky), 182
History of the Civilization of England (Buckle), 68–70
History of the Common Law (Hale), 64
History of the Criminal Law of England (J. F. Stephen), 75, 81, 85, 96, 201, 208, 210
History of the Rise and Influence of the Spirit of Rationalism in Europe (Lecky), 182
Hobbes, Thomas, 19, 26, 27–36, 41, 67, 71, 99, 132, 214
Hobhouse, Sir Arthur, 116
Hobhouse, L. T., 147
Holdsworth, Sir William, 74, 104
Holker, Sir John, 204
Holloway, John, 14
Holmes, Oliver Wendell, 64, 156, 165
Holyoake, G. J., 23
Home Office, the, 197
Home Rule (Irish), 99, 116, 191, 193
Homicide Law Amendment Bill (1874), 202
Hooker, Richard, 26, 174
Horae Sabbaticae (J. F. Stephen), 5, 26–7, 211
Humboldt, Wilhelm von, 135
Hume, David, 30, 61, 67, 71, 174
Hunter, W. W., 105, 187
Hutton, R. H., 6, 160, 188, 189
Huxley, T. H., 37, 167, 172, 188, 209
Hyde Park riots, 23–4, 38

Ilbert, Sir Courtenay, 93, 105, 115, 204, 208, 231 n. 14
Ilbert Bill, 115
Iliad, 189
India, ix, xi, 13, 20, 90, 92, 93, 95, 97–125 *passim*, 153, 187, 191, 194, 198–20, 217
India Office, 197
Indian Contract Act, 103, 104
Indian Councils Act, 101, 105
Indian Evidence Act, 90–2, 103, 104, 202
Indian Law Commission, First, 100
Indian Law Commission, Second, 101
Indian Law Commission, Third, 101
Indian Mutiny, 101, 113
Indian Penal Code (Macaulay), 100–1, 103
Indian Statute Book, 103, 105
Industrial Revolution, 77
'Influence on Morality of a Decline in Religious Belief' (J. F. Stephen), 209
Insanity as a Defence in Criminal Law (Weihofen), 228 n. 35
Institut de France, 205
Institutes (Coke), 33, 64
Ipswich, 211
Ireland, 175
It Is Never too Late to Mend (Reade), 224 n. 3
Iyer, R., 230 n. 7

Jacobinism, 40, 215
Jamaica, 37–8
Jamaica Committee, 37
'James Fitzjames Stephen' (Roach), 230 n. 9
James, Sir Henry, 205'
James, William, 181
Jenkins, Edward, 192
Johnson, Dr Samuel, 125
Jones, Ernest, 23
Joshua, Book of, 212
Jowett, Benjamin, 172
Juridical Society (London), 84
jus gentium (law of nations), 65
jus naturale (natural law), 65

Kant, Immanuel, 81
Keble, John, 176
Kingdom of Christ, The (Maurice), 170
King's College (London), 2, 170
Kingsley, Charles, 37, 50, 68, 175, 177
Knowles, John, 188

Lapsus Calami (James Kenneth Stephen), 211
Laski, Harold, 165
Latter Day Pamphlets (Carlyle), 15, 126
Law Journal, 96
Law Magazine and Review, 95
Lawrence, Sir Henry, 101, 102, 111
Leben Jesu, Das (Strauss), 172
Lecky, W. E. H., 41, 154, 182, 191
Lectures on the History of France (Sir James Stephen), 46
'Legislation under Lord Mayo' (J. F. Stephen), 231 n. 15
Legislative Council, India 119
Leviathan, The (Hobbes), 27–8, 99
Lewes, George Henry, 4, 6, 56
Liberal Party, 7, 23–4, 99, 120, 191–4
liberalism, ix–x, 1, 7–9, 16, 32–3, 37, 41, 60, 66, 82, 120–1, 127–8, 138–9, 143–7, 165–6, 191–3, 215–17
'Liberalism' (J. F. Stephen), 7–9
'Liberalism and the Victorian Intelligentsia' (Roach), 237 n. 132, 241 n.1
Liberty, Equality, Fraternity (J. F. Stephen), xi, 6, 13, 26, 31, 32, 116, 118, 121, 122–66 *passim*, 167, 192, 194, 213
'License of Modern Novelists, The' (J. F. Stephen), 50
Life of the Earl of Mayo (W. W. Hunter), 105
Lincoln, Abraham, 133
literature, politics of, 49–60
Little Dorrit, 52, 54–5
Little Nell, 56–7
Livingstone, Edward, 201
Locke, John, 28, 30, 39, 68, 71, 127, 143, 147, 215
Louis XIV, King of France, 40

Louis XVI, King of France, 72
Lowe, Robert, 13, 23, 191
Loyola, St Ignatius, 168
Lush, Lord Justice, 204
Luther, Martin, 168
Lyall, Sir Alfred, 99
Lycurgus, 120
Lyell, Charles, 171
Lytton, Earl of, 110, 113–14, 119, 191, 209, 211
Lytton, Sir Edward, 54

Macaulay, Thomas B., 11, 17, 64, 71, 97, 100–1, 120, 207
Machiavelli, Niccolo, 219, 67
Macmillan's Magazine, 176, 177
M'Naghten rules, 82–5
Madame Bovary, 59
Madras, 100, 115
Magna Carta, 32
Maine, Sir Henry, 2, 3, 4, 6, 31, 62, 65–7, 86, 91, 101, 108–9, 120, 152, 154, 191, 211
Maistre, Joseph de, 40, 216
Maitland, Frederic, 4, 208
Manchester, 13
Manchester Liberals, 147
Mandeville, Bernard, 158
Manning, Henry (Cardinal), 184–6
Manon Lescaut, 58
Martineau, James, 209
Marx, Karl, 54
Masson, David (critic), 58
Maurice, Frderick Denison, 170–1
Maybrick, Mrs, trial of, 206–7, 211
Memoirs (Mark Pattison), 61
mens rea, 78–9
Metaphysical Society, 188–9
Metaphysical Society, The (Brown), 241 n. 85
Michels, Robert, 154
Midlothian campaign (Gladstone), 192
Mill, James, 28, 71, 109
Mill, John Stuart, ix, x, 2, 6, 9–13, 19, 22, 27, 31, 37, 39, 51, 61, 63, 69, 71–2, 82, 84, 89, 91, 98 104, 117, 120, 122–66 *passim,* 167, 170, 194–5, 198

Milton, John, 10, 143
Minutes on the Administration of Justice in British India (J. F. Stephen), 110–12
'Mr. Arnold on the Middle Classes' (J. F. Stephen), 21
'Mr. Dickens as a Politician' (J. F. Stephen), 50
'Mr. Matthew Arnold and his Countrymen' (J. F. Stephen), 19
'Mr. Mill's Doctrine of Liberty' (Morley), 164
Mohammedans, 113, 119
Molesworth, Sir William, 28
Montesquieu, Baron de, 215
More Nineteenth Century Studies: A Group of Honest Doubters (Willey), 238 n.24
Morley, John, 5, 6, 40–1, 123, 124, 135, 153, 162–4, 188
Morning Chronicle, 4
Mosca, Gaetano, 154
'My Countrymen' (Arnold), 20
'Mysteries' (J. F. Stephen), 188

Napoleon I, 46, 72
Napoleon III, 17, 215
'National Apostasy' (Keble), 176
National Association for the Promotion of Social Science, 84
natural law, 65
'Necessary Truth' (J. F. Stephen), 188
Newcastle Education Commission (1858), 12, 74
Newman, John Henry (Cardinal), ix, 175–81, 186, 212
Newton, Sir Isaac, 20
New Zealand, 205
Nicoll, Sir William Robertson, 225 n. 26
Nineteenth Century, 188, 203, 209
North, Lord, 42
Norton, Charles Eliot, 5, 165

Oakeshott, Michael, 32
O'Connell, Daniel, 57
Old Curiosity Shop, The, 57
Old Regime, 45–6

Index

Old Regime and the French Revolution, The (Tocqueville), 45
Oliver Twist, 52
On Heroes and Hero Worship (Carlyle), 15
On Liberty (J. S. Mill), x, 9–13, 22, 99, 122–66 *passim*, 195
On Liberty and Liberalism: The Case of John Stuart Mill (Himmelfarb), 235 n.80
Origin of Species, The (Darwin), 171, 184
Orwell, George, 51
Osborn, A. M., 223 n. 47
Othello, 59
Oudh, 101
Oxford Apostles (Faber), 239 n. 45
Oxford movement, 61, 175–8, 186
Oxford University, 18, 68, 205

Paine, Thomas, 26, 39, 40
Palestine, 143
Paley, William, 174
Pall Mall Gazette, 5, 6, 25, 98, 122, 161
Palmerston, Lord, 25
Papal Aggression (Pius IX), 186
Paradise Lost, 59
Pareto, Vilfredo, 154
Parker, Theodore, 183
Past and Present (Carlyle), 15, 16
Pattison, Mark, 4, 61, 172
Peacock, Sir Barnes, 101
Peel, Sir Robert, 16, 82, 83
Philippe, Louis, King of France, 211
'Philistines' (Arnold), 18, 20, 21
Pickwick Papers, 52
Pius IX, Pope, 184, 186
Plamenatz, John, 158
Plato, 187
Politique tirée de l'Écriture Sainte (Bossuet), 40
Pollock, Sir Frederick, 74, 104–5, 110, 204
Pontius Pilate, 142
Poor Law, New, 20
Pope, Alexander, 158
'Populace' (Arnold), 21
Popular Government (Maine), 154
Positivism, 123, 157–9, 162, 167, 209
Pound, Roscoe, 94

Powell, Baden, 172
Prévost, Abbé, 58
Principles of Geology (Lyell), 171
Principles of Morals and Legislation (Bentham), 28
Principles of Political Economy (J. S. Mill), 11, 147
Privy Council, 174–5, 196
'Proof of Miracles' (J. F. Stephen), 188
Province of Jurisprudence Determined, The (Austin), 28, 62–3
Punjab, 100–1, 102, 103, 111, 153
Pusey, Edward, 175, 176

Quanta Cura, 184
Quarterly Review, 165
Queensland, 205

Radzinowicz, Sir Leon, 75, 104, 203, 204, 205–6, 208
Rationale of Evidence (Bentham), 90
Reade, Charles, 50, 224 n. 3
Red Sea, 122
Reflections on the Revolution in France (Burke), 45
Reform Act of 1832, 1, 44, 74, 100
Reform Act of 1867, 3, 13, 24, 120, 123, 147, 162, 191, 194
Reformation, 130, 174, 186
Reform League, 23, 24
Reform Union, 23
'Relation of Novels to Life, The' (J. F. Stephen), 51
religion, 167–90 *passim*
Religion of Humanity, 123–4, 157–9, 167
Ricardo, David, 62
Richardson, Samuel, 51
Roach, John, 230 n. 9, 237 n. 132, 241 n.1
Robespierre, Maximilien, 15
Robinson Crusoe, 51
Rockingham Whigs, 42
Roebuck, John Arthur, 54
Rogers, Rev. William, 12
Roman law, 65, 95, 208
Rousseau, Jean Jacques, 30, 40, 41, 51, 68, 157
Rousseau and Burke (Osborn), 223 n. 47

Royal Titles Act, 194
Ruskin, John, 37, 170, 175, 188
Russell, Lord Arthur, 189
Russell, Sir Charles, 206
Russell, Lord John, 7, 23
Russia, 113, 194

Saturday Review, 3–4, 7, 10, 14, 19, 20, 26, 41, 50, 57, 64, 74, 93, 119, 165, 175, 177, 178, 189, 211
science of society, 61–73 *passim*
Scott, Sir Walter, 54
Second Treatise on Civil Government (Locke), 28, 39
Seeley, J. R., 183, 188
Semmel, Bernard, 222 n. 34
Sermon on the Mount, 160, 171, 183
Shaw, G. B., 54
'Shooting Niagara: And After?' (Carlyle), 24
Sidgwick, Henry, 165, 188
Sikhs, defeat of, 100
Smith, Adam, 62, 159
Smith, George Murray, 5
Smith, Goldwin, 68
Social Science Association, 200
Solon, 120
Spectator, 56, 160
Speech on American Taxation (Burke), 42
Speech on Conciliation with America (Burke), 42
Spencer, Herbert, 37, 197
State, theory of, 26–48 *passim*
State Trials, 204
Statute Law Revision Act, 199
Stephen, Dorothea (daughter of Fitzjames), 98
Stephen, James (grandfather of Fitzjames), 2
Stephen, Sir James (father of Fitzjames), 2, 46, 168–9
Stephen, James Fitzjames:
 Anglo-Indian legislation, principles of, 105–12
 appointed a judge, 205
 appointed Legal Member of Council in India, 97
 on Arnold (Matthew), 18–23
 on Austin, 62–4, 75
 on Balzac, 58–9
 birth, 6
 blunt manner of expression, 125
 British rule in India, principles of, 112–19
 on Buckle, 68–72
 on Burke, 40–6
 called to the Bar, 3
 on Calvinism, 12–13, 136–8
 candidate for Parliament, 191–2
 on capital punishment, 82
 on Carlyle, 14–17
 Cornhill Magazine, begins to write for, 3
 on criminal law, 74–96
 on criminal liability of the insane, 83–5
 on criminal procedure law, 86–8
 on culture, ix, 1–25 *passim*, 49, 60, 214, 217
 on democracy, ix, 1–25 *passim*, 32, 36, 48, 49, 75, 96, 129, 131, 139, 146–7, 153–6, 167, 190, 191, 214–16
 on Dickens, 50–7
 dies at Ipswich, 211
 education, 2–3
 and Education Commission, 12
 on English Ultramontanism, 185–7
 on equality, 32–3, 122–3, 146–56, 166
 on equality between the sexes, 150–2
 on Flaubert, 59
 on fraternity, 156–61 *passim*, 166
 and the Governor Eyre case, 37–9
 on Hobbes, 26, 27–36
 honours, 205, 211
 and India, ix, xi, 13, 20, 91, 92, 93, 95, 97–125 *passim*, 153, 187, 191, 194, 198, 199, 200, 217
 Indian Evidence Act, 90–2
 Indian legal codification, 102–5
 on law and morals, 78–83
 on Lecky, 182
 on legal codification, 92–5, 102–5, 199–205, 217

on legal punishment, 80–3
and liberalism, ix–x, 1, 7–9, 16,
    32–3, 37, 41, 60, 66, 82, 120–1,
    127–8, 138–9, 143–7, 165–6,
    191–3, 215–17
on liberty, 32–3, 126–45 *passim*, 166
on literature, 49–60
on Locke, 39
on Macaulay, 17, 100
on Maine, 65–7
and Maybrick trial, 206–7
and Metaphysical Society, 188–9
on Mill (J. S.), 10–13, 122–66 *passim*
Mill's (J. S.) obituary, for *Pall Mall Gazette*, 161-2
on Newman, 175–81
Pall Mall Gazette, begins to write for, 5–6
on parliamentary government 16–17, 194–9
physical appearance, 125
professor of common law, 203
on religion, 167–90
resigns from judgeship, 211
reviews Mill's essay *On Liberty*, 10–13
and Rowland Williams case, 74, 172–5
on rules of evidence, 88–92
Saturday Review, begins to write for, 3–4
on a science of history, 68–71
on a science of society, 61–73
on Seeley, 183
on the State, 26–48
on Thackeray, 57
on Tocqueville, 45–6
Stephen, James Kenneth (son of Fitzjames), 211
Stephen, Leslie (brother of Fitzjames), x–xi, 4, 5, 6, 7, 24, 26, 27, 41, 56, 61, 74, 110, 122, 141, 156, 161, 167, 169, 170, 172, 174–5, 185, 187, 188, 206
Stephen, Mary (wife of Fitzjames), 3, 97–8
Stephen, Rosamund (daughter of Fitzjames), 98

Sterne, Laurence, 51
Stokes, Eric, 230 n. 7
Story of Nuncomar and the Impeachment of Sir Elijah Impey, The (J. F. Stephen), 207
Strachey, Sir John, 116
'Study of History, The' (J. F. Stephen), 69
Subjection of Women, The (J. S. Mill), 124, 146, 150–1, 163
Swift, Jonathan, 21, 51
Sybil (Disraeli), 50
'Syllabus of Errors', 184
System of Logic, A (J. S. Mill), 11, 19, 39, 51, 61, 69, 71, 72, 84, 89, 104, 124, 170

Tale of Two Cities, A, 55
Tasmania, 205
Taylor, Harriet, 152
Taylor, Jeremy, 174
Temple, Frederick, 172
Ten Commandments, 210
Tennyson, Alfred, Lord, 37, 188, 211
Tennyson, Ruskin, Mill, and Other Literary Estimates (Harrison), 237 n. 139
Thackeray, W. M., 7, 57
Thayer, James Bradley, 90
'Themistes', Homeric, 65
Theological Essays (Maurice), 170
Thirty-Nine Articles, 173, 176
Tillotson, John, 174
Times, The, 114–16, 193, 203
Times Literary Supplement, 165
Tocqueville, Alexis de, 9–10, 45, 147, 215
Torch, 192
Tory Democracy, 194
Tract XC (Newman), 176
Trafalgar Square, 23
Trollope, Anthony, 4, 6, 7, 56
Twelve Tables (Rome), 65
Tyndall, John, 188

Ultramontanism, 184–7
United States, 235–6, 114
University of London, 3, 63
Usher, Archbishop, 171

Utilitarianism (Benthamism), ix, 13, 15, 16, 19, 27, 28, 41, 42, 43, 50–1, 52, 53, 61, 67, 80, 93, 98–9, 107, 122, 124, 157, 161, 171, 214
Utilitarianism (J. S. Mill), 124, 146, 148, 157
'Utilitarianism and All That' (Iyer), 230 n. 7
'Utility of Religion, The' (J. S. Mill), 167
'Utility of Truth, The' (J. F. Stephen), 188

Vanity Fair, 57
Vatican Council, 185
Venables, G. S., 119, 211
Venn, Jane Catherine (mother of James Fitzjames Stephen), 2
Venn, John, 170
Vestiges of Creation (Chambers), 171
Via Media (Newman), 176
Victoria, Queen of England, 67, 194
Victorian age (England), ix, x, 1, 2, 4, 6, 13, 15, 17, 19, 25, 33, 49, 52, 58, 68, 96, 125, 147, 151, 152, 167, 188, 206, 212, 214–17
Victorian Church, The (Chadwick), 238 n. 24
Victorian Sage, The (Holloway), 14
Village-Communities in the East and West (Maine), 108–9
Voltaire, 41, 47, 174

Walpole, Spencer, 23–4
Warburton, Bishop 174
Ward, W. G., 176, 179, 184, 188, 209
War Office, 197
Weihofen, Henry, 228 n. 35
Wesley, John, 168
Westbury, Lord, 94, 199
Western Australia, 205
Westminster Confession (1643), 173
Westminster Review, 68
Whately, Richard, 174
'What is a Lie?' (J. F. Stephen), 188
What, Then, Does Dr. Newman Mean? (Kingsley), 177
Wigmore, John Henry, 90
Wilberforce, Samuel, 172, 175
Wilberforce, William, 169
Wilde, Oscar, 57
Willes, Mr Justice, 95
Willey, Basil, 238 n. 24
William III, King of England, 80
Williams, Rowland, 74, 172–5
'Will to Believe' (William James), 181
Wilson, H. B., 172
Wilson, J. Dover, 221 n. 84
'Wisdom and Innocence' (Newman), 177
Wiseman, Cardinal, 184–5
Wolfenden Report, 143
'Women and Scepticism' (J. F. Stephen), 183

GPSR Compliance

The European Union's (EU) General Product Safety Regulation (GPSR) is a set of rules that requires consumer products to be safe and our obligations to ensure this.

If you have any concerns about our products, you can contact us on

ProductSafety@springernature.com

In case Publisher is established outside the EU, the EU authorized representative is:

Springer Nature Customer Service Center GmbH
Europaplatz 3
69115 Heidelberg, Germany

www.ingramcontent.com/pod-product-compliance
Lightning Source LLC
Chambersburg PA
CBHW071702100426
42873CB00017B/388